EMPOWERED

The Fan ReVOLution That Changed College Football

Celina Summers
Tom Mattingly

Afterword by Dr. John Staley, Jr. M.D.

CONTENTS

DEDICATION

John Ward

He gave us moments to remember over the course of his Tennessee broadcast career (1968-99 in football and 1964-99 in basketball), as he told the story of young men accomplishing great things for Tennessee on the gridiron and hardwood. His broadcast style was light years ahead of its time, a staccato baritone many have tried to emulate, but no one has ever duplicated. Over the years, listeners heard Ward's calls of the great plays in Tennessee football and basketball, peppered by such famous phrases as "It's football time in Tennessee!), "Bottom!", "Give it to him!", "Did he make it? He made it!", and "Give him six!" Ward's calls have resonated over the years, not only though the mind's eye, but also through the magic of audio and videotape, and are savored as a part of life wherever Vol fans gather. He defined each great moment for Tennessee fans, who are able to call those memories up at a moment's notice. He was truly a legend, although he never thought of himself that way. When he spoke, Tennessee fans listened.

As we say, "Thanks for the memories," we dedicate this book to the life and memory of the "Voice of the Vols," John Ward (1930-2018).

ACKNOWLEDGEMENTS

IN WRITING a book such as this one, the destination is well worth the journey. We gratefully acknowledge the support we received from Joe McCamish of McCamish Media in Knoxville. He's ridden herd on this project from the word go, through good times and bad, always supportive, always helpful. Each of us is grateful to the other for their advice, counsel, and support, as this manuscript has progressed from a solitary blank page to a finished product.

We are also appreciative of those who shared so their stories so bountifully with us: Larry Pratt, Allan Jones, John C. (Thunder) Thornton, James A. Haslam, II, James A. Haslam, III, Dr. Joseph E. Johnson, Tony Basilio, Jayson Swain, Nathanael Rutherford, Marlin Lane, Mykelle McDaniel, Shawte-Amoure Simmons, Eric Waddell, and Taeler Dowdy.

We also thank our families, who were so supportive during the creative process. Tom remembers the contributions of his wife, Susan, children Sam and Alice, son-in-law Brad McManus, and grandchildren, Gavin Stewart McManus and Eli Thomas McManus. Celina wishes to acknowledge the rebels of the Rocky Top ReVOLution, including Michael Massey, Nathan D. Escue, Bo Ransom, Santa Vol, Spencer Barnett, Josh Parrott, Sam Thompson, Travis Sweat, Larry Hilderbrand, Raynard

Williams, Kevin Cowling, Gina Lee, Brian Gillespie, Jacob Whitehead, Mike L., Jan Teal, Pruitt, Dale Hutcherson, Matthew Hays, Kim Davis, Zack VanMeter, Kyle Schmidt, Nick Hayes, Ken Cowell, Audrey Caylor, and Michael Rose. They epitomize why Vol Nation is the best fan base in college football.

Celina would also like to thank her husband, Shannon. Despite his unfortunate loyalty to Ohio State University, he was always understanding of why the house didn't get cleaned for over a month.

Finally, we thank the players and coaches, who have contributed so much to the Tennessee tradition and enriched each of our lives as well.

So "here's to you, old Tennessee," as the chorus to Mary Fleming Meek's "Alma Mater" tells us. It's been quite a run. We've been with the Big Orange for more than 100 years between us, and we plan on being there for many more.

Knoxville, Tennessee and Lancaster, Ohio

November 11, 2018

INTRODUCTION BY CELINA SUMMERS

November 5, 2018

A YEAR ago today, I couldn't have imagined sitting at my desk to write this sort of book. Sure, I was accustomed to putting my opinions about the University of Tennessee athletic programs down on paper and out there online. But a year ago today, we were still unaware of how thoroughly the UT system was going to break down three weeks in the future. We were unaware of the chaotic atmosphere behind the scenes, of the factions and infighting, and of the total lack of leadership that was steering the course of UT's future.

In some respects, the events that took place between November 26 and December 1 of 2017 were the worst things that could have happened to a major university, and especially the one that Tennessee fans love so much. In others, though, the uprising that began on Schiano Sunday and ended with the hiring of Phillip Fulmer as athletic director was the best thing that ever could have happened at UT.

The Vol ReVOLution.

If nothing else, the world can take away one thing about the ReVOLution. If the hallowed halls of academia are cluttered with agendas and if they cannot right their own ship, fans and alumni of these schools can step in and take the power unto themselves to right the ship for them. Make no mistake: Tennessee fans spoke in one voice against the proposed hire of former Rutgers coach Greg Schiano to replace Butch Jones, and in that voice, they proclaimed, "We are the caretakers now."

We are the caretakers now. What an extraordinary thing for a fan base that's been regularly maligned and characterized as hillbillies by the national media to say. But the fact of the matter is that the hillbillies, the rubes, the ridge runners, the—as CBS Sports' Dennis Dodd infamously said during the uprising—"the Bubbas from the trailer park at Pidgeon (sic) Forge" saved Tennessee that week. Not from a bad coaching hire or media backlash. The fans saved Tennessee from its own decision-makers, preventing them from carrying out yet another horrible plan of action for their beloved university.

And in the process, the fans served as a buffer between that backlash and the university. Because the media was focused on near-universal disapproval of a fan base that had the audacity to say "no", the university was spared the brunt of the repercussions from a nearly catastrophic sequence of events that began in the early 2000s and finally halted in the most publicly embarrassing fashion after those six days in 2017.

The University of Tennessee owes its fans a huge debt.

When Tom Mattingly and I set out to write this

book, we wanted to approach the ReVOLution from two different angles. Tom, of course, is the Vol Historian. He has not only been a fan of Tennessee for over six decades, but he had a twenty-year career covering the Vols from inside the UT Sports Information Department. No one knows more about UT than Tom Mattingly.

As for me, I've loved Tennessee since I was a kid growing up in Clarksville. I am not an alum like Tom is. I've not worked the Knoxville beat as a journalist. My career path has taken me down a far different road. But my fandom began when the Artful Dodger was under center. I was five in 1972, turned six that year on the Third Monday in October, I carried Neyland's Seven Maxims from Tennessee to Florida, to Ohio and New York, to Louisiana and back to Ohio again. And in 2015, I began writing columns for the Orange and White Report about Tennessee athletics as a welcome break from writing and editing fiction full time. I have walked the same path that every other Tennessee fan has walked—including Tom.

But what makes this partnership work is same thing that makes the eclectic Tennessee fan base so vibrant and vital. Tom writes with all the knowledge and old school charm of the great sportswriters from the last half-decade, the golden age of sport journalism. I'm a little snarkier, a little more hardcore and opinionated, with a style that's nowhere near journalistic. And yet, we share the same goals for this story.

Like our fellow fans, we wanted to find out the real story of what happened to Tennessee football...what caused our beloved university to break down in such a public and humiliating fashion. Between the two of us, we wanted to open doors that might not have ever been opened before. And in the process, we uncovered a story that is remarkable for its unique flavor.

A Tennessee flavor.

Make no mistake—the story of the Vol ReVOLution has moments at its core that are uglier, perhaps, than anyone knew or guessed. But there are also moments of joy and triumph and true resolution that uplifted us both.

At the end of the day, the University of Tennessee has provided us with a lot of joy and heartbreak, just like they have for you, most likely. Tom and I wanted to explore those mountaintops and the valleys both. By coming at the ReVOLution from our two differing points of view, we were able to explore the fullness of the entire story in a way I don't think anyone else could have. Tom sets up the historical elements that create the perfect storm of events in the UTAD which resulted in the ReVOLution, and I take the story through the recent history of the football program and the uprising itself.

Together, we are the Tennessee fan base. Our differences epitomize the divide in Vol Nation, but those differences are forgotten when it comes to our love for UT—just like the differences of hundreds of thousands of people were discarded a year ago when we all came together to save UT football.

But then, we veered off the normal path for books like this. For one thing, we let the thought influencers and decision makers around the Tennessee program tell their own stories in their own words. Those interviews are presented verbatim, without editing or journalistic agenda.

For another, the thoughts of the regular Tennessee fan is presented. The importance of those voices was solidified during the ReVOLution last year. Those voices deserve to be heard in this book as well.

After all, it's their story.

Our dual perspective allowed us to see the entire story and relate it to longtime fans and new arrivals in the Tennessee community. The long-time insider, and the only recently heard outsider. The historian and the columnist. The first-hand knowledge that stretches back to the Neyland era, and the observer's eye that's looking to the future. The old school sportswriter and the new school online whiz. Between us, we bridge over six decades of Tennessee fandom.

And just like Vol Nation did last fall, we've come together to illuminate what really happened before, during, and after the ReVOLution.

As I write this, right now on the University of Maryland campus there is a massive student protest regarding the university's lack of oversight regarding their football program and the subsequent death of player Jordan McNair. Last week, the university released its report regarding that fatality, revealing negligent if not abusive practices undertaken by the coaching staff. But then, Maryland incomprehensibly reinstated beleaguered football coach DJ Durkin—only to fire him the following day due to the massive backlash from students, parents, players, and media.

Earlier this fall, Ohio State University football

coach Urban Meyer was caught up in a scandal when one of his assistant coaches, Zach Smith, was accused of domestic violence by his ex-wife, Courtney. As the story unfolded, it became clear that Meyer had been aware of the situation for a decade, dating back to his tenure at the University of Florida, where Smith also was on his staff. Meyer had deleted texts from his phone that allegedly tied him to the case. In addition, the coach kind of threw his own wife under the bus to protect his career when he said that his wife didn't share any of Courtney Smith's text conversations with him. After an abbreviated investigation, Smith was terminated and Meyer was disciplined by being suspended for the first three games of the year.

Tellingly, OSU didn't promote Greg Schiano, the Buckeyes' defensive coordinator and Meyer's top assistant, to serve as the interim coach for those three games. The administration, athletic department, and fan base were all silent about the conduct of the coach and the school. There were no protests in Columbus—save for the one protesting Meyer's suspension—and the athletic director who was so shocked that UT fans would question Schiano because he'd been vetted thoroughly before being hired by the Buckeyes, found himself in a position less than a year later where he had to swallow his own words and give someone else the interim coaching job.

Two other major universities. Two other coaching situations where abuses were revealed. Two different fan bases—one that rose up to demand the school do the right thing, and the other that valued wins over integrity.

Two other moments where the Vol ReVOLution

was vindicated—moments where the uprising on Rocky Top served as a blueprint for the rest of college football fandom.

That's what this book is really about—empowered fans finding their voices, taking back their power, and in the process finding a way to change college football for the better. Not just in Knoxville or Baltimore or Columbus, but every college community. We take a look at the heritage of Tennessee and its fans, the series of events that led to over a decade of problems in the athletic department and beyond, and how the fans at all levels of power and prestige stood up and took their university back. We tell stories that have never been brought to light and reveal the hidden depths of a nightmare that will horrify UT fans when they hear it. We dissect the ReVOLution, because we understand why it happened—something a slew of national pundits should have taken the time to learn before they popped off with their prejudicial stereotypes about a fan base that had endured its last insult.

I'm not the person who was smart enough to first say that the ReVOLution was a blueprint for other fan bases. The person who first said that was Checker Neyland co-founder Spencer Barnett, when I was talking to him about telling this story last winter. But as Tom and I worked our way through this story, we both came to understand that Spencer was right. The ReVOLution *is* a blueprint, and it's already impacting other schools, other programs, other athletes and fans. So it's essential that the real story of the ReVOLution is told from points of view that are not necessarily seen by the rest of the world.

And that includes the fans.

If we're going to create a blueprint, we need to do it right.

So here's the story of the Vol ReVOLution—the empowerment of the fans, the vindication of a beloved coach, and the taking back of a storied university athletic program from those who'd unwittingly steered it nearly to destruction.

Part I | Sowing the Seeds of ReVOLution

By Tom Mattingly

VOLUNTEERS HISTORY

"When you're a Vols fan, you're already halfway to heaven. You are expected to dress louder, yell louder, spend more, suffer more, exult more and care more. You usually go everywhere the team goes. You mix and mingle with friend and foe alike. You revel in victory and die in defeat. But either way, you always come back for more." —Russ Bebb, Three Decades of Big Orange Football, 1964-93

AFTER NEARLY a lifetime of watching, writing, and commenting about sports, especially University of Tennessee athletics and its impact on otherwise sane and sensible people, the time has come to sit down and rationally consider what all the fuss is about.

What stirred my interest in doing this book was the opportunity to examine the reasons the Tennessee athletic program commands such attention from the school's fan base. Why have the past twenty years been so hard on Vols fans? The Vols had been on top of the college football world in 1998 but their fortunes had plummeted since then in a frustrating series of bad decisions, bad hires, and other missteps. The result was a time frame beginning in November 2017 in which the fan base reasserted itself and reclaimed control over the program they have loved over the years.

Everybody has a story about their fandom, how they have stayed ever faithful over the years. Here is mine.

Tennessee football is an event, a happening, even when some fans ended up traveling more than 5,000 miles in September 1981 to see Tennessee lose at Georgia 44-0 and at Southern Cal 43-7 on successive weekends. In the latter game, fans saw Traveler, the famed USC mascot, nearly keel over from exhaustion from circling the field after each score. My friend Doug Jones and I were part of that trip and have never regretted it. Over the years, Vols fans have been there for the highs…and the lows.

Over the years, Tennessee fans have been known to go to great lengths to show their support for their team. One such fan is Knoxvillian Doug (Snapper) Morgan, who was once asked if he'd rather beat Alabama or Florida. His answer was to the point: "Alabama, every day of the week and twice on Sunday." Morgan also has been known to shave and tape his ankles and eat baby food the day of a game. By any measure, those two examples define the term dedication.

I remember walking through a west side gate into what was then Shields-Watkins Field in the early afternoon hours of October 5, 1957. Tennessee was playing Mississippi State in the second game of the season. Bowden Wyatt was in his third season as head coach, and Tennessee fans were worried about two consecutive losses, to Baylor in the 1957 Sugar Bowl and the season-opener against Auburn.

Tennessee was in their uniquely orange jerseys on the east side of the field, while State was headquartered on the west side. The Vols won that day by 14-9, as tailback Bobby Gordon returned a punt fifty-five yards for the winning score, going down the east sideline toward the north end in the waning seconds. I remember the excitement that enveloped the stadium even though the attendance that day, according to the next day's Knoxville News Sentinel, was estimated in the 25,000 range in a stadium with a capacity of 46,390, based on an expansion of 15,000 seats at the south end in 1948.

People have asked me all the time what it was like going to games with much smaller crowds during those long-ago days in the mid-1950s. The answer is that the games were just as exciting as they are today. I always tell them it was a tough trip to Knoxville in those pre-Interstate days from whatever direction a fan might be coming. The 1957 team averaged 35,801 fans in the seats, slightly more than the 33,318 average crowd the 1956 SEC champions had drawn. The 1965 squad averaged 41,951, while the 1967 SEC title team had averaged 53,689. Stadium capacity and attendance numbers have climbed steadily since then.

The action was just as intense, and the fans were into the games much as they are today. In those days, the college football season started, almost without fail, on the last Saturday in September. As the 1960s progressed, games began starting earlier in the month, and there were more of them. The Vols first played a twelve-game schedule in 1970 and have even played thirteen on several occasions since then. The 2007 squad had a fourteen-game run.

The excitement of each game led logically to the next day's coverage, as Tennessee football finally returned to the pages of the city's newspapers after a hiatus that had lasted way too long.

For football fans in Knoxville and anybody else who had access to the newspaper in those pre-internet days, the sports pages of the Sunday Knoxville News Sentinel compiled everything important about the preceding day's game. There was a soothing stability to its coverage.

There was a column about the game on the front page (e.g., "Fans Forget About Vols' Losses in Thrill of Last-Minute Victory" after the Mississippi State game), reflecting the ambience of the day before. On the first page of the sports section, there was a game story by Frank (Red) Bailes or Marvin West (with alternating bold and regular type paragraphs) and a game column penned by sports editor Tom Siler (unless he were covering another SEC game or the World Series).

The main headline was always a classic, e.g., "Gordon's Run Powers Vols in 14-9 Win" on September 5, 1957; "Vols Make a Wreck of Rambling Tech, 22-14" from Nov. 7, 1964; or "SEC Leading Vols 'Curt-tail' Georgia, 17-3" from Nov. 1, 1969.

Many times, a sidebar game story by Roland Julian, among others, gave additional perspective to the main story, also on page one, plus a line score, stat box, and other game notes. The stat box always had a title, such as "Great Scott!" That title came on October 25, 1970, when Bobby Scott threw the ball all over Shields-Watkins Field for 385 yards in a 38-7 win over Florida.

A pithy summary of one of the game's high moments was in a box near the bottom of the page. For example: "Coach, Officials Differ: LaSorsa's Run Looked like Fumble...Bryant," from Oct. 16, 1960, after Alabama's Bear Bryant disagreed with the call on a defensive touchdown scored by Vols captain Mike LaSorsa in a 20-7 Vols win.

There was also a regional summary of all the Saturday scores.

Page three yielded a full dose of game photos. These pictures often included little paste-on cartoons, showing the ball and the path the running back or pass receiver was taking down the field. Many times this path would stretch across three pictures. There was a female cartoon cheerleader who signaled "Touchdown!" when someone scored. Some people liked this novel touch. Others didn't.

KNS cartoonist Bill Dyer's DyerGram was the dominant feature on page four, along with the "jump" of the first page game story.

Dyer's magnum opus was a masterpiece of sports cartooning. "Dyer chronicled the games in pen and ink with a touch of whimsy thrown in for good measure," the late former Vols fullback and UT professor Andy Kozar has written. "Over the years, journalists have told the story of sports in a number of different ways. Bill Dyer did it with cartoons interspersed between the play-by-play of the game."

While he had a seat in the press box at home games, Dyer relied on George Mooney's and John Ward's Vol Network broadcasts for games away from Knoxville and filled in the gaps as best he could.

Dyer had rookie Vols mascot Smokey in tears after the 1953 Mississippi State game (State 26, Tennessee 0, on Sept. 26). The 1965 UCLA game (Tennessee 37, UCLA 34, on Dec. 4) had to have worn Bill out.

Dyer had to keep pace with the ebbs and flows of ten touchdowns, a field goal, and a two-point conversion: "UCLA took the stage first at the Rosebonnet a-go go…then the Vols danced the next three numbers to intermission. UCLA got the action and routines got wilder and wilder. The older generation never saw the likes of such head knocking! When it was over, there were broken records all over the joint!"

Dyer covered the Vols from the 1934 North Carolina game through the 1976 Florida game. He died during the open week between Florida and Memphis State.

In those days, the News-Sentinel also provided a participation chart, listing every player who got into the game by position. A reporter interviewed future opponent scouts and other dignitaries in the press box.

I also remember the Hold That Line show on WATE Radio, when Vols fans called 524-4657 after each game. The Slippery Rock University score was always much in demand, almost as much as the Tennessee score. The program would be a snoozer today, given that only the on-air talent's voice could be heard and no one could vent, however exercised they might have been.

Over the years, fans were treated to many great programs, like the 50-Yardline show with Chuck Ketron or Grandstand Quarterback with ex-Vols player Freddie Moses. Pigskin Predictions with Russ Bebb, E.L. "Tip" Tipton, Ben Byrd, and Ed Harris was another classic look at college football in those days. Those programs were a delightful prelude to the Tennessee game.

During the 1968 Georgia game, someone called

the Neyland Stadium press box (telephone number supposedly unlisted) during the 1968 Georgia game and reminded whoever answered the phone, likely the school's beloved Sports Information Director Haywood Harris, that quarterback Bubba Wyche's name was "Why-ch" not "Witch," as Chris Schenkel and Bud Wilkinson had been saying on ABC. As they do today, Vols fans are always paying close attention to the broadcast, whether on radio or television.

Reading the News Sentinel coverage of Vols contests on the Knox County Public Library Web site or on microfilm at the University of Tennessee library is a trip through time. There's always something special about remembering those long-ago games, the games of our youth.

And the way sportswriters and photographers covered them.

My father was a minister, and there were always men in the church who had tickets, mostly on the west side of the stadium, more likely than not in Section V. Men wore coats and ties to the game, and women were dressed in their Sunday finest. As the years passed, I remember listening to Mooney calling the games from 1952-67, assisted by former Vols wingback Bob Foxx on the Texaco Radio Network. "This is the Texaco Radio Network. Get ready for the kickoff!" was Mooney's tag line.

Ward came along in 1968 staying through 1998, and the Vols program continued to reach for the stars. These were fascinating times, whether I was at the game, in the front yard raking leaves, or listening to the game in the car while going somewhere else. The Vols were *my* team, and life revolved around their fortunes. And still does. "It's football time in Tennessee!" brings back memories of Ward.

High school students could sit in Section X for a dollar, and that was my location for any number of games before heading off to college in 1966. Doug Dickey was the coach from 1964 through 1969, building the program to the point Vols fans felt comfortable about the Vols' chances of winning every time out.

Season tickets came along in 1972, in Section OO, Row 20. But I sat more often in Section PP, row 14, with friends Doug Jones, Jim Gentry, Bob Sullivan, and Jack Dixon. I went to nearly all the games with one or all of them, and we experienced some wonderful moments. We were there every weekend, wherever the Vols played. There were often early departures on Saturday morning and equally early arrivals home on Sunday morning. Sometimes the trips started early on Friday and continued well into Sunday.

In December 1986, there was a small article in the News Sentinel about athletic department staff member Gibson Smith leaving the athletic department for seemingly greener pastures. He was the editor of a UT publication called VOLUNTEERS Magazine/Smokey's Tale, an athletic department official publication. I received a number of calls from friends about the position and remember Harris calling one day about "doing some writing," and my course was set.

I was on staff with UTAD from January 6, 1987, on, through April 30, 2005. My future wife, the former Susan Compton, and I had gone to games in 1985 and

1986, with my having a parking pass proving significant as a winning edge while dating. That opened the door to a wonderful relationship, now numbering more than thirty years, starting January 29, 1988. Once I went to work for the Sports Information Office in early 1987, however, I was in the press box that fall, and on through the years, and she and our family, Sam and Alice Compton, watched the game from Section OO, Row 8. Grandsons Gavin and Eli McManus are now often part of our travel squad to Neyland Stadium.

My office was next to a two-seater restroom in Stokely Athletics Center, a location that allowed me to meet a number of interesting people. My first day, Lindsey Nelson, a Tennessee alum who made it big in radio and television sports, was among the first, as was head football coach Johnny Majors.

Here's word about his first name. His mother, John Elizabeth Bobo Majors, once told me that she sent sons John, Bill, and Bob to Knoxville, and they became better known, at least for publicity purposes, as Johnny, Billy, and Bobby. Johnny Majors tended to introduce himself as John. She was not happy with that turn of events.

One of my most interesting and intriguing assignments, other than producing a weekly newsletter and a quarterly magazine, involved working with the visiting team under the south end where the dressing room was located in the football stadium and near the visitors' quarters at Thompson-Boling Arena in hoops. I was charged with running the interview room and procuring a post-game statement from the opposing coach.

Most Tennessee fans have seen the visiting teams

trot onto the field to a scattered chorus of boos, but that's just part of the story. There's drama underneath the south end after each game precious few people get to witness.

The current visiting team area dates to the 1948 stadium expansion at the south end, with a couple of additions in the more than seventy years since. This area is a continuous hub of activity on a number of fronts after the game, the corridor often being crowded with training supplies as well as food for the post-game trip to the airport and the plane home.

The sound of cleats on carpet laid down over concrete dominated the area, with the uniquely football sights and smells of blood, sweat, and grass. Trainers doled out pills of one kind or another, making notes as to who received what. Players grumbled to themselves over missed tackles, dropped passes, and bad calls. If the opponent was Alabama, Florida, Georgia or Vanderbilt, there were occasional obscenity-laced tirades directed their way by "fans" exiting the stadium down a maze of ramps.

After the 1990 Notre Dame game, Lou Holtz talked to Dick Vitale and Regis Philbin in the tunnel before going to his post-game interview. A gaggle of priests greeted Fighting Irish players as they entered the dressing room, regardless of the game's outcome.

When Tennessee defeated Florida in 1998, there was a massive celebration under the goal post near the visitor's tunnel. There were a number of injuries, and the media room was converted into a mini-infirmary. Steve Spurrier did his post-game media conference in a small boiler room and seemed flummoxed by the set-up.

Occasionally, coaches' comments were more for local media consumption. In 1999, Memphis, formerly Memphis State, once known to most Vols fans as Tiger High, lost a 17-16 decision on Homecoming Day. Rip Scherer, the only Tigers coach to defeat Tennessee (21-17 in 1996), tore into Memphis beat writers for doubting the courage and character of his team.

After the 2001 South Carolina game, when there had been a malfunction with the game clock, Holtz told the media how easy it was to keep the time: "One thousand one, one thousand two, one thousand three."

Two years before, when the game ball had been delivered to midfield by a paratrooper, Holtz reminded everyone that he too had jumped out of a plane, one of the hundred or so things on his adult life to-do list—like eating dinner at the White House, being head coach at Notre Dame, winning a national championship, etc. He always had something pertinent to say, whatever the situation.

Then came the 2002 season, when Alabama dispatched the Vols 34-14. Tide Coach Dennis Franchione did his post-game interview perfunctorily, looking very much like the loneliest man in Neyland Stadium, while his team celebrated loudly in the next room. Coach Fran, as he was known, requested that the media refrain from reporting on the language being used in the dressing room next door. I later found out he had been making plans to change his address from Tuscaloosa to College Station, Texas.

Kentucky coach Guy Morriss's post-game comments after the 2002 game were impressive. The game with the Vols had come three weeks after a real downer for the Wildcat program. The so-called Bluegrass Miracle, when Morriss was doused with Gatorade seconds before LSU completed a 74-yard Hail Mary pass to steal the win from UK, was a complete and total blow to the solar plexus.

I told Kentucky AD Mitch Barnhart, a former colleague, how well Morriss had done in the media room, noting that Guy was a definite keeper. Mitch seemed surprised at my remarks, and, a few days later, I found out why when Morriss left Lexington to become head coach at Baylor.

UNLV head coach John Robinson was holding court after his team lost in the 2004 season opener. In the midst of his remarks, former USC and Cincinnati Bengals offensive tackle Anthony Munoz tried to ease into the room, as if someone his size—6-foot-6, 278 pounds—could do so anywhere. His son, Michael, was an offensive lineman for the Vols. After spotting Anthony, Robinson, who had coached him at Southern Cal where he was an All-American selection in 1978-79, stopped in mid-sentence and told the assembled media, "There's the greatest offensive lineman ever to play this game."

After the 2006 LSU game, I remember walking into the media room and spotting someone being interviewed who looked suspiciously like an offensive tackle. "Which one of the linemen is that?" I queried. The LSU rep said it wasn't a lineman; he just looked like one. Actually, it was quarterback JaMarcus Russell.

Sometimes it was a shock when the inside door opened and coaches such as Spurrier or Mark Richt strode into the room. Spurrier always had a one-liner at the ready, something about "God looking after the Gators" after the controversial finish of the 2000 game. One media cynic said afterwards it wasn't really the Almighty who had aided Florida. The SEC official who ruled Jabar Gaffney had caught the game-winning TD pass was actually the culprit.

On the other hand, Richt was generally more restrained, considering every word, speaking in measured coach-speak. Media representatives generally got better copy from Spurrier.

There was never a dull moment after the game under the south end. The Vol Network is not likely to make a video of great moments in the visitors area, but that should not diminish in the least what goes on there. After all, it takes two to tangle on the gridiron.

Another dominant recollection from across the years was the Friday afternoon walk-though at an opposing stadium. The team charter landed, generally with a loud thump, and the buses went quickly to the stadium, whether it was Florida Field, Legion Field, Jordan-Hare Stadium, or any one of a number of other venues.

On those Fridays, everything was quiet at the stadium, but the storm was building as kickoff approached the next day and continued until the buses left for the airport and the trip home.

In 1990, the storm was amazingly real, when Auburn partisans rocked the team buses on their arrival at the stadium. Not with real rocks, mind you, but with a concerted effort to push the buses back and forth, maybe even push them over.

In 2000, Georgia fans were so ecstatic with a 21-10 victory, their first over the Vols since 1988, they nearly destroyed the famed hedges that surrounded the field at Sanford Stadium. Georgia was always an interesting trip, particularly the trip home, when team buses once traveled through post-game traffic for more than an hour to Atlanta to meet a Delta charter for a 30-minute flight home. Now the team flies hone from Athens on three smaller jets.

If you were at LSU, you could go to the southeast end and see where Steve DeLong and pals made the stop in the 1964 game that ended 3-3. Nearby, a real tiger in a cage surveyed its domain, located near the end zone and the visitors dressing room.

If you happened to be standing on Legion Field, there was always a visit to the west side, north end. If you went to the thirty-one yard line, west side, north end, you could stand where Albert Dorsey took in the last of his three interceptions off Ken "The Snake" Stabler in the fourth quarter for a score to give the Vols a 24-13 victory, its first over Bama since 1960.

That game so caught the attention of the fan base to the point that one gentleman called the News Sentinel Sports Department with the following question.

"A bunch of us fellows were wondering about Coach Dickey's return from Birmingham. Does he intend to come up on the plane with the team, or will he just walk up the river?"

He was serious. Big wins tend to have that type impact on Tennessee fans. That happened on Saturday night, October 21, 1967.

You could also go to the east side, south end, thirty-four yard line, and see Alan Cockrell as he checked off at the line of scrimmage and sent Johnnie Jones around left end on a play officially known as "49 Option," sixty-one yards for a score. The year was 1983, and my memory of Jones emerging from the press box shadows into the bright sunshine at the northeast corner where the Tennessee fans were sitting is fresh.

In 1980, Vols fans were suffused with victory, this time over Georgia Tech, and wrote a check they weren't able to cash when Alabama was up next on the Vols' schedule.

Near the end of Tennessee's 23-10 victory, Vols fans in the southeast corner began an ominous chant: "We want Bama! We want Bama!" The Vols and Tide played in Knoxville the next Saturday, and the game was hyped to the heavens. Alabama showed up the next week and the Vols had them right where they wanted. Or so they thought. On a very rainy day, the final score was Alabama 27, Tennessee 0.

If you were at the Orange Bowl in Miami, you could find the spot near the 33-yard line, west end, from which Karl Kremser lined up the potential game-winner against Oklahoma on New Year's Day 1968. That boot faded to the right, although Vols signal-caller Dewey Warren, never a shrinking violet, has contended over the years the kick was good.

The Vols pulled off a major upset there in 2003. That game triggered a major emotional outburst from

Canes tight end Kellen Winslow, Jr. that made national headlines, but there was an untold story going back to the Vols' arrival at the stadium. Sometimes you win a game before you win it. There are times that seemingly little things make a difference.

Tennessee showed up at the Orange Bowl for the first time in more than thirty-five years for a contest with Miami. The Hurricanes had defeated the Vols 26-3 in Knoxville a year earlier in a game that wasn't that close, and Vols fans had mentally chalked up the 2003 contest as a loss in their preseason analysis.

That early November day, the Vols surprised everybody but themselves. When the Vols came to the stadium early that morning, at ten am or so, several of the players had a prayer circle on the field as was their tradition to help prepare them for the game. That was something Mitchell started and, it grew and grew.

The Vols players were subject to some remarks of an uncomplimentary nature, and that's putting it mildly, from Miami fans in that area of the field, but they didn't buckle, didn't back down, or get otherwise deterred from accomplishing their intended business. They stayed right where they were and never flinched.

Leaving the field, team chaplain James "Mitch" Mitchell looked at one of them and said, "That's spiritual warfare. That's what I've been telling you about."

The Vols took it to heart and took an upset win by 10-6, one that no one really expected. The Orange Bowl is not there anymore, having been demolished in 2008. The memories still linger, however.

At Bryant-Denny Stadium in Tuscaloosa, you could go to the near corner at the north end and see the spot where in 2003 Jason Allen, an Alabamian playing for Tennessee, knocked down a final toss that cinched a Vols victory. The final that day was 51-43 in five overtimes. The series had returned to Tuscaloosa in 1999, and the Vols had won that season and in 2001 and 2003.

If the game was at Notre Dame, you'd hear Johnny Majors talk about games against the Fighting Irish when he was at Pittsburgh in the mid-1970s. He once said the grass at Notre Dame Stadium was, "Higher than an Iowa corn field." And he was right. Artificial turf now adorns that famed greensward, for good or for bad.

I found it fascinating to be in the tunnel in which Miami and Notre Dame once slugged it out in the famous Catholics versus Convicts game on October 15, 1988. I found it equally fascinating to be in the visitor's dressing room, the one with the television monitor. The area looked as if it hadn't seen a wet rag since the days of Knute Rockne and George Gipp.

The Vols won 28-18 in 2001. With the game on the line, quarterback Casey Clausen led the way, scoring the clinching touchdown right there in front of the shadow of Touchdown Jesus.

At Florida Field, you could stand on either one-yard line and visualize a ninety-nine-yard touchdown drive, one that happened quickly from south to north in 1977, as Kelsey Finch went ninety-nine yards for the score on third and ten. The other was a more workmanlike drive in 1971, headed north to south, capped by a TD pass from Phil Pierce to Stan Trott.

You could also go to the northeast corner, where officials adjudged a Florida punt going out of bounds inside the Tennessee one yard-line. Bill Battle earned one of the shortest penalties in the history of the Vols program by debating the call...vociferously. Game officials assessed the unsportsmanlike conduct foul by picking the ball up and setting it down. The ball didn't move. It was that close to the goal.

If you were at Auburn, you could go to the south thirty-three yard line and imagine a sixty-seven yard TD run by Jamal Lewis that was a thing of beauty, happening shortly before he banged up a knee and was lost for the season.

You could also go to the north one-yard line, where Vols defenders stopped Auburn four consecutive times after a fumble had placed the defense in serious jeopardy. Auburn had four tries at the end zone, but all the Tigers earned was grass stains. Raynoch Thompson led the Vols' defensive charge in one of the most memorable moments of that national championship season... or any other time.

There were other amazing times in the late 1990s and early 2000s.

During those times, collegiate publishers also made a beeline to my office in the now-vacated Stokely Athletic Center on campus. Charley Kiger of UMI Press in Charlotte, North Carolina, arrived in mid-1999, seeking someone to write the Archie-authorized collegiate biography of Peyton Manning.

He walked by my office three times before I corralled him and had him sit down. It didn't take long to get my name on a contract. The book was titled *Peyton Manning: The Tennessee Years.*

Here are a couple of notes about Peyton's book. My mother was never a great football fan, but, once the book came out, she became one of Peyton's biggest fans, calling my office after each of Peyton's games to discuss his performance that weekend.

Shortly after the book came out, the phone rang, and there was a familiar voice at the other end of the line. "Tom, this is Archie Manning. I just wanted you to know you did a fine job on Peyton's book." I remember saying thanks or something similar. The call ended quickly.

"Well, bye," he said.

And that was that.

In 2003, Mike Hamilton called and suggested a story on the fiftieth anniversary of the contest that brought Brooks' Blue Smokey to campus as Tennessee's Bluetick Coonhound mascot. That was for VOLUNTEERS Magazine. That ultimately led to a book published by the University of Tennessee Press called *Smokey: The True Stories behind the University of Tennessee Famous Mascot,* co-authored by Earl Hudson, brother-in-law of Smokey's original owner, Reverend W. C. Brooks. The Brooks and Hudson families have cared for the ten dogs that have represented the school over the years. The book version of the Smokey story came out in 2012.

In 2005, Charlie Anderson, formerly of Knoxville's Anderson News, found me outside Neyland Stadium one spring day in 2005 and offered me the chance to do a history of Tennessee football that became the first in a series of *Vault Books* published by Whitman Press in Atlanta. That one came out in 2006, the Monday after the season-opening triumph over California.

Tom Payton of Hill Street press in Athens, Georgia, offered me the *Tennessee Trivia Book* that same year, which arrived at bookstores in 2007.

A second version of the Tennessee Vault came out in 2009, right after the hiring of Lane Kiffin as Tennessee's head coach, with a sticker attached reading "Welcome Lane Kiffin." A great many of those stickers disappeared quickly when Kiffin bolted to Southern Cal in January 2010. Vols fans were very unforgiving when Lane left, particularly with the timing of the move.

Starting in 2007, the Knoxville News Sentinel gave me the opportunity to write about the players, coaches, administrators, and others who have been associated with Tennessee orange over the years. These efforts have been in the form of columns, blogs, and/or more than 150 obituary stories, ranging from tributes to Harris, Ward, Bill Anderson, Ben Byrd, W. J. Julian, and Russ Bebb, to A.W. Davis, Austin Denney, Bob Davis, Jimmy England, Doug Atkins, Kathleen Elam, and all points in between. My nom de plume was the "Vol Historian." That led to me becoming an honorary T-Club member in 2009, thanks to the efforts of Charles Davis, a former Vols defensive back.

If you listen carefully, the echoes of those Saturday afternoons and evenings past can be carefully discerned. There is enough history in the air to satisfy the most hardened observer.

Mention any game and a flood of remembrances

of the good times following players wearing orange and white comes quickly. Following the Vols, home and away, has brought me a lifetime of memories. That's the beauty of it all, that the memory banks really don't have to work overtime. That's the power of history, the power of watching and listening carefully. Fans remember the good and the bad... and that's good.

It's been a good run for more than sixty years.

There's one game, however, that stands out above the rest. That game was played on January 4, 1999, in Tempe, Arizona.

A NIGHT TO REMEMBER

"I want to tell you again, guys, that I love every one of you, love what you stand for, love how you've gone about your business this year and grown as a football team. You have an opportunity tonight that doesn't come around every day. It's been forty-seven years since Tennessee football players have pulled on that orange jersey and had a chance to compete for a national championship. It doesn't get any better than this. Lay it on the line. You do not have to play perfect, but play your butts off. Take a lot of pride in those orange jerseys as you hit the field tonight." —Phillip Fulmer, Fiesta Bowl Pre-Game Speech, January 4, 1999

FOR TENNESSEE football fans, wherever they might have been, the night of January 4, 1999, created all kinds of memories. While Vols fans had experienced many big moments over the past fifty years, this was the only mountaintop experience.

The 1998 season saw everything fall into place, as the gods of football smiled on the Vols at exactly the right times. The Vols won with "great team chemistry, luck, talent and a powerful mixture of fire and ice," wrote the Knoxville News Sentinel's John Adams.

Over the years, the 1982 Alabama game which broke an eleven-game losing streak to the Crimson Tide, the 1986 Sugar Bowl game against Miami, and the 1991 comeback win at Notre Dame came close to creating this type of excitement across Big Orange Country. But the 1999 Fiesta Bowl game topped them all.

The number one-rated Vols and the second-ranked Florida State Seminoles were playing for the first Bowl Championship Series (BCS) national title at the Fiesta Bowl, at Sun Devil Stadium, in Tempe, Arizona. The Vols entered the game with a 12-0 record, winners of forty-four of their last forty-nine games, while the Seminoles came in at 11-1, winners of forty-three of their last forty-eight.

On November 7th Michigan State had defeated Ohio State 28-14 to move the Vols to the top of the polls. Tennessee was ranked number one for the first time since November 17, 1956.

Although the Vols topped the national wire service polls, the Seminoles were still a betting favorite at five and a half points, despite having reserve sophomore quarterback Marcus Outzen at the helm in only his third start. Fellow sophomore and starting signal-caller Chris Weinke, now a member of the Tennessee coaching staff as the running backs coach under head coach Jeremy Pruitt, had been injured in Florida State's game against Virginia and could not play.

The national media were likewise convinced the Seminoles would be too much for the Vols to handle. The pundits, the self-proclaimed intelligentsia of college football, decreed that Florida State had too much history, too much big game experience, and too much Bobby Bowden on the sideline to lose to Tennessee. That's the aura that Bowden's Seminoles brought to the game. There were two other reasons the experts came down on Florida State's side. The Seminoles had the nation's top-rated defense, allowing only 214.8 yards per game, and also had a brilliant wide receiver in Peter Warrick.

This was the same media who had also predicted that Tennessee would be hard-pressed to match its 11-2 record from a year earlier. Sports pundits believed that Tennessee had too little big-game experience, too many ill-timed chokes, and too many question marks. The year before, the Vols had lost quarterback Peyton Manning, defensive back Terry Fair, and wide receiver Marcus Nash to the first round of the NFL draft. Defensive end Leonard Little, center Trey Teague, wide receiver Andy McCullough, and defensive back Corey Gaines had also departed for the professional ranks.

The Vols were replacing Manning with an untested junior: Tee Martin. Martin had seemed like a can't-miss prospect when he'd arrived on campus, but Manning's imposing shadow had loomed large over the Tennessee program in Martin's first two years on Rocky Top.

There were a great many doubters, including quite a few in the fan base, harkening to the memory of the 42-17 loss to Nebraska in the Orange Bowl on January 2, 1998. That beat-down the Vols had recalled almost daily through winter workouts, spring practice, and fall camp.

"Nebraska embarrassed us on national TV," wide receiver Peerless Price said in a story by David Williams of The Memphis Commercial Appeal on New Year's Day. "We didn't know how the big dogs play. We had to have a sense of urgency. If not, we wouldn't be here today."

Over the course of the season, the Vols defied the experts, however, defeating eight bowl teams, including six January bowl teams, four top ten teams, and three BCS bowl-bound teams en route to Tempe. As the season progressed, tickets were hard to come by no matter where the Vols had played.

Tennessee's schedule had been a gauntlet of near-misses, including hard-fought games against number seventeen Syracuse in the season opener at the Carrier Dome in upstate New York, an overtime win over then-second ranked Florida in the home season opener, a major comeback against tenth-ranked Arkansas in early November, and another close call in the SEC title game against twenty-third ranked Mississippi State.

The Vols also faced back-to-back road games against Auburn and number seven Georgia in early October. The Vols played their traditional Third Saturday in October game against Alabama on the fourth Saturday that season, thanks to the SEC's indifference regarding the date of one of football's traditional rivalries. The Vols played on the second Saturday in 1995 and on the fourth Saturday thirteen times between 1996 and 2018.

When Tennessee went to Nashville for the season finale against Vanderbilt, regular game excitement peaked when more than ten thousand fans showed up for the Vol Network's Kickoff Call-In Show in Centennial Park across the street from Vanderbilt Stadium. Fans came from across the state and beyond in such numbers that longtime Vols Network broadcaster John Ward, was moved to tears as he and sidekick Bill Anderson came on the set and saw nothing but fans dressed in orange as far as the eye could see. The stadium was also enveloped in orange that day, to the point that even Vandy players noticed the scope of Tennessee fan support.

The team had a quiet aura of confidence about it. Head coach Phillip Fulmer said his squad handled success in a mature and even-keeled manner. The bigger the hurdle, the better the Vols responded.

Throughout the season, the Vols lived by all of General Robert R. Neyland's seven Game Maxims, but found Maxim Three—"If at first the game or the breaks go against you, don't let up—put on more steam."—to be particularly relevant. The Vols might have been down at times, but they were never out. Somebody, or any number of somebodies, always seemed to make a big play, exactly when needed.

For example, the Vols had lost starting tailback Jamal Lewis, a freshman All-American selection in 1997, for the season with a knee injury during a 17-9 win at Auburn. Fellow running backs Travis Henry and Travis Stephens, a part of the Vols' 1997 recruiting class like Lewis, filled in for him admirably. The Vols were obviously a T-E-A-M in the best sense of the word.

"We always said we didn't have to be the best team in the country," Fulmer told the Sporting News' Tom Dienhart. "We just had to be the best on each Saturday."

Going into the game, the Vols were a tradition-rich program that had consistently competed at the highest levels of collegiate football over the course of decades of previous seasons. Tennessee's all-time record is now 837-388-53 as of Nov. 3, 2018, ranking tenth all-time in wins among NCAA Division I programs.

Tennessee fans had seen their team do nothing but win since the Vols first hit the gridiron in 1891, the year before Neyland had been born in Greenville, Texas.

But there was one nagging doubt, one elephant lurking in the room, that had plagued the Vols since early in their history. There was always seemed to be that one game—season-ending tie games with Kentucky in 1928, 1929, and 1931; the 1950 loss at Mississippi State; the 1952 Sugar Bowl loss to Maryland; the 1957 Sugar Bowl loss to Baylor; the 1967 UCLA game; the 1970 loss to Auburn; the 1995 loss to Florida; and particularly the 2001 loss to LSU in the SEC Championship game—that left fans wondering what might have been. Fans feared each game, worried that one misstep might unexpectedly arrive on the scene, but kept encouraging the team, coming to watch them play despite the way their muscles tensed up at every game…on every play.

Vol Nation's faith was rewarded when the Volunteers met every challenge.

Tennessee fans were in a heady state of mind heading to Arizona. The 1998 season had been the answer to uncounted dreams and prayers across Big Orange Country. Vols fans had always traveled well, but this one was special. No one used the word destiny, but it had to have been in the back of everybody's mind.

Fulmer wrote in *A Perfect Season* with Jeff Hagood: "After the Mississippi State game, a gentleman stopped me, wished me well, and said, 'I can't really afford to go Tempe, but my wife and I are going anyway. I want to be a part of history...I want to see the Vols win this national championship.'"

Vol Nation had waited anxiously for this moment and fans were going to make the most of it. The stage was set, and Tennessee fans were up to the challenge of helping their heroes grab the brass ring.

One night during game week, at an establishment outside of Tempe called Rawhide, the opening strains of *Rocky Top* were played. Vols loyalist Trey White hopped onto a table, put his hand over his heart, and exclaimed, "Ladies and gentlemen, our National Anthem!"

He then led the multitudes in a rousing, maybe even raucous, rendition of that amazing song.

As game time approached, Vols fans, gussied up in every shade of orange imaginable, found nearly every nook and cranny in the stands in Tempe. Fans lined the players' path to the stadium gates with a Fiesta Bowl version of the Vol Walk. Grown-ups felt what a young Vols fan, aged nine, had told his parents the day before the game:

"We'll never have another unhappy day, because tomorrow night we'll be national champions!"

Such was the exuberance of youth.

Such was the exuberance of the fan base.

Football fans, particularly those who grow up in the south, make critical and life-changing decisions about team allegiances in their most tender years and live with the impact of those decisions the rest of their lives.

The 1998 team had its share of stars, with five all-

SEC players, sophomore offensive guard Cosey Coleman, senior placekicker Jeff Hall, junior linebacker Raynoch Thompson, junior defensive tackle Darwin Walker, and senior linebacker Al Wilson. Offensive tackle Chad Clifton, defensive back Dwayne Goodrich, and wide receiver Peerless Price were second team selections.

Wilson, a native of Jackson, Tennessee, was a consensus All-American, a player who caught everybody's attention wherever he was on the field, with a forceful leadership style that separated him from the pack. Wilson's motivational abilities had come to the fore on December 6, 1997, when Tennessee trailed Auburn 20-10 at halftime of the SEC title game.

Wilson took over the Vols locker room, challenging nearly everyone, including captains and All-American selections Manning and Little, to step up their games. From that point on, everybody instinctively knew who the team's leader was.

"You need to know that Wilson spoke boldly, clearly, loudly," wrote former Knoxville News Sentinel and Scripps-Howard sports editor Marvin West. "His high-pitched voice cut through all other sounds. It would ring in your ears and make a fast break to the brain. When Wilson spoke, it sounded like he meant business."

He obviously meant business because the Vols rallied to win, Tennessee 30, Auburn 29.

Wilson was a dominating defender, whom West called a "fierce hitter with an overflow of intensity," one who had no quit in him. He was the glue, the man who held the team together. He missed three games due to an injury that season, but was always there on the sidelines, wearing his jersey # 27 and waving a towel. No player ever felt disposed to cross Wilson, and from that night in Atlanta on, no one ever did.

In the always-critical game against Florida on September 19, 1998, Wilson had responded by making twelve tackles and causing a school-record three fumbles in a 20-17 overtime win. No one had ever put up numbers like that on Shields-Watkins Field in a game of that magnitude.

One teammate later said that if he were called on the carpet and had a choice between Fulmer or Wilson wielding the sword, he would rather take his chances with Fulmer.

Such was Wilson's influence.

Wilson was one of the few former Vols whose name could be mentioned in the same breath with linebacker Steve Kiner, the two-time consensus All-American selection (1968-69) and 1999 College Football Hall of Fame member. In 1997, comparisons to Kiner came quickly when Wilson played outside linebacker and roamed sideline to sideline on his way to All-SEC recognition.

A year later, when Wilson anchored the middle, comparisons to 1969 All-American Jack "Hacksaw" Reynolds seemed to be more appropriate. When fans and media alike mentioned Wilson anchoring the defense, they meant the term literally and figuratively.

"As one of the team captains that year," Wilson told the University of Tennessee's Haywood Harris and Gus Manning in *Six Seasons Remembered: The National*

Championship Seasons of Tennessee Football. "I took it on myself to assume the leadership role that had been vacated when Peyton Manning and Leonard Little both graduated. Nobody knew who would step up and take over. I decided I was going to lead the team to be the best we could be."

In a *Sports Illustrated* cover story after the game was in the record books, Tim Layden added, more accurately, "Wilson seemed to scare his teammates into succeeding."

"We were a team," added Wilson. "We weren't separated by offense and defense. My role was to lead the entire team, not just the defense. It was my job to go out there and lead by example with the hope that the entire team would feed off it. We didn't have any stars. So what we did was jell and play like a unit.

"The coaches treated me as a leader. We trusted one another. I told them what I thought would work in a situation, and if they thought so, too, we would use it. We worked off one another."

No one knew it at the time, but the Vols had won a significant battle just before the game kicked off. Florida State has been traditionally renowned for its gamesmanship, getting in opponents' head even before the game started.

"Something important happened before we took the field. A gentleman tried to stop me at the door and told me we had to wait for FSU to go to the tunnel first," Fulmer said. "That made no sense to me. They were going to go by our dressing room, make us wait, and probably taunt us as they went by. This was my first decision of the night, and the game hadn't even started. No, we were going to go to the tunnel first, and the Seminoles would have to wait for us. He didn't like it, but we went. Our team loved it as I told the guy to move or he might get run over. We went first, FSU waited for us. To me, logistically, it made all the sense in the world, and strategically we had struck the first blow."

The key moment came with just under ten minutes left in the game. A Fiesta Bowl record crowd of 80,470 on a clear and cool early Monday evening in the Mountain Time Zone was in full voice. Mike Strange of the Knoxville News Sentinel termed the Vols fans in the crowd "an orange-tinted majority."

As the strains of the Florida State War Chant echoed across Sun Devil Stadium, one Vols fan, obviously irked by hearing the cheer over and over, had asked an FSU booster if they were singing the "first verse or the second verse."

Vols fans remember where they were when this play took place. Fans can almost recite the play call from memory. The play was called 69 All Go.

Ward's voice was in full flower across the width and breadth of the Vols Network. He had a marvelous ability to set the scene, to punctuate the moment. How good was John? He was so good that he made the standard broadcast disclaimer, "This broadcast is authorized under broadcast rights granted by the University of Tennessee through the Vols Network..." into an epic form of poetry.

The ball was on Tennessee's twenty-one yard line, third-and-nine. The Vols were one for twelve on third-down conversions for the game, and this play would be the one. The score was 14-9, Tennessee. Here is Ward's memorable call, not diminished in the least by the passage of time.

"Peerless Price is the wide receiver returning to the Vols huddle with the clock showing 9:45 to go in this game. This is John Ward and Bill Anderson sending you the action from the Fiesta Bowl in Tempe, Arizona.

"Tennessee will come to the line with Travis Stephens as the running back. There are two flankers to the left, one to the right. Florida State in a five-man front. They're going to blitz this time! Martin back, steps up, struggles, going to throw the ball long, long down the field to Peerless Price. Caught at the forty-five! He's at the forty... thirty-five... thirty... twenty-five... twenty. Just give it to him! No flags on the field. Touchdown, Tennessee!"

The touchdown reception went for seventy-nine yards. Price, who had come to Knoxville from Dayton, Ohio, had four catches for 199 yards, the ninth all-time mark in Tennessee history and best for the Vols in a bowl game. He also had a seventy-six yard reception that led to Tennessee's first score.

For his part, Peter Warrick ended up with one catch for seven yards.

When the Vols had won 23-16 after a few tense moments in the final frantic minutes, Ward told his listeners, "The national champion is clad in Big Orange!" while Anderson added his own cogent comment, saying quietly in the background, "What a year!"

The two Tennessee legends were doing their last broadcast together on the Vols Network. Ward, an award-winning Knoxville advertising executive, was the architect of the school's landmark media strategy, calling play-by-play for the Vols Network in football from 1968-98 and in basketball from 1964-99. His broadcast style was light years ahead of its time, and he presided over football and basketball coaches' shows that were equally trailblazing.

Anderson, a Knoxville insurance executive who died on April 18, 2017, had lettered three years (1955-57) under head coach Bowden Wyatt as a wide receiver and defensive back, playing at 6-2, 190 pounds. He had played professionally for the Washington Redskins and Green Bay Packers (1958-63), had a one-year tenure under Doug Dickey as ends coach at his alma mater in 1964, and had returned to the Packers for two years (1965-66) before embarking on his radio career with Ward two years later. He played in Super Bowl I.

They described the great moments of Tennessee football, from the rally against Georgia to salvage, maybe even steal, a 17-17 tie in the 1968 season opener, through the excitement of winning a national championship and all points in between. Ward often said Anderson's supposed weakness of not being a professional announcer became his strength. Vols fans hung on their every word.

For Tee Martin, a native of Mobile, Alabama, the season had been a once-in-a-lifetime opportunity as he demonstrated how to follow in the footsteps of a Tennessee legend, one selected by SI as the SEC's best quarterback over the years.

Martin seemed unruffled by the pressure and

hoopla associated with playing quarterback at Tennessee. He got his chance and made the most of it, with a little help from his predecessor.

"I was like this great big sponge while Peyton was here," Martin told SI's Mark Bechtel. "I tried to soak up all the knowledge I could."

For his part, Martin did quite well for himself, setting an SEC record with twenty-three consecutive completions against South Carolina. He was 22-3 (.880) as starter and was a co-captain of the 1999 team. His picture adorned the cover of SI's Special Commemorative Issue ("Perfect: Tennessee Volunteers 1998 National Champions"). After his career was over, the street behind the south end of Neyland Stadium was renamed Tee Martin Drive. When the Vols coaching job opened up in November 2017, many Vols fans brought up Martin's name for the top job, or, at minimum, for the offensive coordinator position.

He and Manning were also honored in Tennessee's Hall Fame Exhibit with life-size wax replicas that looked so real that one player saw them lying on the floor before they were installed. He was convinced the real duo had been the victims of foul play. The figures disappeared during Lane Kiffin's tenure in 2009 and have not been seen since.

For his part, Price made the cover of SI's January 11, 1999, issue. The cutline read, "No doubt about it: The Vols are Peerless." Price and Vols linebacker Eric Westmoreland made the magazine's All-Bowl Team.

On the ABC telecast, Keith Jackson provided one significant insight into Tennessee football history and tradition. Late in the game, when the Vols seemed to have the game in their back pocket, Jackson paid tribute to the legendary George Cafego, who had died in Knoxville on February 9, 1998.

A Hall of Fame tailback from the vintage years of the late 1930s, Cafego had coached kickers under head coaches Bowden Wyatt, Jim McDonald, Doug Dickey, Bill Battle, and Johnny Majors.

"Phillip Fulmer went to see George Cafego, who is an absolute legend in Tennessee football history, two days before he passed away," said Jackson. "George said, 'Good luck. I'll be watching.' Good night, George…and thanks. Nobody's name rests higher in Tennessee football than George Cafego."

For the Tennessee Volunteers, the path to the 1998 national championship was a circuitous one, with a number of potential stumbling blocks along the way that might have decimated a lesser team. Powerful critics were poised on the edge of their seats, waiting for the Vols to fold, to prove their time on the national stage was a mirage.

They didn't.

The 1998 season was a delightful time. When the team was honored at the 2018 Florida game, Vols fans responded, coming to their feet quickly. The memories were still something special, not dimmed in the least by the passage of time. The fan base has always loved the Vols program and has done so for years. Love of school and love of tradition across Big Orange Country has never waned, never died.

No Vols supporters at the game or listening or watching—with a great many of them turning down their televisions to hear Ward's radio play-by-play—could have surmised what was in store for the University of Tennessee in the ensuing years.

The twenty-year period that followed would test the mettle, grit, and spirit of Tennesseans who loved the university with all their hearts, but found, to their dismay, that the university would not—or *could* not—love them back in appreciation for being part of their hopes and dreams. A course was being set, little by little, indignity by indignity, trying moment by trying moment, for a fan revolt the likes of which college football has never seen.

What follows is the story of a meaningful and challenging period in the history of the University of Tennessee.

I WILL GIVE MY ALL FOR TENNESSEE TODAY

VOLS FANS historically have been an amazing and impressive group that have followed the fortunes of the school through good times and bad, always present, always loyal, always a part of the ambience of the school that has generated so many memories for them over the years. They have walked the rolling hills of the Tennessee campus, sat in the classrooms, supported the institution financially, and taken the school's message to their communities, states, nations, and world.

The University of Tennessee is representative of a state—about 150 miles wide north to south and more than 400 miles long east to west—known historically for World War I hero Sergeant Alvin York (1887-1964) from Pall Mall, a small community in Middle Tennessee's Fentress County in the Wolf River Valley. Former Vice-President Albert Gore, Jr. (1993-2001) of Carthage (Smith County) also called the Volunteer State home, as did Democratic Vice-Presidential candidate Estes Kefauver of Madisonville (Monroe County) in 1956.

According to a story by athletic department historian Nathan Kirkham in the 2018 University of Tennessee Media Guide, the United States War Department requested 2,800 volunteers to go to Texas during the Mexican War but was overwhelmed when 30,000 Tennesseans showed up ready and willing to go. As a result, Tennessee became known as the Volunteer State.

As far as the school nickname Volunteers goes, often shortened to Vols, the school yearbook adopted the name Volunteer in 1897. The Atlanta Constitution was first to use the term in their reportage of a Tennessee-Georgia Tech game in 1902, but the Knoxville Journal reported in March 1905 that, "One of the admirers of the old school has suggested 'the Volunteers.' The name sounds good, and it is likely the name will stick."

The state has also laid claim to the Grand Ole Opry and numerous country music stars including, but definitely not limited to, Dolly Parton and Kenny Chesney. Jack Daniels sipping whiskey originated in Lynchburg and Moore County. A delicacy known as Moon Pie traced its origins to Chattanooga in East Tennessee.

Charles Moore, the captain of the 1892 team, promoted orange and white as school colors from a flower, the common American Daisy that "grew in profusion" on the hill above the north end of the stadium. That's part of the legend of the University of Tennessee.

Not true, wrote Knoxville News Sentinel columnist Sam Venable recently. That was part of the legend propounded over the years.

"Dr. Mark Windham teaches and does research at the University of Tennessee's department of entomology and plant pathology," Sam wrote. "Nope, says Windham; there ain't no such plant. Never was. And this comes from a guy who has spent his career studying flowers. As close as I can tell, they were wild black-eyed susans, which look somewhat like daisies. Usually they have yellow petals, but I've seen some with orange petals."

Regardless, some type flower did exist on campus that nearly exactly matches the color of the Tennessee orange jersey.

The Hill, as it is formally known, has had an important role in the history of Tennessee football. The scoreboard and game clock—a real clock complete with minute and second hands—remained next to Alumni Gym until a 1966 addition to the north end brought a countdown clock and scoreboard high above new bleachers. One long-ago observer said with the Hill at the north end and the Tennessee River at the south end, the visiting team didn't have an escape route or a chance at winning.

One campus fraternity used to shoot off a cannon located high on the Hill after every Tennessee score. When the SEC skittishly outlawed the practice, members of the same fraternity held up a large and sarcastic sign that read "BANG!" in response when the Vols found the end zone.

Before 1921, the Vols had played on campus at a venue called Waite Field, at the northeast corner of Cumberland Avenue and 15th Street, known in later years as Stadium Drive and today as Phillip Fulmer Way. Players from that era told stories about combing the field the day before the game to remove any number of rocks that were embedded in the playing surface. Earlier Vols squads had also played at Baldwin Park off Asylum Street/ Western Avenue in downtown Knoxville and at a field in Smithwood, a community located north of the city.

Today, Neyland Stadium surrounds Shields-Watkins Field, a venue named for its 1921 benefactors Colonel William Simpson Shields, president of Knoxville's City Bank and a school trustee, and his wife, Alice Watkins-Shields. The campus hosted a workday on March 16 and into March 17 where students prepared the field under the tutelage of Dean Nathan Washington Dougherty, the namesake for Dougherty Hall on campus.

Shields-Watkins Field was first used for a baseball game on March 19 and for the 1921 football season opener on September 24 against Emory & Henry, with the Vols winning 27-0. Colonel Shields is estimated to have given more than $40,000—estimated at more than $560,000 in 2018 dollars—to the stadium's building fund.

Ninety-seven years ago, stadium capacity was 3,200 spectators on seventeen rows on the west side, but the stadium has grown over the years to seat 102,455 fans, becoming the fifth-largest stadium in the country. The Tennessee gridiron remains one of the nation's most recognizable fields with orange and white checkerboard end zones and the orange Power T at midfield. No one has ever confused the Tennessee greensward with any other field, collegiate or professional.

The stadium memorializes legendary Brigadier General Robert Reese Neyland, the man who built Tennessee's winning tradition in three eras between 1926 and 1952, with two interruptions for military service, 1935 in the Canal Zone and 1940-46 in World War II. An engineer by trade, he developed the master plan for future expansions of the stadium that bears his name.

To all concerned, General Neyland made his mark

on his city, state, university, and his country.

"And let me say that the influence exerted on me by General Neyland has never left," Lindsey Nelson wrote in his 1985 autobiography, *Hello, Everybody, I'm Lindsey Nelson*. "At present, I live in a condominium in Knoxville, Tennessee, after twenty-seven years of living in New York and pursuing the life of a sports announcer. My townhouse is high on a bluff, and at sunset the view is spectacular. In the far distance is a mountain range.

"Nearer one looks out on the sprawling campus of the University of Tennessee, bathed in the setting sun and so enriched and expanded in the fifty-odd years since that young army captain reported to the ROTC department and, incidentally, to the athletic department. Workers on their way home drive along a broad boulevard. They call that Neyland Drive.

"Lifting one's gaze only slightly, the last towering thing one sees on the horizon is a rising silhouette of a magnificent football stadium with a capacity of more than ninety thousand. They named it Neyland Stadium.

"I look at that scene and I often think of the day I first met him and he threatened me. I think of all his achievements, of the many lives he touched for the better, the man who valued loyalty seemingly above almost all other virtues."

As you read Nelson's words, you can almost hear the *Spirit of the Hill* playing softly in the background and witness the great moments of Neyland's thirty-seven years as a Volunteer passing in review.

"I think of that and I always smile," Nelson said.

"And, sometimes, when no one's looking, I salute."

Neyland's name was added to the stadium on Oct. 21, 1962, at the Alabama game, just a few months after Neyland died on March 21 at the Oschner Clinic in New Orleans. Funds were raised at the game to begin the Neyland Scholars program—academic scholarships for non-athletes—the scholarship fund being Neyland's special dream.

The visual aura of Tennessee football is credited to Roy Striegel, known as Pap to his friends, who convinced head coach M.B. Banks to outfit the team in orange jerseys in 1922, the year after the Vols christened Shields-Watkins Field. The previous jersey of choice had been a black shirt with orange piping.

More than forty years later, at a time when the future of Tennessee football seemed to hang precipitously in the balance, Striegel, a native of tiny Perryville (Decatur County), proved to be a moderating and thoughtful influence, convincing his colleagues on the Athletics Board, weary of wrangling over the hiring of a new coach, to let Athletic Director Bob Woodruff make the choice. That choice was Arkansas offensive coordinator Doug Dickey.

On Labor Day, September 6, 1926, that morning's Knoxville Journal contained a note on page nine, a relatively obscure item. It didn't really foreshadow the excitement we see on campus today, but, in retrospect, it was a seminal moment in Vols history. The Vols were on their way to the big time.

"Coach Bob Neyland will gather his Vols at Shields-

Watkins Field at eight o'clock and start the Orange and White aspirants on the rocky road to glory."

There were twenty-five prospective Vols present that day. No one knew what the years ahead might hold, but one thing had become clear. The road to glory might have been rocky, but Neyland established a simple plan for gridiron success.

"Men, we will practice two and one-half hours each day," Neyland said. "That's all. Each practice will be organized. We will know what we want to accomplish each day, and we will work full speed. Any questions? Let's go."

Neyland became the eleventh coach in school history and brought stability to the position. He became a legend, a Hall of Fame coach, with a career record of 173-31-12. His teams had 112 shutouts in 216 games. After his time at Tennessee was finished, he was favorably compared with Notre Dame's Knute Rockne.

A Bluetick Coonhound, a breed native to the state of Tennessee, has occupied a place near the southeast corner of the field at every game since 1953. Since his arrival on campus, Smokey has led the Vols onto the field though the T formed by the Pride of the Southland Marching Band just before kickoff. The dogs were the product of a 1953 search for a mascot conducted by the school's Pep Club at the season-opening game against Mississippi State.

Reverend Bill Brooks was from (ironically) nearby Mascot. His dog, Brooks' Blue Smokey, was the last contestant paraded in front of the students at the Mississippi State game that last day of September. Smokey won a bark-off paws-down. Brooks promised to have a dog at every game, the product of a handshake agreement with Pep Club president Stuart Worden in October. The Brooks and Hudson families, related after Bill and Mildred Hudson's marriage, have kept up the tradition, with the dogs missing only two games in their sixty-five-year tenure entering 2018.

The line of hounds became known individually and collectively as Smokey, a name suggested by Vols fan Hubert Duncan of Kingsport, Tennessee, and reported in the Knoxville News Sentinel on September 27, 1953. Each dog is named Smokey, from the inaugural Smokey I, all the way through the current mascot, Smokey X.

When the world lost its bearings and young men went off in defense of their country, the program was characterized by great triumph, accomplishment and occasional moments of tragedy dotting its history since those first tentative steps from 1891 into the next two centuries. Four Volunteer players—#32 Bill Nowling, #49 Rudy Klarer, #61 Willis Tucker, and #62 Clyde "Ig" Fuson—have had their numbers retired because of their service and loss of life in World War II. Their names are emblazoned on the facade in the southeast corner of Neyland Stadium.

In 1962, UT broadcaster George Mooney wanted to avoid the traffic jams associated with his trips down Kingston Pike to and from Neyland Stadium on game days. The trip into campus was neither quick nor easy.

Since his home on Cherokee Boulevard in West Knoxville backed up to the Tennessee River, he took a quick look at his boat—"a little runabout," he called it—

and made plans to hit the water. He didn't know he was making history and creating a tradition.

There was no dock, as no one ever imagined anyone parking a boat on the Tennessee River near the stadium, but Mooney was undaunted. "We had to tie the boat to a tree and climb over the rocks and weeds."

His idea caught on. More than two hundred boats, eighteen feet long to luxury liners, dock just off Neyland Drive, many of them well before game day. There was even a Vols Navy Boaters Association. Neyland Stadium turned into one of four major college football stadiums where fans can arrive by boat, later joined by McLane Stadium at Baylor University in Waco, Texas, Heinz Field in Pittsburgh, and Husky Stadium in Seattle.

Many in the Vols Navy head to the stadium when it's game time, while others, happy with life on the waterfront, are content to stay aboard, tailgating and watching the game on big screen televisions.

The campus takes on a life of its own on game day, as fans from across Tennessee and across the country travel to Knoxville. Everybody somehow gets into town, gets parked, and is able to get home after the game, even by the standards of the most unreasonable fan. Knoxville has a multitude of places to eat, drink, and sleep. The city is a good host.

Where else could you consistently find more than 100,000 people at one venue for an American sporting event?

That's something important to consider, particularly when many NFL franchises, located in much larger and allegedly more sophisticated urban areas, average 20,000-30,000 fewer fans through the gates than several collegiate venues, including Tennessee.

The iconic state song *Rocky Top*, played by some estimates more than fifty times a game, maybe more, was the product of Nashville-based songwriters Felice and Boudleaux Bryant and was written in fifteen minutes in 1967 at the Gatlinburg Inn. Boudleaux came up with the chorus and then wrote the verses jointly with Felice.

Haywood Harris and Dr. Julian, the latter often referred to as Doc, came on board in 1961 as sports information director and director of bands, respectively, followed in 1963 by Doug Dickey as head football coach.

The Volunteers program was reaching for the stars, and each of them had their fingerprints all over the growth and development of the program.

"When Coach Dickey came to Tennessee, he was very interested in the band," Dr. Julian said. "He thought we should have a little more hype. He's actually the one who designed and opened the T. I remember the week we practiced on it that he had the team come so they could practice running through the T.

"If the band didn't form the T, there would be a lot of complaints."

Rocky Top was first performed at Neyland Stadium at halftime of the 1972 Tennessee-Alabama game. It is not a fight song, as some have suggested, but one of ten songs that have helped define the landscape of the state. It was adopted by the General Assembly in 1972.

Under Julian's leadership, the Pride of the Southland Marching Band became one of the best in the nation, with a spit-and-polish pre-game and halftime show. The pre-game show has varied little from week to week, but fans wouldn't have it any other way. There is nothing like the moment the band opens the T, first from the east side of Shields-Watkins Field starting in 1965 and then beginning from the north end in 1983.

As befits both Julian and Dickey, each of them gave the other the credit for a longtime tradition that has continued into the 2018 season.

Julian was single-minded where the band was concerned, obsessive about the smallest detail of the band's operation, loyal to the university, and a man whose name will be written large when the next history of the University of Tennessee is penned.

How does all this add up to the excitement that envelops campus during the fall months?

There's a different feeling about college football from any other version. You can't create it and nobody really knows how to define it, but we all know it when we see it, know it when we feel it, especially in the Southeastern Conference.

Tennessee fans are something special, wearing orange of all description to the games, gobbling up season tickets, and traveling in great numbers to the venues wherever the Vols play.

It's not uncommon to see Vols fans on the road, in Los Angeles, South Bend, Birmingham, or any number of venues where the Vols might be playing, ready to take on all comers. It doesn't matter how they get there. They always get there. It's a matter of pride and honor.

The fans have brought a unique perspective, a unique frame of reference, to the games, because they grew up watching their school play, might have attended the games with their future spouse, and wouldn't dare dream of rooting for any other team, despite the occasional ups and downs they might have experienced over the years.

They might know a player as a neighbor, one related to someone in their Sunday School class or as a classmate of one of their children. In addition, while many Vols players have come from across the country, the fan base has adopted them, each as one of their own. Many of these players have stayed well past the end of their collegiate careers, making their mark on the fabric of Knoxville society.

Over the years, young men were brought into the fold who did great things for the Volunteers. On the flip side, there were a few who got away, young men who did great things for other schools and, occasionally, did in the Vols.

When you think about it, it's sometimes hard to imagine that a decision a young man makes at age seventeen or eighteen can have such historic import for a school, community, and state, but that's exactly what happens. Think about Steve Spurrier and Steve Sloan spurning the Vols for Florida and Alabama, respectively, in the 1960s, decisions that carried over into Tennessee history into the second decade of the twenty-first century.

All of this history illuminates why the names,

dates, and places of Tennessee football, all of which are important to developing the entire picture, highlight the conversations Vols fans engage in wherever they might be—on church steps, in barbershops, factory breakrooms, corporate boardrooms, on talk radio, or on social media. The stories might even get exaggerated ever so slightly over the years, but, regardless, college football, especially at Tennessee, has a wonderful feel to it.

Every time the Vols hit the field, there were those brief but memorable moments when young men in orange and white made history in the time it took to return a kickoff, to throw or catch a touchdown pass, or to break a long run from scrimmage.

In the Southeastern Conference, which Tennessee joined as a charter member in 1933, events on the field sometimes carry over into everyday life, all part of the rivalries, some ancient, dating a hundred years or more, with others of more recent occurrence.

Coaches tell fans over and over that, "There's no 'I' in team." Over the years, teams have been composed of a group of young men who seemingly had nothing in common except a desire to excel.

There were a number of memorable storylines emanating from the 1968 season opener, when number nine-ranked Tennessee and Georgia squared off at Neyland Stadium for the first time in thirty-one years.

One story was artificial turf. Doug's Rug, as it was popularly known, was installed on Shields-Watkins Field and stayed in some version for twenty-five years. The venerable stadium grass had been ripped up during the summer on 1968 and replaced initially by something called Tartan Turf, a product of 3M. There were a number of different artificial surfaces on the field until grass made a triumphant return under turf guru Bobby Campbell's leadership in 1994.

That game was when John Ward and former Vols wingback and 1957 co-captain Bill Anderson made their debut on the Vols Network. Sometime in the second half, Ward thought to himself he and Anderson might make it as a broadcast team, and history has proved his assessment was correct. John and Bill stayed through the 1998 season and the national championship game against Florida State.

There were the days over the years, as might be expected, Tennessee lost when, perhaps, the Vols should have won. Likewise the Vols won, perhaps, when the team should have lost.

On November 15, 1969, the third-ranked Vols journeyed to Jackson, Mississippi, to play the number eighteen Ole Miss Rebels. That game became known as the "Jackson Massacre" for good reason. Vols fans wore "Archie Who?" buttons to the game that day—the product of a pre-season comment by linebacker Steve Kiner about the famed Rebel quarterback Archie Manning—and lived to regret it. There have been few days longer than that one. Former Vols defensive back and 1970 captain Tim Priest once observed that, if Tennessee hadn't showed up, the Rebels would have lined up and gotten after each other.

The "Jackson Massacre" was part of a lost weekend in Tennessee football, and that's putting it mildly. Rarely had a weekend been so bleak in Big Orange Country. The

Alabama freshmen had defeated the Vols rookies 35-0 in Knoxville the day before. But despite an occasional bump in the road every now and then, there was always another game, another weekend, for Vols fans.

General Neyland knew that feeling well. When things were going bad in the late 1940s, a Vols fan on the elevator at the Chisca Hotel in Memphis said some disparaging things about the General after a lopsided loss to Ole Miss at Crump Stadium. Two weeks later, after a win, the same fan said, "There's the greatest coach in the country."

Neyland, who had overheard both conversations, said simply, "That's not what you were saying two weeks ago."

But history can take a number of strange turns.

After their respective collegiate careers were over, Manning and former Vols signal-caller Bobby Scott, on opposite sides of the field in 1968 and 1969, ended up as teammates on the New Orleans Saints, became close friends, and watched their respective families grow up.

Out of the wreckage of that late 1969 November afternoon, in the time heals all wounds department, fast forward nearly twenty-five years to February 2, 1994, the day a younger player named Manning signed scholarship papers to come to Knoxville. No one thought that it could ever happen, but, thanks to a number of twists of fate, it did.

Peyton Williams Manning, Archie's second son, wore orange and white jersey #16 and led the Vols to glory from 1994-97. He took #16 because junior defensive back DeRon Jenkins, now co-starring on HGTV's "Flip or Flop Nashville" with ex-wife Page Turner, had the famed Manning #18. No one could imagine Peyton being selfish enough to want an upperclassman's number. His second choice was #12, but fellow rookie Marcus Nash wanted that one. So #16 it was.

Peyton became one of the most decorated players in Tennessee history, complete with a street named in his honor—Peyton Manning Pass—a study area in the Thornton Student Life Center, the Peyton Manning Locker Complex in Neyland Stadium, and his number being retired at the South Carolina game on October 29, 2005.

Tennessee quarterback Rick Clausen, the second Clausen brother, had worn the #16 jersey during the 2004 and 2005 seasons. On the night of the South Carolina game, however, he showed up in jersey #7, retiring the famed #16 a game or two early. Jersey #7 was also his brother Casey's number during his Tennessee career. Vols fans fondly remember how Rick led the way in a 38-7 win against Texas A&M in the 2005 Cotton Bowl and an overtime comeback win at LSU that September.

A whole generation of children were born in the late 1990s and beyond named after Manning, either Peyton or Payton. He was definitely something special.

There were also great wins over the years, games that took your breath away, games that have always seemed to be at the ready in the mind's eye. In the pantheon of sports, the mind's eye tops the charts. Fans can recall at a moment's notice exactly where they were and what they were thinking when significant events happened. They can see them happening and experience them again and again.

On the flip side of the "Jackson Massacre," one of the greatest comebacks in Tennessee history came during the 1991 contest at Notre Dame. The Vols visited South Bend for the 300th game at Notre Dame's storied stadium. The Vols had underachieved to that point of the season, despite winning the previous two SEC titles, while Notre Dame was in the national championship hunt as always and apparently headed toward a big bowl game.

A crowd of 59,075 was in attendance, Notre Dame's one hundredth consecutive sell-out. NBC was there for the national telecast. The Vols had to deal with the psychology of it all, the aura surrounding Notre Dame football, the ghosts, the echoes, the Four Horsemen, and all that. Many teams were beaten long before the game started because of all the hoopla surrounding Notre Dame and Notre Dame Stadium. Johnny Majors had been there before as head coach of the Pitt Panthers. The game encompassed the history of college football, with teams descended from the lineage of Knute Rockne and Bob Neyland, squaring off on the famed Irish greensward on a cold but otherwise perfect November day.

Touchdown Jesus stood majestically above the field at the north end as the Irish and Vols battled. Initially, it seemed as if Notre Dame were going to win handily, leading the Vols by twenty-four points in the second quarter, 31-7.

Just before halftime, the Vols began to rally, as Daryl Hardy blocked a field goal and Floyd Miley took the pigskin seventy-six yards for a score. It was 31-14 at the half, and the Vols had a glimmer of hope. Remember Neyland's Maxim Number Six? "Press the kicking game. Here is where the breaks are made."

The Vols continued to rally in the second half, cutting the margin to 34-28 in the fourth quarter. The strains of *Rocky Top* strongly challenged the *Notre Dame Victory March* as the game neared its finish. *Rocky Top* was the bane of opposing coaches, particularly Notre Dame's Lou Holtz, who'd had the song blaring over and over in practices during Tennessee game week.

The Vols were headed to the north end of the field facing second down at the Irish twenty-six yard line. With the Fighting Irish blitzing both safeties, quarterback Andy Kelly found Aaron Hayden in the left flat with nothing but green in front of him, heading "down to the end zone," as Ward said.

"We knew they tended to blitz in that area of the field," said Kelly, a cool customer under center all day. "They stuck to their tendency, and we executed. Aaron had a clear shot to the end zone. I saw the linemen in front of him. I saw there weren't any blue jerseys for a long way."

Hayden wasn't so sure about the play, at least initially, although game tapes show Aaron with the pigskin under his arm full tilt to the end zone. "To be truthful," he said, "I didn't know if it was going to work. I didn't think it was a very good call. Then I got the ball, and it was perfection."

Ward told the uncounted multitudes across the expanse of the Vols Network and whoever might have been listening while watching on television it was the perfect call. Placekicker John Becksvoort, who was kicking for Red Bank High School in Chattanooga, Tennessee a year earlier, said he had dreamed of beating Notre Dame with a field goal. In this case, however, an extra point was plenty. The clock showed 4:03 to go.

No one expected the Fighting Irish to fold their tents and give in. And they didn't. Notre Dame rallied and headed goalward, as the game came down to the final seconds. Placekicker Craig Hentrich had been injured earlier in the half, so sophomore walk-on kicker Rob Leonard of Decatur, Georgia, was thrust into the spotlight. Every eye in the stadium focused squarely on him.

It was a chip shot, twenty-six yards, from the near hash mark.

"It has come down to a final field goal try by Decatur, Georgia's Rob Leonard," Ward intoned as the game was on the line. Leonard had been so far down on the depth chart that spotter Bob Kesling, Ward's successor in 1999, had a hard time finding him on any piece of Notre Dame publicity material.

"The pressure will be on this young sophomore," Ward said, the intensity rising in his voice. "Four seconds remain in the game. Holding will be Sexton. Snapping will be Johnson. It will be right at twenty-seven yards. This will be Rob Leonard."

"The kick is up. The kick is good—"

Check that. Check, Check, check, as Johnny Majors always said when something went awry in practice. Hearts stopped wherever Vols fans were. Then came Ward's make-up call.

"No! It is no good! It is no good!"

Vols fans likely looked for a flag on that play, given that penalty flags seemed to appear as if by magic at Notre Dame when the Fighting Irish were in trouble. None appeared from the SEC crew officiating the game.

What happened was something unusual, something rarely seen in the annals of football, collegiate or professional. Vols defensive back Jeremy Lincoln, lined up on the right side of the defensive formation, had blocked the kick with his rump to save the come-from-behind triumph. He got there so quickly that he almost overran the kick. Lincoln, who had come to Knoxville from Toledo, Ohio, just down the turnpike from South Bend, thanked his mother after the game for the size of his backside.

There are stories, some apocryphal, some not, about Tennessee fans who left the game early, maybe even before halftime, and headed home, the deficit being too much for them to handle. Down US 31 and I-65 they went. They couldn't believe Notre Dame would blow a big lead at Notre Dame Stadium. Rockne wouldn't have allowed it. They couldn't even consider that possibility

About the time they were probably passing Indianapolis, inching ever closer to Louisville, the realization hit. They were probably arguing about whose decision it was to leave. They had missed a memorable piece of Tennessee history.

The post-game sight was surreal.

Notre Dame students were still singing the *Notre Dame Victory March*. "*Cheer, cheer, for old Notre Dame, Wake up the echoes cheering her name..."*

NBC analyst Bill Walsh walked out of the press box ashen-faced, not really believing he had seen and described what had just transpired.

Down on the field, fans in orange were celebrating a glorious victory. Ward 's remarks were vintage.

"Tennessee beats Notre Dame 35-34. The Volunteers go home victorious. Notre Dame goes with the sophomore replacement kicker. It is no good, off to the right. The coaching staff to our left is jubilant, as are Tennessee fans. You...could...not...write... this...script."

Even today, the game ranks near the top of the list of great Tennessee victories.

That day was the day the Vols would shake down the thunder from the sky to add a significant chapter to the history of the Tennessee football program. Time has not diminished the game's impact. Not in the least. Games like this define the reasons fans are fans. Fans don't get that many chances to go into a tradition-laden venue and see their heroes pull off an improbable comeback.

On that day, they did—and there were others.

Rumor claims that ghosts dwell under the turf in Neyland Stadium, apparitions capable of causing fumbles, false starts on offense, or other dastardly occurrences for visiting teams. No one can say for sure. But you'd have to think there were... and still are.

Check out the 1981 game against Wichita State. With the game tied 21-21 in the fourth quarter, Shocker tight end Anthony Jones caught a pass over the middle and when two Vols in pursuit collided, he looked to be off to the races toward the south end zone. A Homecoming Day loss seemed imminent. But for no apparent reason, Jones started veering ever so steadily to his right toward the west sideline.

"I was sitting there with former Vols baseball player Robbie Howard," said grass guru Bob Campbell, the late caretaker of the Shields-Watkins Field turf, then a Knoxville high school baseball coach. "We saw him heading our way, and Robbie said, 'He's going to run out of bounds.' And he did."

Three plays later, the Vols intercepted a pass and marched to the game-clinching field goal.

In the rain-soaked 1998 Arkansas game at Neyland Stadium, with his team trailing 24-22 and hope gradually leaving Neyland Stadium along with many in the crowd, defensive tackle Billy Ratliff caused a fumble and gratefully scooped it up, just as he had promised quarterback Tee Martin when Tee left the field mere moments earlier. The Vols had looked dead in the water, but miracles can happen when least expected.

Vols fans who had left the Arkansas game early for whatever reasons were huddled in the rain around tailgate televisions with total strangers, united in their desire to see the Vols pull off a miracle finish.

A closer look at the play showed that Ratliff caused the collision and made the play possible. That may be the reason former Vols defensive line coach Dan Brooks once called Ratliff "the best lineman I ever coached."

The ball lay on the turf for what seemed an eternity.

The play has been ensconced in Tennessee gridiron history as the Stoerner Stumble.

The Vols scored in five running plays, totaling forty-three yards, all by tailback Travis Henry ("They need to give it to Henry!" Ward said) to take a look-what-I-found 28-24 win, a victory every team has needed to experience at least once to win a national title. We all know the football gods have to be smiling at exactly the right time, one of those magic moments when one team looks unstoppable, while the other appears to be barely hanging on.

Fans wondered how close the Vols would have to get to be in position for a game-winning field goal from the ever-dependable Jeff Hall, thinking a 25-24 victory would be sufficient.

After Henry's first run, one thing was certain. There wouldn't be a field goal. Champions go for touchdowns, and this bunch had the look of champions, even when things looked darkest.

When the Vols went to Gainesville, Florida, on December 1, 2001, for their annual matchup with the Gators, they were double-digit underdogs in a game played for all the Eastern Division marbles. The game had been postponed due to the tragedies on September 11.

Tennessee had more than a few arrows in its quiver. Travis Stephens, the senior tailback from Clarksville, Tennessee, rushed for 226 yards and the Vols hung on at the end, denying the Gators a chance to tie. Defensive back Buck Fitzgerald broke up a two-point conversion pass to Gator wide receiver Jabar Gaffney, and tight end

John Finlayson recovered an onside kick. The final was 34-32.

Casey Clausen led the way under center, proving to be the ultimate road warrior. During his time at Tennessee, he won twice at Alabama, twice at Florida, at Notre Dame, at Arkansas, at Miami, and in the 2002 Citrus Bowl game against Michigan. The game also was Spurrier's last at Florida, as he left for the NFL Washington's Redskins. He would return to bedevil the Volunteers at South Carolina in 2005. That night, he took great pleasure in knocking off the Vols the night the school retired Peyton Manning's jersey.

Of such moments are legends made, legacies created. There were a number of times opponents were hopeful of victory, but, in the parlance of Vols football, Tennessee was more than hopeful. The Vols were certain, even as prohibitive underdogs.

Fans have special memories of Condredge Holloway (1972-74), the "Artful Dodger" or "Peanut," as Bill Battle called him. Condredge was the first African-American quarterback in the SEC, weaving his way through opposing defenses and helping to blaze the trail for the wonderfully talented athletes who would follow him to campus. When Condredge was asked how he felt being the first African-America quarterback in the SEC, he said, "I don't know; I've never been a white one."

Bill Battle was someone who knew. He once said the only way to describe Condredge was "indescribable." He was right. Give Battle the credit for giving Condredge his chance under center during those uncertain times when others wouldn't. Bear Bryant, for example, said "no," that Alabama wasn't ready for an African-American quarterback. Without Condredge, UT would never have had a Jimmy Streater, a Tony Robinson, a Tee Martin, or a Joshua Dobbs under center.

During an injury-plagued senior season, Battle had offered Holloway the chance to leave the team, so as not to affect his future in professional baseball. Condredge's response was to the point: "I have to be at practice."

Fans can look back and remember Holloway's game-winning two-point conversion pass to wide receiver Larry Seivers in the 1974 Clemson game at the south end of Shields-Watkins Field or two enthralling runs to the north end against Georgia Tech a year earlier. They watched Condredge somehow get the ball to Haskel Stanback near the south goal line in the fourth quarter of the 1972 Penn State game, leading to a score that helped keep Joe Paterno's team at bay.

Condredge was always a leader at Tennessee, both on the field and off it. For those of us who were there, a profound moment in Sylva, N.C., exemplified his character and influence, when time stood still momentarily and everything about him came into clear perspective.

Word came on Friday, February 20, 2004, that Jimmy Streater had died in Asheville, North Carolina. Willis James Streater III, a co-captain of the 1979 Vols squad with Roland James and Craig Puki, was forty-six when he left this earth, having literally been to the mountaintops and through the valleys, experiencing nearly every emotion a man can deal with in two score and six years.

The next Monday, Streater once again played to a

packed house at his services at the Liberty Baptist Church, near the railroad on Hospital Street in his hometown of Sylva, North Carolina.

The tiny church was packed to the rafters not only with his family and friends, but also full to the brim with the requisite, albeit occasionally sidestepped, virtues of faith and forgiveness. Jimmy's family had been offered the sanctuary of the much-bigger First Baptist Church uptown for the services, but he had wanted to be home, where he had been a part of many of the important things in his life.

"Strong stuff, touching moment, powerful message," former Knoxville News Sentinel and Scripps-Howard sports editor Marvin West wrote February 20, 2006, the second year after Streater's passing. "Tennessee never forgets a Volunteer, even when he hits the wall."

Everyone there had their own special memories of the small town youth who carried Sylva's torch to the University of Tennessee, and yet who always retained the love and adulation of those who knew him best.

At the service, Holloway had attached a T-Club pin, the emblem of the school's Lettermen's Association, to Jimmy's lapel, calling it the "hardest thing I've ever done."

Condredge Holloway always exhibited class, grace, poise and a whole bunch of other similar adjectives in large doses. Like most pioneers, he took a whole bunch of arrows, but lived to tell the tale.

But consider this, just for perspective: There wouldn't have been a Condredge Holloway at Tennessee without a Lester McClain, the ultimate pioneer of his day. There also wouldn't have been a Lester McClain at

Tennessee without Dickey. Lester's career had begun on that September 14, 1968 season opener against Georgia, on a newly christened Tartan Turf, in front of a record crowd and millions more on ABC. John Ward and Bill Anderson were making their debut on the Vols Network. Lester made a key catch on Tennessee's final drive and helped the Vols earn a 17-17 tie.

When Vols fans get together to discuss the great leaders in Tennessee football, several famous names come to mind.

Bowden Wyatt, an All-American end at Tennessee in 1938 and a man possessed with movie star good looks, had won conference championships at Wyoming and Arkansas and was the people's choice to take over for the 1955 season after Neyland had dismissed Harvey Robinson, the coach who was unfortunate enough to follow in Neyland's footsteps.

At a team banquet shortly after his arrival in Knoxville, Wyatt made a dramatic presentation of a coin he won as 1938 team captain to Jim Beutel, 1955 team captain. Wyatt had kept it to give his first captain if he ever became head coach at Tennessee.

Wyatt's team won the SEC title in 1956, and Vols fans looked forward to more of the same. However, he never found his way to the top of the conference again. After the 1957 Gator Bowl season, the Vols hit a rough patch, and Wyatt was out in June 1963. Vols football was mediocre at best, but the tipping point came for the coach when Wyatt pushed a sportswriter into a swimming pool at the SEC meetings in Atlanta.

Doug Dickey, who had arrived for the 1964 season, put the swagger back in Vols football, with considerable assistance in the early days from Jim McDonald, the man who preceded him as head coach. Once Dickey had sorted things out in his first season and put his systems in place, the sky was the limit for the Vols program. There were numerous times during his tenure when Dickey stood tall, earning respect from thoughtful people.

When three assistant coaches—Bill Majors, Bob Jones, and Charley Rash—were killed at a railroad grade crossing in West Knoxville in October 1965 early on the Monday morning after a 7-7 tie against Alabama, Dickey held the team together under exceptionally trying circumstances.

In March 1966, he did likewise when two players, linebacker Tom Fisher and lineman John Crumbacher, died in a traffic accident and a third, offensive guard Gerald Woods, was injured near Benton, Tennessee, south of Knoxville. Whether during his tenure as head coach or as athletic director, Dickey was a man with broad shoulders, a man you wanted on your side in a crisis situation.

Dickey brought the T-formation to Knoxville and led the Vols to glory from 1965 through 1969, during which Vols fans were convinced their team would win nearly every time out. A Hall of Fame athletic director, Dickey brought the Vols back from the dark days of the late 1950s and early 1960s.

McDonald was the bridge between the two eras, a man who didn't seem to worry about what might have been but helped ensure the Vols program got back on the right track and stayed there. He introduced Dickey to a number of prospects, notably linemen Bob Johnson and John Boynton, three-year starters each, and leaders on the 1967 team that brought the SEC and the Litkenhous national title home to Knoxville.

Thirty years later, Vols fans watched as Dickey provided an emotion-laden introduction of McDonald at an honors banquet, mentioning McDonald's role in those early days as one of the keys to his success.

When Dickey left for Florida in early 1970, Woodruff turned to Bill Battle, a twenty-eight year-old ends coach, who had been on the staff since 1966. He had played for Bear Bryant at Alabama and was part of the Tide's 1961 national championship team. Many Vols fans had found it hard to accept that Battle had stood on the west side of Shields-Watkins Field as an Alabama player in 1960 and 1962 and, just a few years later, would be there as Tennessee's head coach.

His teams were 31-5 his first three years, 8-4 in his fourth year, but the Georgia game on Homecoming Day 1973 turned out to be his Waterloo. Neither Georgia nor Tennessee had stopped each other that day, and the Vols, leading 31-28, faced fourth-and-three when Battle opted for a fake punt. The move failed, the Bulldogs scored, and the fans never really warmed to Battle from that point on.

Johnny Majors came home in 1977 after a national championship season at Pittsburgh to continue a Tennessee career that began in the mid-1950s as an All-American tailback and ended with him being Heisman runner-up in 1956. He rebuilt the Tennessee program with from the ground up. "Follow me to Tennessee!" was his byword, and the Vols program was, once again, reaching for the stars.

Not far removed from the excitement of the 1976 national championship season and a Heisman Trophy winner named Tony Dorsett, Majors had found himself in January at Trousdale County High School in Hartsville, Tennessee, located midway between Carthage and Gallatin on Tennessee Highway 25, the following January, speaking at the team's honors banquet in the school cafeteria.

In attendance were local prospects Donnie Oldham and Reggie Harper, both of whom would later become Vols. The sight of a coach coming off winning a national championship eating off school lunch plates and sitting on those round metal seats attached to the table was memorable. By the way, both local products signed with Tennessee. Harper was an All-SEC tight end, while Oldham banged up a knee and never played after the 1977 California game.

You couldn't ask for bigger moments than the 1986 Sugar Bowl win over Miami, the streak-breaking win over Alabama in 1982, smashing triumphs over Auburn in 1985, 1989, and 1991, and the previously-chronicled comeback at South Bend against Notre Dame in 1991. He was and still is a Tennessee legend and the first hero for a number of Tennessee fans. The Vols garnered SEC titles in 1985, 1989, and 1990. He also started the school's Vol Walk in 1990, as the team walked to the stadium while thousands of cheering fans lined the route to the stadium.

The 1992 season was Majors' last, and it had to have been one of the strangest in Tennessee football history. Majors had health issues in May. Longtime trainer Tim

Kerin died in early August of a dissecting aortic aneurysm. There were many in the Vols camp who believe history would have looked a great deal different had Kerin lived, given his straightforward relationship with Majors. Majors missed a Monday practice a week or so later, media being told it was for a doctor's appointment. Fans found out the next day that he was undergoing open-heart surgery and would miss the start of the season.

Phillip Fulmer was named the interim coach and would coach through the Southwestern Louisiana, Georgia, and Florida games—all wins that caught the attention of the fan base.

Majors returned unexpectedly the Sunday night after the Florida game. The Vols defeated Cincinnati and LSU and then lost to Arkansas and Alabama in successive weeks. In a rare scheduling quirk, they had an open date the week before and the week after a trip to South Carolina. The Vols lost at South Carolina by 24-23, and the atmosphere surrounding the program was not good. Stories began to circulate that a coaching change was in the works.

The announcement came in Memphis on Friday, November 13. Majors resigned, saying, "Since I have not been given the opportunity by the UT administration to remain as head football coach past this current season, I am, effective December 31, 1992, relinquishing my duties connected with the University of Tennessee." Fans gathered at the hotel or around television sets to watch the Vols legend step down, many with tears streaming down their faces. It was the same way at the game the next day.

"His programs were widely regarded as one of

the nation's best," Bebb wrote. "To many people, he was Tennessee football. Majors might have painted himself into a corner. But no matter what he might have done to bring on his ouster, no matter what demands he might have placed on the administration, he deserved a far nobler farewell."

Fulmer, a member of championship teams as a player, assistant coach, and head coach, had promised to take the Vols to the next level when he was named head coach on November 29, 1992, and he did just that. Vols fans fondly remembered the thrill of a first-play touchdown in the 1995 Alabama game ("Eighty yards... Joey Kent... on play... Number One!" was the way Ward called it) when the series turned around. Again.

This is what it means to be a Tennessee fan, what it's always meant to be part of Vol Nation. This history, these legacies, the memories of players and coaches and games past—all of this combines and melds with the souls of people whose hearts begin to sing with the first words of *Rocky Top*. Winning has always been a big deal, but Vols fans will tell you that there's something special involved. Following the Vols is an essential part of life across the expanse of Big Orange Country.

That's one reason Knoxville radio talk show hosts Tony Basilio and Russell W. Smith have done post-game radio call-in shows that last into the wee hours of the morning, patiently answering questions about every aspect of the game just played.

But several salient questions arise when we consider the fan experience, the aspects of college life that draw us all to campus and what happens on Saturday afternoons and evenings during the fall.

If Vols football has been historically been about winning and nothing else, why do we have school colors, alma maters, Homecoming celebrations, checkerboard end zones, and the ambience of game day?

Why have fans made special efforts to get tickets and parking passes, often for a king's ransom, prepare the tailgate, and fought the good fight to get to the games eleven or twelve Saturdays a year, home and away?

Why have Tennessee and other schools continually constructed or added to stadiums much larger than those of twenty-five or fifty years ago to further serve the fan base?

Why has Tennessee expended the effort to build a Letterman's Wall of Fame with the names of those who have gone before etched into stone?

Why have fans visited the wall and paid silent homage to those who have led the way on the gridiron and other fields of play?

Why have sportswriters and other journalists written books that have recapped the exploits of their favorite college football teams, Tennessee being one, in great detail?

Why have sports talk radio, the newspapers, social media, or message boards become so popular?

Why have long-term rivalries been fought not only on game day, but also throughout the year, often day after day?

Why have these endless and wonderful debates over the best players and the best teams at nearly every school in the country?

Why have fans worried about the fortunes of every potential recruit who has been mentioned as a possibility to play for a particular school?

Why have athletic teams at these schools if not for the fans? If it weren't for the fan experience, what would the pages of the Knoxville News Sentinel or any other newspaper across the state look like? Would there have even been a Knoxville News Sentinel worth reading without its exhaustive coverage of the Vols and other area sports teams?

The fans cherish their season tickets and live for the excitement in and around the stadium. They have all types of orange gear in their closets and for three hundred and sixty-five days a year, the team is always in their thoughts.

Without a doubt, Vols fans are demanding. Winning football has been engrained in their hearts and souls. They've experienced the Promised Land, been to the mountaintop, and seen the other side. If fans don't see that happening or getting ready to happen, a great many questions arise in all types of media, and more than a few empty seats appear inside the big stadium.

Or worse, seats occupied by hordes of visiting fans.

If you don't believe that, think about the second half of the 2008 Alabama game, final score Alabama 29, Tennessee 9, when Neyland Stadium became Bryant-Denny Stadium north, with the crimson and white in the stadium overwhelming the orange and white.

That's why the orange sign in the shape of the state of Tennessee above the door in the Tennessee dressing room, home and away, says it best (and most simply, in a mere eight words). These are expectations and requirements surrounding Tennessee football:

I will give my all for Tennessee today.

Wherever Tennessee plays, that message is the last thing the players see as they leave the dressing room to go to the field. The sign is a silent motivator, a statement of purpose from those who have gone before.

From the earliest days of the program, the young men representing the University of Tennessee on the gridiron have faced that challenge, day-in and day-out, week-in and week-out, year-in and year-out. More often than not, the Vols have been up to maintaining the legacy that comes with tradition and heritage.

Leonard Coffman and Marvin West were perceptive observers of the history of Tennessee football. They came from differing perspectives, player and sports journalist, respectively, yet they found a common thread in their assessments.

"To play for Tennessee," said Coffman, a longshoreman disguised as a UT fullback from Greeneville, Tennessee in the glory days of 1937–1939 and thought by Tennessee historians and players of his day to be one of the toughest Vols ever. "To play for Tennessee, you have to get wet all over."

The Tennessee experience, Leonard was saying,

was not something to be taken lightly. It was and is a total commitment, a way of life. There are great expectations and great rewards.

"Some would say it is a religion, full of faith," West wrote about the Tennessee fan experience. "Clearly ritual and worship are involved. And inspiration. And fire and brimstone. Hymns about homes in high mountains played on tubas and bass drums."

This is Tennessee football, where the future is not tomorrow, but today.

PHILLIP FULMER: A TRUE SON OF TENNESSEE

WAS PHILLIP Fulmer destined to be a scholarship football player, the head football coach, and later athletic director? Was his leadership written in the stars, a certainty to happen from the outset? Were there events that foreshadowed what was to happen to him in the years to come?

No one knows for sure, but there were some early indications of that possibility during his undergraduate years at Tennessee (1968-73). If you check the 1970 Volunteer, the school's yearbook, Volume 1, pp. 9–10, there's a special article that Fulmer penned about his sophomore season in the fall of 1969, one in which the Vols had won the SEC title and played in the Gator Bowl. He was then a few months short of his twentieth birthday (September 1, 1950) and just ahead of becoming the father of Phillip E. Fulmer, Jr., born March 25, 1970.

The team had also lost its coach after the season, given that Dickey ended up at Florida for the 1970 season, to be replaced by twenty-eight year-old Bill Battle, University of Alabama alum and Tennessee's wide receivers coach.

Fulmer's thoughts are illustrative of his approach to and love for the game. He was, it seems, ahead of his time, already a perceptive observer of what it took to be successful on and off the gridiron. The article was a primer on leadership, an explication of what it takes to succeed on the gridiron…and beyond. He seemed wise beyond his years.

"The beginning of a football season is always an unusual time for me," he wrote. "I look forward to the games, the bid for the SEC title, and the chance to go to a bowl game. But sometimes I dread those long, hot practices, the running we have to do, and, I guess, a million or more things.

"But after a game, and I'm talking about a winning game or after the season is over, I actually miss the work we went through to make our season a successful one. Sure we go through hell in spring practice, but if for one minute I didn't think it was worth it, I'd quit. Let's face it. I love football."

The young offensive lineman understood what it took to make the team and have a significant impact of the team's fortunes.

"On the first day of practice, you can generally tell the people who are going to have the best chance of making the team," Fulmer wrote. "They're the ones who are always at the beginning of the line to do the wind sprints or the first ones to volunteer to do some kind of drill. In other words, they're the ones with the most desire. The only way you're going to impress your coach is to be as gung-ho as possible, even if it kills you. Pride, and a great deal of it, is what you need if you're going to make a good football team like ours."

His freshman days seemed so far away, fifty years

ago in the fall of 1968. Freshmen weren't eligible in those days, but Fulmer came in ready for the challenge.

He had come to the University of Tennessee from Franklin County High School in Winchester, Tennessee, on the Tennessee-Alabama line. He wanted to be a linebacker, maybe even a tight end, but ended up an offensive guard, sharing time his first two years with Don Denbo of nearby Pulaski, and starting in his third.

He came to Tennessee as part of an exceptional 1968-69 recruiting class that included Bobby Majors, the last of the Majors brothers to play for the Vols, Curt Watson (the "Crossville Comet"), Carl Johnson, Jackie Walker, Phil Pierce, Gary Theiler, Tom Bennett, Anthony Edwards, Roger McKinney, Ray Nettles, Sonny Leach, Joe Balthrop, Richard Earl, and Frank Howell.

There were two All-American selections in that class—Walker and Majors—and four All-SEC selections (Watson three times, Walker and Majors twice, and Nettles). Balthrop was a three-year starter. Johnson started in 1970 and 1971. Howell stared in 1971. Leach started in 1972. So it was a special group.

There was a pitched recruiting battle between old rivals Alabama and Tennessee for Fulmer's services, what with Winchester having a substantial Alabama presence. The Vols won out when assistant coach Ray Trail convinced Fulmer that Tennessee needed the best players to stay in the state.

"Phillip, you are a Tennessee boy," Trail told Fulmer. "If anything good is going to happen to you, it's going to happen at Tennessee. It's not going to happen at

Alabama. If anything good is going to happen at Alabama, it's going to happen to a boy from Alabama."

His time at Tennessee was one of the best periods in school history, a 30-5 record with two bowl wins in three tries, an SEC title and 9-2 record in 1969, and an eleven-win season and Sugar Bowl championship in 1970. He was also named an alternate captain of the 10-2 1971 team.

"I wasn't a great player, but I hoped people realized I was a team guy," he said.

Think about that statement when you consider that, when things might not have gone as well as they could have during his coaching career, Fulmer would say something like, "The name on the jersey was more important than the T on the helmet."

That was his way of saying that somehow the letter "I" had gotten into the word "TEAM." And that wasn't good.

Shortly after his graduation in 1972, he began his journey up the coaching ladder, with tenures at Tennessee (1972-73) as a student coach, Wichita State (1974-78), and Vanderbilt (1979), before returning home under head coach Johnny Majors in 1980.

In his graduate assistant stint at Tennessee, he was charge of the freshman team's defense and linebackers. During that time, the legendary assistant coach and All-American tailback George Cafego taught him the abilities it took to scout the opposition. It became a key development in Coach Fulmer's future success. He then took those experiences to heart and coached five seasons at Wichita State and one season at Vanderbilt before returning to Knoxville in 1980 for thirteen years as a Tennessee assistant, the last four as assistant head coach and offensive coordinator.

He coached the offensive line (1980-88), was offensive coordinator (1988-1992), and interim head coach (for the first three games of the 1992 season), before being named head coach on Nov. 29.

His first official game as head coach was a 38-23 triumph over Boston College in the Hall of Fame Bowl in Tampa.

The Hall of Fame Bowl was an indicator of the good things that lay ahead for the Vols. Two days before the game, David Cutcliffe had told Heath Shuler that the first play would be for all the marbles, bombs away. And it was. Shuler hit wide receiver Ron Davis down the left side to the BC one-yard line, and the Vols ran away with the game, 38-23 in a game that wasn't as close as the score.

The gauntlet had been thrown down.

Every Saturday was an adventure. When Fulmer was interim coach in 1992, fans seemed to realize there was something special going on. Many saw a great deal of Doug Dickey's influence in the way Fulmer coached and the Vols played.

The Vols defeated Southwestern Louisiana, Georgia, and Florida during his three-game interim tenure. When the twentieth-ranked Vols defeated the number fourteen Bulldogs in the second game of the season, even the most casual observer in the Vols dressing room could have noticed the camaraderie between Fulmer and his offensive line charges.

There was an unmistakable respect between coach and players. Tempers flared at times on the practice field, necessitating that offensive and defensive linemen needed to be separated. When Fulmer stepped in, the combatants instantly stepped back. He was rapidly ascending the coaching ladder, and Vols fans intuitively took note of Fulmer's prospects in the category of "unfinished business."

When he was introduced as head coach on November 29, 1992, he promised to take the Vols to the next level. He hit the ground running and the record reflects that he meant what he said.

There were a number of magic moments over the course of his stewardship of the Volunteers. The Vols finished number three (AP) in the 1995 season behind sophomore quarterback Peyton Manning, rolling up 413 points in twelve games and beating Ohio State in the 1996 Florida Citrus Bowl. The Vols won SEC titles in 1997 and 1998, and the national crown that latter year.

Fulmer produced eighteen All-American selections, seventy first team All-SEC selections, and ninety-one NFL draft choices. The Vols won ten or more games in nine of those seasons. There were only two losing seasons during his tenure, 2005 and 2008. His teams played in fifteen bowl games, winning eight. He coached four Jacobs Trophy winners as the SEC's best blockers: Harry Galbreath (1987), Eric Still (1989), Antone Davis (1990), and Aaron Sears (2006).

He had thus won conference championships as a player, assistant coach, and head coach.

Over the years, Fulmer had a 12-5-1 record against Alabama.

There was a 45-5 run from 1995-98, when the Vols won again and again and always seemed to have something special when it was needed most. Neyland Stadium was a House of Horrors for visiting teams, while the Vols went on the road with confidence and won in some of the toughest venues in college football.

Vols fans celebrated the wins with swagger typical of the history of Tennessee football. Opposing venues were dotted with orange, as Vols fans followed the team wherever it went, from Notre Dame to UCLA, from Miami to Dallas.

Vols fans are split on the time the wheels fell off during Fulmer's coaching tenure. Significant losses to Nebraska in the 1998 Orange Bowl and 2000 Fiesta Bowl were mitigated by the Vols' national championship season in between.

There was a tough-to-take loss in the SEC title game in 2001, the week after a memorable 34-32 win at Florida that exorcised a great many demons. There was a hastily arranged celebration at Tom Black Track when the team charter arrived home that evening. Many players were carrying roses, symbolic of their hopes of playing in the Rose Bowl in the national championship game.

It was a magic moment, a celebration of a great moment in Tennessee football history. In the back of their heads, however, fans had to wonder whether the news of the excitement in Knoxville made its way to Baton Rouge, Louisiana, where Nick Saban's LSU team lay in wait.

Somehow, the Vols had handed the Tigers a tremendous motivational edge.

The euphoria lasted a week. An injury-riddled LSU squad, down to a back-up quarterback and back-up running back, took advantage of two critical second half Tennessee turnovers to steal a 31-20 win that sent shockwaves across Big Orange Country. That loss still haunts many in the fan base years later.

There were two lopsided losses in the Peach Bowl, to Maryland and Clemson, and two other losses in the SEC title game. The 2005 and 2008 seasons were a couple of body shots. Somehow records seen as successful in his earlier tenure were no longer perceived to be good enough, particularly in the early 2000s.

The arrival of Mark Richt at Georgia in 2001, Urban Meyer at Florida in 2005, and Saban at Alabama in 2007 also complicated matters.

How could two Tennessee teams defeat Florida and Alabama and win ten games in each of 2003 and 2004, yet have the seasons somehow be perceived as a disappointment or, for lack of a better word, as underachieving?

That's exactly what happened to Tennessee teams that each compiled 9-4 and 10-4 records overall, went 13-3 in the SEC, and played in the SEC Championship game that latter season, yet left fans wondering what happened or what might have been.

In 2003, the Vols had won at Florida and at Alabama and had pulled off a major upset at Miami, but in the minds of many Vols fans, it somehow wasn't enough, especially when an unranked Clemson team dominated the Peach

Bowl.

The 2004 team defeated Florida and Alabama at home and won at Georgia, but lost twice to Auburn, once at home and once in the SEC title game, and somehow lost to Notre Dame a few weeks before Irish head coach Tyrone Willingham was let go. The Tennessee game was Willingham's last victory as Notre Dame head coach.

An injury to Vol freshman quarterback Erik Ainge in the final seconds of the first half against the Fighting Irish sidelined Erik for the season, a week after fellow freshman quarterback Brent Schaeffer had broken his collarbone in a game at South Carolina. The Vols won the 2005 Cotton Bowl, 38-7 over Texas A&M, but, in many minds, even with benefit of hindsight, the seasons after the 1998 national championship somehow didn't measure up.

The 2005 season was one of those years that saw a number of close games get away sometime during the fourth quarter. There were lingering rumors of a lack of discipline within the team. There had been a remarkable comeback at LSU in the third game of the season, when the Vols won 30-27 in overtime in a surreal setting brought on by the aftermath of Hurricane Katrina.

The Vols had flown to Baton Rouge and home again the same day because there was no place for them to stay, given the number of evacuees in the area. The Vols were in a no-win situation relative to game day preparations but managed to win after trailing by 21-0 in the second quarter.

That victory was overshadowed by tight losses at

Florida, at home against Georgia, at Alabama, at Notre Dame, and at home against Vanderbilt in Tennessee's first loss to the Commodores since 1964. A picture of a dejected Fulmer, coaching cap and headset askew and hands on his knees on the sideline at Notre Dame, summed up the entire frustrating season. The Vols grabbed a consolation prize of sorts, winning at Kentucky in the season finale.

Offensive coordinator Randy Sanders left the team in November and line coach Jimmy Ray Stephens and receivers coach Pat Washington left after the season finale was in the books.

The 2006 season got off to a good start with the return of David Cutcliffe as offensive coordinator and a resounding win over California, 35-18.

Air Force's triple option offense gave the Vols all they wanted, but Xavier Mitchell recovered an onside kick inside the final minutes to save a 31-30 victory. That game was overshadowed by a serious injury to defensive back Inquoris (Inky) Johnson, who suffered a career-ending injury that left him paralyzed. Johnson afterward became a motivational speaker, specializing in the areas of leadership, teamwork, or perseverance

After a 21-20 loss to Florida, the Vols knocked off Marshall, Memphis, came from 24-7 down at Georgia to win 51-33, defeated Alabama 16-13, the last win over the Tide, then won a tough one at South Carolina.

The Vols lost at home to LSU and on the road at Arkansas yet came back to defeat Vanderbilt and Kentucky. The Outback Bowl against Penn State, tied 10-10 in the fourth quarter, got away when the Nittany Lions had an

88-yard fumble recovery for a touchdown just when it appeared the Vols were ready to take the lead.

In 2007, the Vols lost decisively at California, Florida, and Alabama and lived dangerously against South Carolina and Kentucky, with both games going into overtime. Vanderbilt had a shot at a game-winning field goal, but it misfired to the left.

Ainge had two critical picks in the SEC title game against LSU, in a game dominated by off-the-field news that Tiger coach Les Miles might be headed home to Michigan. The Vols recovered to beat Wisconsin in the Outback Bowl and things looked rosy going into 2008.

A season-opening overtime loss at UCLA set the tone for the season in 2008. The Vols looked as if they might be able to put the game away, but several turnovers proved decisive. The Vols lost six of eight games from that point on, to Florida, Auburn, Georgia, and Alabama, where Crimson Tide fans took over the stadium.

The South Carolina game also got away, and AD Mike Hamilton seemingly tipped his hand in the News Sentinel the next day. When asked about Fulmer's future, he said, "I don't want to comment, out of respect for Phillip."

Fulmer was let go the next day as word leaked out well before a Monday press conference. The Vols sleptwalked through the next game, the Homecoming contest against Wyoming, losing 13-7 to a Wyoming team whose coach would also be fired at season's end.

There was a fortuitous open date the next week, allowing Fulmer to rally the troops for contests at

Vanderbilt, a 20-10 win, and a 28-10 win over Kentucky the next week.

Underdog Tennessee led Vandy at the half 20-0, causing Joe Biddle, sportswriter from The Tennessean, Nashville's morning newspaper, to look at no one in particular at halftime and ask the following question. "If this is Vanderbilt's best team in twenty-six years and Tennessee's worst, why is the score 20-0, Tennessee?"

The rain and cold at the Kentucky game somehow symbolized the season, but Fulmer left the field on the shoulders of his players to the applause of the crowd.

Fulmer's final record was 152-52. He joined the ranks of former Vols who had played and coached at Tennessee and somehow found their way to the wrong side of the fan base: Robinson, Wyatt, and Majors. Dame Fortune is one fickle creature. It's really tough, however, when it's one of your own.

"I never thought the firing would happen," Fulmer told Fox Sports' Clay Travis in *On Rocky Top: A Front-Row Set to the End of an Era*. "Picture this in the last twelve months. We play LSU for the conference championship until the final couple of minutes, won the bowl game for our tenth win (a victory over Wisconsin in the Outback Bowl), I'm inducted into the Knoxville Sports Hall of Fame, got a new contract, won my hundred and fiftieth game, and got fired in the same year. It doesn't add up."

At the end of his tenure at Tennessee, Fulmer had the second-highest number of wins of any head coach in Tennessee history, twenty-one behind General Neyland. Fulmer also was the third Tennessee head coach to win a national championship. He was considered by many to be an icon of college football, especially one of institutional loyalty.

In recognition of his accomplishments at Tennessee, Fulmer was inducted into the College Football Hall of Fame in 2012, joining colleagues Jimmy Johnson at Oklahoma State (1979-83) and at Miami (1984-88), and R.C. Slocum at Texas A&M (1989-02). Since leaving as head coach with a six million dollar buyout in hand, Fulmer was a sports analyst on the CBS SEC Postgame Show, as well as various programming on the CBS College Sports Network. He had also played himself in the 2009 movie Blind Side.

He won the Robert R. Neyland Award from the Knoxville Quarterback Club and had served as a special assistant to the athletic director at East Tennessee State University, helping reestablish the school's football program. On June 20, 2017, Fulmer was named as a special advisor to the University of Tennessee president Joe DiPietro. He was selected as the 2018 University of Tennessee Legend, to be honored at the SEC Championship Game December 1.

Things were changing markedly on the University of Tennessee campus in Knoxville. Nobody knew it across the expanse of Big Orange Country, but the year 2017 would be the most tumultuous in the institution's history. There were a number of issues that demanded attention almost on a daily basis, and no one was ready when the powder keg blew. The results would be unprecedented and have very real implications across the collegiate landscape.

SYMPTOMS AND DIAGNOSIS OF UT'S DOWNFALL

By Celina Summers and Tom Mattingly

"Our Tennessee family is united in its goals but divided in the right path to get there. I love Tennessee too much to let her stay divided."

AT FIRST glance, the statement above looks like something anyone intimately associated with the Vol ReVOLution would have said in 2017, when the University of Tennessee's dirty laundry was raked over and turned into a punch line by the national media. After all, the remark was a perfect summation of what was happening within the Volunteer family, with the in-fighting and power plays exposed to the world in glaring detail.

Only…

Only those words had been uttered on November 3, 2008 by Phillip Fulmer during a farewell press conference as he prepared to leave the University of Tennessee football program he'd coached for seventeen years. These words represent a fascinating insight from a man who was being ousted as the *root* of Tennessee's problems only to vindicated and brought back in triumph nine years later as a last-ditch effort to find a *cure* for the problems that truly began when he'd been fired.

Some wise people claim that our memories are subjective, colored in our mind's eye by emotions rather than the clarity of perfect recall. I was surprised when I looked up the historical weather data for November 3, 2008, that the old saying was one hundred percent correct. Despite my recollection of a slate-gray sky spitting out a desultory freezing drizzle in a bitter cold wind, in fact November 3, 2008 was an unseasonably warm day in central Ohio. The sun was out that afternoon and the temperature ultimately rose to seventy-five degrees. Despite a morning fog, there were no clouds and barely a wisp of a breeze.

I know why my perceptions of that day were skewed. So do you. The day that the University of Tennessee took its first step toward disaster and fired Phillip Fulmer in the middle of the season will always be a day that I, for one, associate instinctively with my least favorite kind of day.

Fulmer's firing, to anyone who loves University of Tennessee sports and football, in particular, was one of those significant days whether you agree with the firing or not. UT is almost a decade to the day removed from that afternoon in Knoxville where a tearful Fulmer bade farewell to Vol Nation. Although the seeds of the Volunteers' fiasco were sown after former athletic director Doug Dickey's retirement in 2003, that November afternoon in 2008 saw the first of them bear fruit.

All Tennessee fans have their own memories, colored by their own perceptions, about that day. Many focused on the catch in Fulmer's voice; the rather smug expression on then-athletic director Mike Hamilton's face when he took the microphone back after Fulmer's farewell address; a smirking assistant AD hovering in the background who'd impact UT disastrously several years later; and the ten seconds immediately after Hamilton took the mike. That's when the then-current Tennessee football players in the room stood up, turned their backs on the AD, and marched from the room.

"He ain't got nothing to say to us!" one of the players yelled on his way out the door, as reported by ESPN journalist Chris Low, a University of Tennessee graduate who'd just joined the sports media giant.

Of all the ways to bring a legendary coach's career to an end, Tennessee chose a remarkably classless and ungrateful manner of forcing Fulmer out of the football office doors. Fulmer had taken the Volunteers to the pinnacle of college football success, to heights the Vols had barely glimpsed since the departure of General Neyland. But instead of allowing him the dignified departure that his accomplishments had merited, UT chose to humiliate him, and show him the door mid-season with brutal unconcern for Fulmer, his former and current players, the fans—

And, as it turned out, the consequences.

UT has dealt with the repercussions of that awful decision for a decade. With unimaginable turnover in the administration and athletic department of the university, the future of Tennessee sports—which had looked so promising for two decades—plummeted into the stranglehold of first, mediocrity, and finally, embarrassing ineptitude. The reason for that fall was crystallized by

Phillip Fulmer during his farewell press conference.

Funny, isn't it?

"Our Tennessee family is united in its goals but divided in the right path to get there. I love Tennessee too much to let her stay divided."

If only UT had paid attention to Fulmer's diagnosis of the problem in 2008. If they had, then Schiano Sunday would not have been necessary. But in the nine years between Fulmer's removal and his appointment as the athletic director at the University of Tennessee, not only did the actions of the decision-makers render the Vol ReVOLution necessary, but day-to-day communication between fans and the university they supported underwent such a rapid and stunning transition that the ReVOLution became unavoidable.

And even harder to overcome was the incontrovertible fact that the seeds of the ReVOLution had actually been planted in titles in 1985, 1989, and 1990. Those years brought great moments when the sky was the limit on the field, with SEC titles in 1997 and 1998, a national championship in football in 1998, but they also brought on an inexplicable time frame—from 2008 on—where nothing good happened, something that pumped up the alumni and fan base, without a corresponding gut punch.

There was a crisis of leadership on campus, with a revolving door of presidents, chancellors, athletic directors, and coaches. Financial buyouts of head coaches and administrators have become the norm, a part of the cost of doing business. It wasn't quite the gang that couldn't shoot straight, but it was close. The university has faced nearly every imaginable crisis since 2008 with the impacts still being felt on campus.

But Tennessee's downfall really began in 2003, when UT was still one of the top athletic programs in the country.

Doug Dickey had arrived in Knoxville forty years earlier as a thirty-two-year-old head coach from Frank Broyles's staff at Arkansas. Dickey had been in the athletic director's chair in Knoxville since 1985, overseeing a Tennessee athletic program that many had considered a model program.

Dickey was a known quantity, a Tennessee loyalist, and a major player in the biggest decisions on campus from the time he was head football coach through his time as leader of the department. Dickey had broad shoulders and could handle a crisis situation. When he talked, thoughtful people listened.

Dickey stepped down June 4, with a final and emotional appearance before departmental staff. Moments of transition are interesting things—sometimes sad, many times poignant, always intriguing. As one career passed into history and another regime began, the gamut of emotions can be wide-ranging.

For those on staff, what you could call the changing of the guard came that morning in the team room in the Neyland-Thompson Sports Center. If those attending hadn't been paying attention at the meeting, they might have missed it.

Sometime after 9 am, Dickey talked for a few moments about the athletic department, its past, its present, and its future. There were really no surprises as he discussed facilities, revenue streams, and cash flow, as well as his remembrances of people he had come to know and respect. He discussed UT competing against schools like Ohio State, Texas, Florida, and Georgia and the dynamics of supporting coaches and student-athletes in their quest for excellence. He talked about the ability of the athletic department to put on events, calling it a "pretty good, fan-friendly place."

The Volunteer Athletic Scholarship Fund (VASF) was founded in 1986, with revenues of $1,436,271. In 2003, he added, the amount to date was $12,148,645. It had been a period of steady growth, peaking in the late 1990s, hitting $10 million in 1999, $12 million in 2000, $12.4 million in 2001, and $12.5 million in 2002.

He praised VASF donors, the people, he said, "who make the program go.

"They've been the winning edge. We've have been able to raise the money we need for scholarships and facilities and use the earnings to run the department. I have always been aware of the progress we have made through the VASF, and it's been thrilling to watch the growth generated by so many of you who have not only contributed but have enrolled new members as well. The winning edge can come from a lot of places. For us, over the last fifteen years, each of those VASF members has been the winning edge."

He talked briefly about the great athletes and great moments, the thrilling moments of his career, and the incredible dynamics that helped make the University of Tennessee a great place.

"We don't know where the next great athlete is coming from," he said, "but the bottom line is that it's still all about the teams and the student-athletes and how we manage the Tennessee scene. That's the important thing for us."

His last words to the staff as AD were vintage Doug Dickey: "I have a comfort zone about what you've helped accomplish."

With that, he introduced Mike Hamilton as his successor and quietly left the room. The transition was complete.

That was then.

This is now.

It seems so long ago, the days former coaches ran athletic departments, long before the business model came into vogue and bean counters were elevated into positions of responsibility.

With all apologies to Felice and Boudleaux and the House of Bryant, how does a great institution go from *Rocky Top* to rocky bottom? How have fans reacted to such a precipitously quick decline and what could they have done to stem the tide?

Over the years, the hiring of Tennessee football coaches had rarely been the product of a search committee. Tennessee just didn't do things that way. Dean Nathan

Dougherty had wanted to hire Bob Neyland, then an assistant coach under M.B. Banks, all along, but let the local media think there was a search. Neyland was his man, and he got him in December of 1925, after Banks left to go to Central High School. He was the second Tennessee coach to go from the university to a local high school. John R. Bender had gone from Tennessee to Knoxville High School after the 1920 season.

After he stepped down just before the 1953 Cotton Bowl on doctor's orders, Neyland hired assistant coach Harvey Robinson, holding out the possibility he might return in 1954. He never did return, but also had to fire Robinson two years later after a 10-10-1 record, saying, "I just didn't know how to handle the situation. It was the first time I ever had to do anything to hurt any of my boys."

Neyland then hired Bowden Wyatt, the Vols' captain in 1938 and two-time selection to the College Football Hall of Fame, who had won conference titles at Wyoming and Arkansas. That was a no-brainer. He was literally the people's choice. Vols fans wanted Wyatt and no one else.

Jim McDonald was an interim coach in 1963 as the Vols were scrapping the single-wing and heading to the T formation.

There were appearances of a coaching search in December 1963 with all kinds of names being floated in the press, but Bob Woodruff wanted Arkansas offensive coordinator Doug Dickey and hired him in early December. Dickey had played for Woodruff at Florida in the early 1950s, and Woodruff had kept a watchful eye on him ever since.

When Dickey left in 1970, Woodruff wanted someone already on staff, and that choice was Bill Battle. Johnny Majors was the clear-cut favorite in 1977, as was Phillip Fulmer in 1992 after Majors stepped down.

Heading into Fulmer's last season as head coach, glaring cracks had been exposed within the fan base. For one thing, Fulmer had always been slightly controversial since the transition between former head coach Johnny Majors and himself. For another, Fulmer was in his seventeenth year at head coach and there was a growing sense that he no longer had the flexibility as a coach to take the Vols back to the top of the college football ladder. Vols fans were divided, and the ones who were lobbying for a new head coach were just as vociferous as the ones who weren't prepared to oust Fulmer after a 2007 campaign that took the Vols to the SEC Championship game.

But the firing of Fulmer—and primarily the disrespectful way that UT officials handled the midseason coup—drove the biggest spike between factions within Volunteer Nation and the university, and ultimately laid the foundations for the nine years of chaos that followed. The idea that any school, particularly a tradition-laden school in the South, would fire a SEC and National Championship-winning head coach mid-season was incomprehensible to many, and the sight of a man who'd given thirty-one years to the University of Tennessee as a player, GA, assistant, and head coach tearing up as he said farewell was a staggering indictment of UT's leadership.

Fulmer's departure had detrimentally impacted the program with an immense obstacle that had to be overcome during subsequent coaching hires: how could any big-name head coach trust UT to deal with them fairly when it had been so easy for the school to rid itself of a Tennessee legend?

Obviously, no coach could.

As a result of the ouster, Fulmer was succeeded by a precocious brat-savant in Lane Kiffin, whose losing record and antagonistic manner caused his expulsion from the Oakland Raiders' head coaching job. He compiled a mediocre 7-6 record, insulted every school and coach the Vols played, then bolted from Knoxville to USC in the middle of the night like a thief fleeing the scene of a crime, leaving NCAA violations scattered behind him like he was Johnny Appleseed with a new bag of seeds to sow. Kiffin departed a few weeks before National Signing Day, calling recruits to follow him to USC. As he drove through the campus, he was heckled on his way to the airport by fans, burning couches and any Kiffin paraphernalia they could get their hands on.

They can be forgiven, perhaps, for enjoying the story of Kiffin's ouster from USC on the airport tarmac a few years later just a little too much.

The timing of Kiffin's departure proved to be a real problem for Hamilton because National Signing Day was less than a month away. He selected Louisiana Tech head coach and athletic director Derek Dooley, who had a losing record at a much smaller school. Rumor has it that Will Muschamp, who faced the Vols at Florida and South Carolina and is undefeated in seven tries, declined the position, but recommended Dooley.

So Kiffin was succeeded by the woeful Derek Dooley, who despite his record and poor in-game coaching decisions, was well-liked by his players. He was the creator of the Vols For Life program, an initiative that was intended to assist both current and former players and strengthen their ties to the program. But that was pretty much the only thing fans appreciated about the young coach with a law degree and a vaunted SEC pedigree as the son of legendary UGA coach, Vince Dooley. Dooley left the Vols after a 41-18 loss at Vanderbilt and a 15-21 record. The coach was reviled on his way out of town—orange britches notwithstanding—after three lousy seasons.

Dave Hart was now in the AD's office. He brought Butch Jones to Rocky Top, after Jones had previously followed Brian Kelly to Central Michigan and the University of Cincinnati. Jones came in with a boatload of slogans and gimmicks that initially energized the fan base.

But in Ohio, one journalist with ties to both the Bearcats and the Volunteers expressed strong reservations about the hire. Eric Waddell, who'd covered Jones at Cincinnati, stated unequivocally that Jones was a bad fit for UT.

"I never saw him as a winning hire. He was not a fit to the Tennessee fan base. He didn't have the experience for a job like this. There is a different level of pressure at UT. I was concerned there would be rough times with the media," Waddell remarked. "I thought he would bring tons of energy and work hard on the recruiting trail, but he didn't know how big a deal football was and would get in more trouble with his mouth than what happened on the field. I was concerned with the attitude he had at Cincinnati. He was a brusque, midwestern type guy. He seemed more interested in recruiting skill players than the guys up front. What worked in the MAC or Big East wouldn't work here. I believed that wouldn't endear him to Tennessee fans. He was incredibly stubborn and didn't have a grasp of the depth of the knowledge of Tennessee fans."

His thoughts turned out to be remarkably prescient. His diagnosis of what would happen was almost eerie in its accuracy.

"Cincinnati had one beat writer. There's just not the same type scrutiny. My gut feeling was that he wasn't prepared. The truth is I had hoped he would prove me wrong. He has a reputation for being hard-headed. He doesn't always learn from his mistakes. There was a ceiling level he could get to and once he reached it, he couldn't get higher. When Tennessee played Cincinnati, people connected with the program told him not to play press coverage against receivers who went on to the NFL. He didn't take their advice, and Tennessee smoked 'em all day. The next week, they played Akron, played zone, and shut them out. When reporters asked him about the change in defense, he said they didn't change anything."

Initially, Jones seemed to do everything right. Every year, his recruiting classes were highly ranked. The talent of the players he brought to Tennessee masked his deficiencies as a coach. But fan sentiment began to turn against him, especially when the Vols crashed and burned after blowing a 17-0 lead against Oklahoma in 2015 (losing

31-24 in OT) and then losing at Texas A&M 45-39 in 2016, also in overtime and amidst a hail of turnovers.

Moreover, fans were incensed that Jones showed the inability to pull the trigger on tough decisions, kicking a field goal on fourth-and-one near the Sooners goal line and kicking an extra point in a similar situation to tie the 2016 game against A&M, when the Vols were within a yard or so in the shadow of the Aggie goal.

After a win over Florida and stealing a last-minute win at Georgia on a Hail Mary pass in the 2016 season, his tenure was never the same. He never recaptured the magic of those victories and losing three out of five games, two in Knoxville, to in-state rival Vanderbilt didn't help, either.

But the football program hadn't been the only element integral in creating a rift between UT and its fan base. The same pattern of controversy arose in other men's and women's athletic programs, amplified by a growing tendency of tone-deafness by the UTAD toward Tennessee fans. Mike Hamilton had hired Bruce Pearl as the head basketball coach, brought in at the behest of former Vol All-American Ernie Grunfeld. Pearl broke every dish in the house with a fast break offense that led to Tennessee hoops becoming a can't-miss proposition for the fans.

However, an anonymous letter sent to the NCAA and transmitted to Tennessee on April 11, 2011, included a picture of a recruit at a barbecue at Pearl's home. That picture became a smoking gun when Pearl was confronted with the photo and was not forthcoming about the circumstances under which it was taken.

During that season, when Pearl was suspended by the SEC for eight games, whatever network was telecasting the game took more than a few minutes reviewing Pearl's NCAA dossier. Pearl was fired on March 22 after Hamilton threw him under the bus even as his team prepared for the NCAA Tournament. Pearl ended up with a three-year show cause order keeping him out of coaching until he was hired by Auburn in 2014. Pearl has since built that program up the same way he had the Vols, sharing the SEC regular-season championship with the Vols in 2018.

Cuonzo Martin, whose Southwest Missouri team had played the Vols earlier that season, was hired to replace him. Many observers believed he was the anti-Pearl and would work hard to avoid any hint of impropriety with the NCAA. But despite a run to the Elite Eight and a one-point loss to Michigan in his final season, Martin was never really accepted by the fan base. Early in his career, about 25,000 fans signed a petition calling for his removal. After the NCAA run, he left for California and is now at Missouri.

Then AD Dave Hart made a disastrous coaching hire, compounding the woes on Rocky Top. Donnie Tyndall came to Knoxville with all kinds of NCAA baggage and lasted a year before being fired.

But Hart somehow hit the jackpot when he hired former Texas coach Rick Barnes after he had been let go in Austin. Barnes was merely pedestrian in his first two seasons but hit the jackpot by sharing the SEC title with a Pearl-coached Auburn in 2017-18. The program now appears to be on solid footing and is ranked in the top ten in the fall of 2018.

Baseball also proved troublesome after Rod Delmonico was let go in 2007. Todd Raleigh, who came from Western Carolina, didn't make the NCAA Tournament in his four seasons. His successor, Dave Serrano, fared no better, and was relieved after six seasons. Current coach Tony Vitello came along in 2017-18, and the program is now showing signs of life.

But the real wedge was driven between the UTAD and Vol Nation over the Lady Vols.

Hearts were saddened when Pat Summitt, who had led the Lady Vols basketball program to eight national championships in thirty-eight years, and 1098 victories, made the announcement on May 24, 2011, that she had early-onset dementia/Alzheimer's. That diagnosis shook Big Orange Country to its foundations.

Fans and media alike had noticed that Summitt wasn't herself but didn't know exactly what was going on and didn't know exactly what to do. Summitt still had a seat on the bench, with Holly Warlick, her long-time assistant, effectively acting as head coach.

"The legendary coach who never had a losing record in thirty-eight seasons, shocked the sports world in May, 2011 when she announced she would continue at the University of Tennessee despite the diagnosis," Erik Brady of CBS Sports wrote. "It was as if she were staring down her disease with the same icy glare she made famous while winning eight national championships and the respect of a nation that didn't pay much attention to women's sports when she was growing up."

The Summitt Stare, highlighted by her piercing blue eyes, became a personal trademark, highlighting her competitive zeal and her desire to have her players be the best players and citizens they could be. Summitt alone boast the distinction of graduating one hundred percent of the young women who played basketball at UT on her watch.

In 2011, athletic director Mike Hamilton resigned and the university took the opportunity to merge the then-separate men's and women's athletic departments into one entity, under the aegis of longtime women's AD Joan Cronan until a permanent athletic director was hired to replace Hamilton. One consequence of the continued effort to merge the two departments was a battle over how the reorganized department would function, given the turf battles that had dominated the days when the men and women's departments each did their own thing. In addition, a new battle arose over the Summitt legacy.

Of particular importance to most fans was a determination that the newly-diagnosed Summitt, who had contributed so much to UT and Knoxville and who basically built NCAA women's basketball out of sheer grit and persistence, should be able to leave the program on her own terms. Summitt's influence extended far and wide, even at least once after a loss where she appeared to gain the moral high ground.

Just when you might have thought the book *Unrivaled: UConn, Tennessee and the Twelve Years that Transcended Women's Basketball* by Jeff Goldberg might have been an unabashed UConn promotional piece, Alysa Auriemma, Geno's daughter, penned a tribute to Summitt that was a masterpiece. She related the day that Pat left Alysa, aged eleven, a voicemail message: "I hear you like orange!"

Later, the legendary coach met Alysa at the 1997 Dayton Regionals.

"I'm positive I was so freaked out I never returned her call," Alysa said. That meeting made an impact on her, particularly when news broke on Aug. 23, 2011, of Summitt's diagnosis…at age fifty-nine. That had to have been hard on an eleven-year-old who idolized her, much the way many young girls and women did over the years.

"What I will mostly remember that this multiple-championship-winning coach on her way to another championship in 1997, called me on the phone, remembered my name, and looked me in the eye as an eleven-year-old with gnarled hair with a gaze that said, 'You are on my level.' But no one is on that level. She's at the Rocky Top."

Goldberg also shared a moment where Summitt seemed to have Auriemma flummoxed, even after a decisive UConn win in the 2004 NCAA Championship game. That may have been a classic athletic example of no good deed going unpunished.

Goldberg recounts that Pat came to the dressing room to congratulate the UConn team on winning the championship. 'I don't think any of us will ever forget it," center Jessica Moore said. "It was pretty darn cool."

Auriemma said he wasn't sure of the "context" of the Summitt visit. He hadn't been there to see it himself. "I always wonder when something like that happens. What is the motivation for doing it? Is it for publicity? To gain some kind of edge? I have no idea. I just thought it was a little odd."

But regardless of what Auriemma did or didn't think, what happened to Summitt immediately after that locker room visit drove a wedge between UT and the fan base that rocked the entire Tennessee system.

Pat Summitt stated in a court affidavit in associate AD Debby Jennings' age and gender discrimination lawsuit against Hart and the University of Tennessee that AD Dave Hart had informed her on March 14, 2012 that she would step down after the season. "This was very surprising to me and very hurtful, as that was a decision I would have liked to have made on my own at the end of the season after consulting with my family, doctors, colleagues, and friends and not to be told this by Mr. Hart. I felt this was wrong."

When Jennings had sent an email protesting the forced resignation, Hart had given her the choice of resigning, retiring, or being fired at the age of fifty-seven.

In the same affidavit, Summit also revealed that Hart had informed her he was doing away with the Lady Vols brand entirely. And although Summitt later said that Hart had told her she'd "misinterpreted" what he'd said, the fan base never forgot—or forgave—Hart for seemingly forcing Pat Summitt out.

They didn't forgive UT either.

Pat Summit's death on June 28, 2016 brought that anger boiling back to the surface after the first wave of sorrow crushed the Tennessee community. Many observers found it interesting that neither Chancellor

Jimmy Cheek nor Athletic Director Dave Hart spoke at or attended Summitt's memorial services. But when Peyton Manning choked up during his eulogy, Vol Nation choked up as well.

Their dislike and distrust of the athletic director and the administration grew.

Holly Warlick had been named Summitt's successor before the 2012-2013 season. She led the Lady Vols to the SEC 2012–13 and 2014-15 regular season title. On March 9, 2014, Warlick coached the Lady Vols to their 17th SEC Tournament Championship by defeating Kentucky 71–70. She has an overall record of 153-54 and 71-25 (SEC).

But it's never as easy to step into the shoes of a giant as it is to stand on her shoulders.

Jimmy Cheek became the seventh chancellor of the University of Tennessee, Knoxville, on February 1, 2009. One of his roles on campus was oversight of the school's athletic program, a responsibility once held by the school's president. In handing him the reins of athletics, the argument was made that athletes were students and the responsibility of campus faculty and leadership.

Cheek's reign as chancellor could be seen as a policy of benign neglect, an attitude or policy of ignoring an often delicate or undesirable situation that one is held to be responsible for dealing with. Cheek appeared exceptionally uncomfortable in an athletic setting, unless it was on television after a bowl victory or accepting or dispersing a check earned by athletics.

But his impact on the athletic department caused outrage and reignited the resentment most fans felt about the way he and Dave Hart had dealt with Pat Summitt's retirement—and the plans they'd unwittingly revealed simultaneously.

In a November 12, 2014 Associated Press (AP) story titled, "Lady Vols For Basketball Only", the University of Tennessee started calling each of its athletics teams, men's and women's, the Volunteers, phasing out the Lady Volunteers nickname for all women's sports other than basketball starting in 2015. The move was part of the process of merging the two departments that had begun when Mike Hamilton retired and been continued under Hart.

The release said women's basketball would be exempt from the move and would continue using the Lady Vols nickname "because of the accomplishments and legacy of the championship program built by Coach Pat Summitt and her former players."

Cheek released a statement, stating that: "Brand consistency across the university is critical." This was part of the "One Tennessee" slogan adopted during the 2012 merger of the two programs.

The controversy resulted in a tough battle that benefited no one. No one knew whether Hart or Cheek wielded the most influence, but the smart money was on Hart. Hart and Cheek had claimed the coaches and athletes in the women's athletic programs had bought into the name change, but the fans weren't buying it.

One loyal fan was inspired to send the following

letter to UT President Joe DiPietro.

"I am SO delighted that you have hired a woman (Dr. Beverly Davenport) to replace Chancellor Cheek. She sounds wonderful. NOW, would you PLEASE re-install the Lady Vols name and logo to where it was before it was taken away? I've been one of MANY Lady Vols supporters who have been collecting signatures on a petition. I mail mine, six pages at a time, to Susan Whitlow in Bristol, Tennessee. She, in turn, mails 500 at a time to you. At the last count, she had sent over 25,500 names to you on the petition to get the LADY VOLS LOGO BACK! I would appreciate your response to my e-mail, and all of us would be thrilled to have the logo back as it once was so we can quit our volunteer job and begin concentrating on the University of Tennessee and the Vols and the Lady Vols again."

The chant of "Lady Vols! Lady Vols!" had echoed across the stands at their games, and supporters had worked overtime to flood the president and the Board of Trustees with petitions requesting, actually in numerous cases demanding, that the name be returned. They left no stone unturned to get their message out that the Lady Vol name and logo were an essential part of Tennessee tradition.

The administration, all the way to President Joe DiPietro, turned a deaf ear to their protests.

On August 1, 2017, the News Sentinel's John Adams said Lady Vols supporters "fought a long and honorable fight. You fought the kind of fight that would have made the late Pat Summitt proud."

He also encouraged them to move on to other matters. That never happened.

As a result of this decade and a half of history, the relationship between the Tennessee athletic department and the fan base disintegrated from a mutual support system to an adversarial and confrontational breakdown of communication. The UTAD ignored the rising agitation of its fans, unheeding of the disaster they were creating as a result. By the time Jimmy Cheek had been replaced by Beverly Davenport as chancellor, and Dave Hart succeeded by one-time Hamilton protégé John Currie, Vol Nation's trust in university officials to do what was best for Tennessee student-athletes, athletic programs, and fans had eroded into outright suspicion.

And within this atmosphere of brooding discontent and swelling outrage, Butch Jones had to make the transition from a 2016 that was loaded with talent to a rebuilding year in 2017 and a fan base that was completely fed up, not only with him but with the athletic department and administration as a whole.

Over the course of late summer and the fall of 2018 as this book was written, one goal was at the top of the list. The entire story of what happened to the University of Tennessee over the twenty years that saw the destruction of the athletic department's habitual success had to be told. For two decades, fans and supporters of UT had demanded answers from a silent and aloof Tennessee administration.

What was going on in Knoxville? Why were the problems surrounding the athletic department compounded instead of being resolved? Why was the school hiring sub-par head football coaches, and bringing in recruits that didn't match up with the historic dominance of the program?

Who was making all those bad decisions?

When there is a vacuum at the top of any organization, something always steps in and fills the space. Usually, whatever takes over for what was intended to lead that organization runs contrary to the plans and processes of the organization.

So what happened at UT?

Two decades of chaotic turnover in the administration meant that no one was actually leading the university. Since the 1998 BCS Championship, the University of Tennessee has gone through seven presidents (Joe Johnson, J. Wade Gilley, Emerson Fly, John W. Shumaker, John D. Peterson, Jan Simek, and Joe DiPietro) and is now headed up by an eighth in Randy Boyd. There have been six chancellors (William Snyder, Loren Crabtree, Jan Simek, Jimmy G. Cheek, Beverly Davenport, and Wayne Davis), five athletic directors (Doug Dickey, Mike Hamilton, Dave Hart, John Currie, and Phillip Fulmer), and five head football coaches (Phillip Fulmer, Lane Kiffin, Derek Dooley, Butch Jones, and Jeremy Pruitt). That instability devastated the chain of command. Instead of actual leadership, UT was crippled by in-fighting between agendas around the university.

Those factions were fighting so hard to consolidate control over Tennessee they didn't realize that between them, they were pulling the school apart.

But outside the circle of administrators, coaches, and boosters that surround the athletic department,

Tennessee fans and alumni were shut out of the decision making processes and given no insight as to what was going on. Vol Nation had been asking questions about how those decisions were made for two decades. We wanted to disinter the answers to those questions.

For the first time, that inner circle has been penetrated in this book. The next section of this book contains interviews with former players, Tennessee administrators, boosters, donors, and media regarding the decline of UT, the ReVOLution, and what that meant for Tennessee and the rest of the college football world.

These interviews are presented in transcript form, without any prejudice or pre-determined agenda that could portray any comments out of context. Every interview is presented verbatim, without editing or authorial slant, save for comments the subjects asked to be kept off the record. Every subject was given the opportunity to go on the record about what, in their perception, has been going on.

Sure, we could have cleaned these up. We could have edited them with an eye to keeping the subjects within a confined stream of narrative. But we didn't, and once readers hear for themselves what these thought influencers around UT have said, perhaps they'll understand why. We left their words 100% intact, not even editing out "um" or "you know" when repeated a lot. Only things they specifically asked us to keep off the record were omitted.

Some of these stories conflict with each other. All of them clarify what the real problem at the University of Tennessee actually was. Pulling back the veil of secrecy that surrounds every major college athletic department has never been accomplished on this scale, and especially not while representing a cross-section of thought influencers that impact decisions made at the University of Tennessee.

We have audio files for every interview, to serve as confirmation that we've presented each subject's word exactly as he said them. But we'll leave the interpretation of these interviews open, so that readers can reach their own conclusion about what really happened before, during, and after Schiano Sunday, when the ReVOLution changed college football forever. We also interviewed a large cross-section of regular Tennessee fans—the side of the Tennessee family that erupted when the university seemed poised to make yet another misstep. Judge for yourselves how essential the Vol ReVOLution really turned out to be.

Part II | Interviews

ALLAN JONES, UT DONOR

"It's A Foot Without A Big Toe"

W. Allan Jones founded Check Into Cash in his hometown of Cleveland, Tennessee, in 1993. Since then, the company has grown into the third largest payday lending company in the nation and has become a billion-dollar-a-year enterprise. Prior to founding Check Into Cash, he worked for nearly twenty-five years in his family's Credit Bureau business before selling it in 1998. Mr. Jones started in business at the age of twenty while a student at Middle Tennessee State University. He was instrumental in helping restore and revitalize the city's downtown business district and beautifying the city's streets by planting dozens of trees to enhance the area's environmental health. The Allan Jones Aquatic Center on the Knoxville campus is named in his honor.

CELINA SUMMERS: And if you're ready to get started. Awesome. Ok just to start off with can I have like a brief kind of bio - what your connection is with Tennessee?

ALLAN JONES: Well my name is spelled A-L-L-A-N, two L's.

SUMMERS: Yes sir!

JONES: And I guess I just became a Tennessee fan... First of all I had a scholarship when I was in high school. I was a wrestler, a good wrestler in high school and went up as a recruit and I didn't actually like the coach and I basically decided not to wrestle in college and so that was kind of my first...

I just grew up a Tennessee fan. And then I got to know Phillip Fulmer back probably twenty years ago. I guess I met coach Fulmer when... Shazzon Bradley, do you remember that football player? Shazzon was a wrestler and another guy coached him to two state championships. He was from McMinn county. They didn't have the wrestling program to take it to that level and I think I met Phillip (Fulmer) when both Alabama and Tennessee were after Shazzon. I was talking to Fulmer and Shazzon paid a lot of attention to me. He thought I was an Alabama football coach and we was dying when he found out I was just this wrestler. So that's when I first met Phillip. Then I got to know him through John Thornton and, you know, we were big fans. So we had funded the aquatic center. Now one of the issues that I don't think anybody really understood is that we had four presidents in six years, you know about that?

SUMMERS: Yes sir.

JONES: So in academia, unlike in business, they don't want to make any big quick decisions. The problem that was causing me was that I'd agreed to fund the aquatic center and we had to come up with a plan. I think it was in November, and they said, "If you'll make your first installment on or before March 1st, they'll start in

April the aquatic center."

So I decided to make my first installment on December 31st to take the deduction and then they had promised to start April 1st. This must have been around 2002 or so and then on April 1st they didn't start, and then the *next* April they had to start it. I called up there and one president would leave and another one would come and then another one would leave and another would come and I would continue making installments but no aquatic center.

In the meantime, Phillip Fulmer started having trouble, he would call me about…He couldn't get his kids in. When we turn over president after president after president what would happen is, in my opinion, is that the provost became too powerful and the department heads became the power source….

How I know that is, no matter what I did is—no matter what I did, I couldn't get them to build that aquatic center! We had a contract, shaken hands.

SUMMERS: And you were paying substantial installments.

JONES: Yes, which leads up to your library (author note—I had mentioned his endowment of the Cleveland Public Library before the interview). That wasn't a donation to the library, that was when I sent a…In December, I had a $500,000 installment due (to UT) and on December 20th the library people walk in and wanted to know if I'd make a $50,000 donation as a lead donation and I thought…

"You know what? Today and today only I'll give you a $500,000 donation."

I couldn't get Tennessee to respond! I had done everything I could—on December 31st, I sent them a *copy* of the check to the Cleveland Public Library instead of the installment. And they finally came down here, John—Dr Peterson. But what was happening by this point...

The reason I couldn't get the aquatic center built is because there was nobody in charge of the chief of police. As I understand it—this is what I was told, I didn't know it for sure—when you don't have nobody for president there's nobody to tell everyone what to do. The police chief reported to the president you see. Nobody could get the chief of police to move out so they could tear down the police center to start the aquatic center. In the meantime the cost of steel went up by $7,000,000 and now they're having to rescale this whole thing way down. I'm real disappointed.

In the meantime, Phillip Fulmer would call me on a Sunday or he would call occasionally and he was having trouble getting his kids in. To Alabama, Georgia, LSU, they're hitting on all cylinders and he would come in and he could not. He would need some special help here, some special help there and they just wouldn't do it. They wouldn't co-operate with him.

Mike Hamilton was not a strong leader; he was a weak leader. Instead of Mike Hamilton, you know, Doug Dickey would go in there and lay the law down and say look, you are required to do this, but Hamilton wouldn't do that. So unless Phillip threw Hamilton out in the hallway for not doing anything, he wouldn't get anywhere. He couldn't get students in. He didn't have the university co-operating with him.

So that's okay for a year, and I was okay for a year not building an aquatic center, and then two years, I was okay two years without an aquatic center. But Phillip was still going in and this thing is catching up to him because he still can't get his kids in. So finally I get the school's attention and we had a big meeting and they all came down to my conference room. I'd had it! They had nailed me for a bunch of money. But it…

I was a victim of what Phillip Fulmer was, you understand?

SUMMERS: Yes sir.

JONES: I was the only one at the time that shared…I was experiencing what Phillip Fulmer experienced. I couldn't get the aquatic center built no matter what I did. You understand? It's a long story but they had to agree to add a student fee onto to the University of Tennessee in Chattanooga to help the wrestling team or I wasn't going to help no more. And they did that.

SUMMERS: I think that story kind of encapsulates what the real problem is there. That's actually knocked out about thirty percent of my questions already.

JONES: Well it wasn't Phillip Fulmer's fault. It was the school's because you've got a world class coach here that we're blaming. And then I remember when he could not get the budget he needed, when he was hiring an offensive coordinator. He would say, "Hamilton won't give me the budget. You know, they're wanting to pay $315,000 and the market's $650,000." And so we went through all that. He couldn't get the offensive coordinator at the time.

SUMMERS: Did that seem like sabotage to you?

JONES: At the time, it seemed like incompetence to me because I'd been through all this just trying to build the aquatic center. I know what you're saying and that did cross my mind but—I do not think he (Hamilton) was strong enough to do that, I think that was kind of the end result of that. I'm not sure it was a deliberate sabotage. I don't know why.

I don't know anything about their budget. I don't know anything about that, but I know if everybody is paying $650,000 or $750,000 or $850,000 then he gets the guy for $315,000? I mean, and then the next year after they fire Phillip, the weight guy makes more than the offensive coordinator, you understand? From one year to the next year, the weight guy makes more than the offensive coordinator!

So then Kiffin comes in and, now Kiffin…

I had no feelings towards Kiffin until about three weeks into his job and I did not like him. Mike Hamilton wanted to bring him down here and I refused to see him. I wasn't mad. I wasn't refusing to see him because of Fulmer. I was refusing to see him because he was bad mouthing all these other coaches and he's yet to win a college game! You understand? He's never been a college coach. Now he was a pro coach. Coaching the pro guys that you hire that walk in the door but he's never…

College is all about recruiting and that's what Phillip Fulmer was: the world's greatest. He's a great recruiter. So, anyway, we go from Phillip not having any money to pay to the next year, you know, and Kiffin's daddy's making a million-six!

SUMMERS: Yeah.

JONES: So I finally get the aquatic center, you know, kicked off. And that thing didn't get built until '08. Now when I donated the money, Phillip Fulmer's daughter Britney, who was a family friend, was a diver on the University of Tennessee team. They promised me that she would be diving there her sophomore year. Well when they finally dedicated it, she had to come back to town to attend the dedication. She was married and had moved off! I mean it was so ridiculous. Crazy.

So anyway, I've been close to the University of Tennessee ever since. But I've been very angry with them. Because I see this whole fiasco coming, and I see the president, we go through one president and then another and then another president and then I see the whole...

You know, if a CEO of a company had gone in up there, we would have started that aquatic center right there, bam, bam, bam. And that needs to be done. But academia doesn't operate that way. They want to sit back and wait and see what happens and they won't make a decision, you know, and it was just like that.

SUMMERS: So do you think the hiring of Randy Boyd as interim president is...

JONES: I think it's a damn good idea because Randy Boyd is results-oriented. Now he's going to pick up the phone and get something done right away. If the aquatic center was supposed to be built and Randy Boyd saw that? He's the type of guy, in the first thirty days of his job he would fix that and get it moving forward. He would take the chief of police and say, "You've got to move out right now." and get it done. But instead it costs the university a lot of money and the grandiose...

That was the nicest aquatic center in the country at the time but it's only a portion of what it was supposed to be when I agreed to do it. So anyway that's kind of the history.

SUMMERS: So what did you think about the job that Dave Hart did coming in after Mike Hamilton?

JONES: I think Dave Hart did a good job. And I thought, "It's about time." He came to Cleveland and visited with me. I thought he did a good job.

SUMMERS: And what about John Currie?

JONES: The two mistakes they made—firing Phillip Fulmer and hiring John Currie.

SUMMERS: What did you think of Currie's managerial style?

JONES: Well, he was part of firing Phillip Fulmer and when you fire Phillip Fulmer, you fired the cook for a bad hamburger that wasn't his fault, okay? I could see through that right away. And have you figured out why they fired Phillip Fulmer?

SUMMERS: I have been sifting through that. I've heard a bunch of different stories.

JONES: Is Hamilton willing to talk to you?

SUMMERS: Doubt it. From what I understand there was a power play involved. That involved some boosters, some you know, like mega fans around the program.

JONES: That wanted rid of Fulmer? Well Celina, he called me, I guess ten years ago this week, or next week. When they fired him. My phone rang at *seven am* in the morning. When Fulmer calls you at seven am on Monday, I thought someone had died. I didn't know what had happened. He told me he had been fired, and it was just devastating to me. And Janie (Jones's wife), Janie and I, he wanted us to come there while he tells the team and Jane and I drove up there and it was…

I was in there but I felt like I shouldn't have been in there. We were in the dressing room, and then we went to Phillip Fulmer's house and he was a wonderful host. It's like a funeral, and the body is walking around serving the food. It was an odd feeling. Because his whole life had been there (at UT) and I knew what had happened. I lived it. I saw it. I couldn't get the aquatic center built; I can't imagine needing some help with a student. Nobody to help. There's no big toe on the foot.

SUMMERS: I live in Ohio and I watched that farewell press conference and I seriously had to question for a few weeks, especially after they hired Kiffin, it's like, "Man he had been loyal to the school for forty years, I don't know if I can support them after this."

JONES: Phillip has a magnetic personality. He's the warmest, he's a girls' Daddy.

SUMMERS: He's a charmer.

JONES: If we hadn't have fired him, he and Nick Saban would be the two biggest celebrities in football history right now, I'm pretty sure.

SUMMERS: I agree with that.

JONES: And he'd be going neck to neck with him.

SUMMERS: I think a lot of people would agree with you on that. What do you think about the vindication of Coach Fulmer? They fired him 2008 mid-season in a pretty classless move and then they have to turn to him last year to salvage the situation.

JONES: Exactly. There wasn't one other person in this world that could've saved us but him.

SUMMERS: I agree. And I said that at the time. Like, as a story, what does that make you think about when you think about them bringing Coach Fulmer back?

JONES: Well, I mean I was rocking along with this thing and I did not care for Currie. But I had loaned them my plane. Kurt Gulbrand (associate UT athletic director) called. Do you know Kurt?

SUMMERS: No I don't.

JONES: He's an assistant AD. This is Sunday I guess, in November. It's a winter day. I was taking a winter nap when Kurt Gulbrand called me at home and said. "I've talked to Bill. We've hired a coach, we need your plane."

My plane was on charter and he wouldn't tell me who it was—which, I didn't ask. I've always respected their confidentiality. And he wouldn't even tell me where they were going except it was two and a half hours away.

So finally I hung up and then finally I called him back and I said, "Wait a minute, Kurt. Two and a half hours away in a Falcon 900? That's the other side of Utah. I need to know about where it's going."

He said, "We're going to Columbus, Ohio."

So I called the plane up and they'd just left Philadelphia so they were in mid-air. I transferred that plane to Columbus, Ohio...I mean I redirected it.

And then about fifteen minutes later, I get a call from Kurt and he says, "All hell is breaking loose. I'm not sure what to do. The students are lighting up the...they're burning the dumpsters around the stadium and we're planning to bring this coach back and announce it at 8 o'clock on Sunday night!"

And I said, "Why are you going to do something at 8 o'clock on Sunday night when no one's paying attention?"

He said, "We were going to bring him back to the stadium but all hell is breaking loose."

And I said, "Well you better ring John Currie."

I'll never forget this. He said, "Mr. Currie is in a real bad mood. I don't want to call him and tell him."

I said, "Oh, God." I'd been asleep, but now I'm dealing with...

I said, "Look, you cannot allow that coach to come back here into a riot!"

And then he told me it was Greg Schiano. And remember, he hadn't told *me* who it was. I don't know how the word got out but in fifteen or twenty minutes, word had got out on the internet.

It's a new world right now, you understand? Because whoever they hire there's a base out there that can respond in twenty minutes with a national voice on the internet. And I saw that happen.

So now I've got my plane entering into a major controversy with my name on the side and so I wasn't sure what to do. I don't pay attention to that. I didn't know Schiano. I didn't know why they (fans) were rioting. I had no idea but it got worse and worse and Kurt could not reach Currie at the time.

So then he called back and said he'd heard from Currie and they have a...no, let me correct that...they redirected it (the plane) in the air, that's right. They redirected in the air from Philadelphia. It was going to Knoxville, to pick up a charter client and I redirected it to Columbus. He (Gulbrand) called back and said that they'd had a contract snag.

I said, "Well, I'm going to go redirect it back to Knoxville, pick up our client, and take him. The flight's going to Birmingham and then we can be on the ground in two and a half hours. He said, "That's fine."

So in the meantime, when all hell breaks loose and he calls me back and says, "I don't know what to do. They're burning down the school."

I said, "You've got to call Mr. Currie."

And he says, "I hate to call him. Mr. Currie's in a real foul mood."

And I said, "You've got to call him. You cannot allow..."

That's when he told me it was Schiano. I asked, "Why are they rioting?"

And he said, "I think he's a…"

What was it, a pedophile? I don't know anything about it. I just know I was asleep and an hour later I'm in a big controversy with my airplane. I didn't know if they were going to attack the plane once it landed, you know. So I was on the phone with Bill Lane like: "I gotta get out of this mess."

Finally Curt called back and said, "I've found another plane that can pick us up a little quicker, is that okay?"

And I said, "Yes, but you gotta make sure he understands what he's coming into."

So Curt called me back again and said, "The whole thing is off."

And this is about five o'clock. Probably three hours had passed and I still didn't get to go back to sleep. *laughs*

SUMMERS: Did you follow the uprising as it was going on online?

JONES: Well, no. I don't do all that, but Bill Lane my chief financial officer did. He was watching it, and he was reporting it all to me, because I just don't even know how to do that. You can tell I'm pretty technical but I don't care to do that. I don't care what people are saying.

SUMMERS: Social media is not your thing.

JONES: No, I don't care about all that. Anyway, and then we get this fiasco going on. People from all over the country was calling…I have never seen a major university screw up so bad in my life.

SUMMERS: It was embarrassing and it wasn't embarrassing for the reason the national media was saying. The fans had no reason to be embarrassed by that. It was the most mismanaged coaching search in the history of college football. It was fumbled from the beginning.

JONES: It was crazy. He was going from one spot to another spot to another spot and…

SUMMERS: Disappearing for a day.

JONES: Disappearing. So, now, I guess John Thornton told you, I mean—here's something else I disagree with. I think the university, that the guy who runs the cash flow for the athletic system, for the number one team in Tennessee needs to report to the president not the chancellor, okay?

So what they had done was they had put Beverly Davenport as chancellor and I should tell you some things…I did suggest John Thornton borrow my plane (during the AD search). "I'll donate my plane if you go up and have dinner with her (Davenport) and tell her how important it is to hire Phillip Fulmer as athletic director."

First thing she (Davenport) had to do was pick an athletic director. And did John tell you that? That they went up there and had dinner?

SUMMERS: No, he didn't tell me that part. We did discuss the fact that she landed on Currie after only a week of being in office herself, which is something I find really odd.

JONES: She didn't have a clue. And I don't want to blame her for any of that.

SUMMERS: Right.

JONES: Because she did not call me and say, "I've decided to hire Phillip." When they did that search, they wanted to see Phillip on a Sunday morning at eight am. Phillip called me to borrow the plane on Friday night at eight pm...I mean he had a meeting Sunday morning at eight am in Nashville. So I had to get them early and get them out and get it done and it was a great interview. And without going into a whole lot of things I don't want to go into, on Tuesday I thought Phillip had the job.

Now, nobody told me that, but I think Phillip thought he had the job. And then on Tuesday afternoon, Currie comes out of the blue. He wasn't on anybody's radar screen. And I tell you what...

It was apparent one person was running everything. And it wasn't the chancellor, you know. And there was no...I don't think the committee knew about it, the committee they put together?

SUMMERS: Yeah, I agree.

JONES: I don't think they knew what was going on and I don't think Charlie Anderson (Chair of the Athletic Committee on the University of Tennessee Board of Trustees) knew what was going on. I don't think anybody...I think it was a 1-0 vote.

SUMMERS: And was that vote inside the university inside or outside of it?

JONES: I think it was outside of it. I'm not saying anymore.

SUMMERS: Understandable. Looking at the

uprising that happened last fall, what was your response to seeing the Tennessee fan base come together, spontaneously, without organization, and within three hours turned this bad hire around the way they did?

JONES: They took control of the university.

SUMMERS: Yeah, they did.

JONES: The fans took control and it was a family coup. There was nothing else to it and I...not wanting to go into a lot with you about that but...there's more. I just don't want to hurt anybody's feelings but it was a coup and Beverly Davenport made that decision on her own.

SUMMERS: To not honor the...

JONES: To hire Fulmer.

SUMMERS: Yeah?

JONES: To fire Currie and hire Fulmer.

SUMMERS: John Thornton said in our interview this morning that Beverly Davenport did the university a huge favor.

JONES: John Thornton and I had no input to her. In fact, when we found out they were making the announcement, Phillip wouldn't return our calls. We didn't know who the athletic director was going to be. We got in the car and rushed up there, me and Janie and John Thornton. John Thornton was driving a hundred miles per hour and Janie's having a fit—she's in the back seat, and he was so mad and I thought, "John, what if we get up there and walk into that news conference and they don't pick Phillip?"

So we got there at the last second and walked in, I had to run to the restroom and there's Phillip, back there by himself. He came to the corner and he just hugged me. And I teared up. He never said a word.

We didn't have an idea. Did he tell you this? Did Thunder (John Thornton) tell you this? I mean we did not know and Beverly Davenport did not tell us. There was no heads up like there usually is with athletic directors. It was totally done. I mean *she* made that decision. About a week later, John Thornton, we had her down to my house for dinner and I was going to present her with a pair of brass balls and I couldn't find any.

laughter

JONES: But that's what it took and that's what she did.

SUMMERS: And do you think that was the best thing that anybody could have done at that point?

JONES: Yes. She saved Tennessee. She made the only decision she could. I mean—she was going to be fired anyway. She was going to be blamed for all this, and she made a drastic, last minute decision and it instantly solved the problem. You saw that.

SUMMERS: Oh yeah.

JONES: It was instantaneous.

SUMMERS: I was reporting that whole week and frankly being an agitator online because that's where the impetus was for this. It was social media. And when Coach Fulmer, when we found out he was going to be the guy at the athletic department, because for a second somebody—and I have my suspicions as to who but I don't have confirmation—was pushing for Currie's number two (Assistant Athletic Director Reid Sigmon) to be named as the interim athletic director. But we heard pretty quickly that Chancellor Davenport went, "Nope, not going to do it."

So the fan base was pretty aware about two hours before the press conference that it was going to be Coach Fulmer, and if it hadn't have been...

JONES: No, I'm going to tell you: they were just *hoping* it was going to be Fulmer. There's nobody closer to Fulmer than me and John Thornton. Fulmer did not know about this until about 10 o'clock that morning. She asked, he said yes; no time for contract. They made an announcement based on a handshake instead of all this bullshit of negotiating and all that stuff. And he was there to step back in and save this thing.

And when Jane and I were up there we were behind him, kind of, because we were late getting there and it was just a dynamic time. I mean, it was just a moment in the history of the University of Tennessee that I had accidentally shared by being there and watched him instantly calm everything down. Now he had a problem with—we had alienated every coach in the country, so...

SUMMERS: Do you think that alienation with the other coaches, top tier coaches, began with the way Fulmer was fired?

JONES: Sure. Who'd want to work for Hamilton? Every coach knew what Phillip's problem was; every coach knew he couldn't pay the prime. They all know all that stuff. They knew he was a good coach so...

SUMMERS: What strengths do you think Coach Fulmer is bringing as athletic director aside from the fact that the fan base trusts him to do the right thing?

JONES: Well I think Phillip has a...People would call me and ask for help to get into the University of Tennessee because I'm a big donor, and I tell them, "I don't know a soul up there. There's not anyone up there in management that went to the University of Tennessee. Now they will know who I am if I explain who I am and I have the aquatic center. They will know of my name. But nobody up there—I don't know them. I can't really help you."

See Phillip...Look at the presidents we had. Over and over and over.

SUMMERS: The one question I did have with naming Mr. Boyd as interim president, it seems like another kind of stop gap measure. Because we've had interims and interims and they did two years here and one year there—how do you think you address that problem within the university? Putting some stability there?

JONES: I don't think this is interim. I think this is the term they're using. As long as he's willing to do it, they'll probably go on letting him try to do it. But you gotta realize we have to get out of academia. I've worked with academia. If you come to Cleveland Tennessee, right here, if you want to win a state championship at wrestling then you're going to have to come to Cleveland, Tennessee to do it. We're ranked number one. Cleveland High School, who I donated the two centers to. If you're going to win a state championship in wrestling, you're going to have to come to Cleveland, Tennessee.

This year Cleveland High School will be in its twelfth final. I say will...*should*. They're so strong now I don't even know who's close to them except Bradley and Bradley's down. so our two schools meet in wrestling each year for the championship state finals. What was I talking about?

I know how to build a championship team, I kind of know what to do, because I got to pick the coaches here and it's all in who you pick. And, what I was going to tell you, is it's been a fight for me, just to keep those two schools on top. It's been a fight with Cleveland High School, it's been a fight with the school board. Now they disagree with me on all kinds of things, academia.

The stream casting, if you see that stream casting right there, that's the Jones Wrestling Center. Nobody knows this—I created the (live) stream casting back in '06 and handed it to the school system. We had 3000 viewers for wrestling matches. But after they (school board) took over they made stream casting so complicated they had zero viewers, but seventeen people are producing the show. And not one person in that school understood that producing a show has nothing to do with it if you don't have viewers. That's the difference between business and academia.

So that's what we were facing before, is that type of mentality. Where somebody like Boyd will figure out it's how many viewers you've got, it's how many people are watching the show. And that's what I think Boyd is going to bring to the table. Because the president, DiPietro, he's a veterinarian?

SUMMERS: I believe so.

JONES: Okay. You talk to him? Do you know if you have a PhD you have less than a four percent chance of working for yourself?

SUMMERS: I never thought of it that way but now it makes sense.

JONES: Now this is not a teaching job, this is a big ass business job, okay? And there's nobody up there who's been president of the university that has dealt with these kinds of budgets. Well Randy Boyd has that budget as his own income budget. Now if you look at his own company, look at the size of it compared to the University of Tennessee, it's probably going to be about the same. He's used to dealing with that. So I'm real hopeful for Randy. And that we start getting away from academia and realize you don't have to have a PhD to run a company.

SUMMERS: I think, and correct me if I'm wrong, I think there's also a tradition at Tennessee with having Tennessee people doing these jobs for the university. Because until Lane Kiffin, every football coach at the university of Tennessee had a former tie, either as a player or as a former assistant coach. We had presidents and chancellors going all the way back that had that same kind of tie. And once we got to the point where we didn't and we're bringing in people from places like Utah and Connecticut, that have no idea of how the people of the state are, that's to me where the disconnect began.

JONES: That's exactly right. That's what I'm saying, I had nobody up there to call. I don't know: who would I call? I mean, I can call the president, it's the new guy—whoever's the president is the new guy—chancellor, we went through chancellor after chancellor.

SUMMERS: It was what...eight presidents, six chancellors? Five ADs, five football coaches. In a decade.

JONES: Right. And before that we had just one. Joe Johnson, we had Phillip Fulmer, we had Doug Dickey. Now Doug Dickey? When he would come here to see me, he would walk through these aisles and everybody would look at him. He was one of those guys that everybody knew who he was here. When Mike Hamilton did the same, they wouldn't have a clue who he was. He'd come to the front desk totally uninterrupted. Debbie wouldn't know who he was, nobody would know who he was. But when Dickey came in, he had that air about him. Phillip Fulmer walks in here, he has that air about him.

I tell you something else...Oh, here's something else nobody knew. I had a guy working for me named Money Mark. He could do videos for me, so we had a social media launch and I was getting ready to launch a social media campaign against...they (UT) were getting ready to hire an athletic director, what was his name, from Chattanooga?

SUMMERS: David Blackburn?

JONES: Blackburn. They were ready to name Blackburn the AD. Now Blackburn, I liked Blackburn. I knew Blackburn, but comparing Blackburn to Fulmer would be like comparing a candle to the sun. Okay?

So she's (Davenport) told to hire Blackburn so I do a video—it's a man on the street interview. We went and started talking to people.

"Hey! Money Mark here! Who is this man right here?" (showed picture of David Blackburn)

"I don't know."

"Who is this man?" (picture of Phillip Fulmer)

"Oh that's Phillip Fulmer."

"What'd he do?"

"He won a national championship."

"Who is this man?" (picture of David Blackburn)

"I have no idea."

"Who's this man?" (picture of Phillip Fulmer)

"Oh that's Coach Phillip Fulmer. Yeah we need to bring him back."

We did that time after time and he said, "That does it! This man? No way. Phillip Fulmer is the only plan."

So I had that video, and I sent that up (to UT) and I said, "I'm going to tell you—no one's controlling this but me. I will launch this. If I need to." So she (Davenport) decided to form a committee and the committee was maneuvered around. You've already learned that about the committee. Have you talked to anyone about the committee to pick Fulmer?

SUMMERS: No.

JONES: They're probably not willing to talk to you.

SUMMERS: I'm running into a problem with some of the people that were on the board of trustees and the university. They don't want to go on the record.

JONES: The committee...they formed that committee and then circumnavigated the committee. So anyway that's kind of the story.

SUMMERS: Now what did you think of Coach Fulmer conducting a real football coach search in six days and landing Jeremy Pruitt?

JONES: I thought it was a...I mean, what could he do? I couldn't believe he could find anybody. And you know, he knows football, and Pruitt was on the best football system in the country. I tell you what made Hart good is Hart had been an Alabama assistant so Hart knew we had to have those provosts cooperating with us. Everybody would be working together to make this thing work and it's just like...do you know who Gary Rankin is?

SUMMERS: No.

JONES: Gary Rankin is the winningest football coach of all time. And I totally saw my battle with our superintendent at city schools when....

He let me pick the wrestling coaches because he didn't want to fool with it. And then he picked the football coach and the wrestling coach I picked. We went on a national search for Cleveland High School...spent $50,000 and interviewed the top wrestling coaches in the country. I picked a guy who was actually the youth director at a church here, and Doctor Denning, the PhD, picked a football coach and three years later his football coach created the worst loss in Cleveland's history in football. He quit on his own and now he's a girls' basketball coach. My coach became the second high school coach in the country to become a D1 college coach from (coaching) high school.

SUMMERS: Wow.

JONES: And they took my entire staff and that's when my wife called Hart down at UTC and chewed his ass out. I peeled a couple of guys back but he had hired my entire coaching staff. So that's when I realized how stupid a PhD can make you. I told Dr. Denning that he should pay his parents back for that PhD because it sure didn't help him none.

SUMMERS: Now talking about coaching searches, I do want to go through this a little bit. How surprised were you, because I've gone through all of the documents that were released from UT during that period—the Freedom of Information Act documents—calls, texts, all that fun stuff. How surprised were you that there was not a single communication with any coach whatsoever within all of that information?

JONES: When Currie was doing the search? I was shocked. You see here's the problem with a recruiting firm. We had recruiters all the time. Your good coaches are working. I'm trying to hire you, Celina. You're going to say a lot of nice things to me but that recruiter I hired? You're going to tell the real thing to the recruiter.

That's why when I was looking for a wrestling coach, I hired Double Pump International who brought in (Bruce) Pearl (to UT) and I paid him $50,000 instead of $25,000 like they (UT) paid (on the search for) Pearl and they brought me...they had a whole top list of coaches and I compared that to what I had. I made a good choice and they earned their money. They were devastated when I didn't hire one of their guys, but they had earned their money. I recommended them, they did a great job. A recruiter is so important.

So when Currie did not hire a recruiter, that showed his total ignorance and arrogance. I know these guys myself but what he doesn't know was what was happening to him. They'd tell him one thing and then do something else. And that's where a recruiter comes in handy to say, "Look—well, he admitted he's not really interested." Recruiters will tell the truth. Recruiters are worth their weight in gold.

SUMMERS: I thought it was interesting that Mike Leach called and left a message for John Currie on October 29th—two weeks before Butch Jones had been fired—and the message was simply: "Mike Leach wants to talk to you about coaching the Vols." And Currie didn't even respond to that.

JONES: It's bizarre. It's so bizarre I have no opinion, okay because...

SUMMERS: What about cutting out the whole athletic committee or the board of trustees, you know, Charlie Anderson calling up, it's his job and they basically...

JONES: I think Charlie's probably rethinking his roles. He's been such a great Vols fan. And you spend all that time and he's probably rethinking what his role really is.

SUMMERS: Tom Mattingly is trying to sit down with Charlie Anderson, which I think...

JONES: He's not going to talk to you.

SUMMERS: So when everything blew up at Tennessee last fall. What was it like behind the scenes with boosters and men you know and deal with things around the program?

JONES: You know, I've got a friend at Palm Beach who's extremely wealthy. And he is a huge Vols fan. He's one of those secret fans you don't know. His daughter played tennis there. I won't mention his name but he's extremely wealthy. He watches every game. Now his daughter went four years there without Tennessee ever knowing who he was. And he's that low key. And he would call me, and he would text me, and he was furious with what's going on. He was shocked at Tennessee; he watches every single game. You don't realize how many secret fans we have like that.

SUMMERS: Oh, I know.

JONES: That are just huge fans. He lives in Malibu and Palm Beach.

SUMMERS: It doesn't matter where you go, I can go into a bar in backwoods Wyoming and somebody would walk in with the power T on the hat.

JONES: And he knows more about Tennessee football than I do.

SUMMERS: That's a lot.

JONES: He went to Navy. And so I know more about Navy football because since he texts me while he's watching his football team, I text him while I'm watching my football team. That winter I was in Palm Beach and my friend down there said, "What is going on with Tennessee?"

They would blame *me* like: "You gotta fix this!" And I'd be like: "I wouldn't know who to call. I don't have anybody to call."

SUMMERS: Nobody to call.

JONES: Nobody to call. That's what I said: it's a foot without a big toe. That'd be a good chapter.

SUMMERS: Oh well actually, I mean every interview is its own chapter so that's what I'm going to call yours.

JONES: But that's what it was. There was just nobody in charge and this huge operation just kind of meandering up until then. With a couple of people making decisions, you know...I think I could have used my nose sometimes and picked a better coach than Currie was picking.

SUMMERS: I would not disagree with you, sir. Not at all.

JONES: Will Currie talk to you? What the hell was he thinking? Somebody had to be backing him, somebody had to be saying, "Good boy." Or "Go here...now do that." *Somebody* had to be talking to him because Chancellor Davenport wasn't talking to him.

SUMMERS: Well, I mean—there's probably an NDA (Non-Disclosure Agreement). Logically, I look at it this way: he didn't communicate with any coaches whatsoever, through email, phone or text at any point prior to the Schiano Sunday deal or after. There were no communications at all. So it makes me wonder...do you think that Schiano was the predetermined successor somehow to Butch Jones and the reason they didn't hire a search firm or include anyone...like Charlie Anderson...

JONES: That's a damn reasonable conclusion.

SUMMERS: Do you think that's the case?

JONES: Well, absolutely the case. Why would it not be the case? You're not going to hire a recruiting firm if you don't need one.

JAMES A. HASLAM III (JIMMY), UT DONOR

"You Cannot Kowtow To The Masses"

Jimmy Haslam began his career at Pilot Corporation in 1976. In 1980, Haslam was named vice president of sales, development and operations. At that time, Pilot operated 100 convenience stores with annual fuel sales of about 125 million gallons. Pilot opened its first travel center in 1981 and by 1996 – the same year Haslam was named president and chief executive officer – the company operated 96 travel centers and 50 convenience stores and its total gallon sales had reached 1.2 billion. The Pilot Flying J network provides customers with access to more than 70,000 parking spaces for trucks, 4,800 showers and 4,300 diesel lanes featuring DEF at the pump. He is also owner of the NFL's Cleveland Browns.

TOM MATTINGLY: Hey Jimmy, it's good to hear from you. We'll start out, the first question we wanted to ask you was: in the week between the failed Schiano hire and Currie's firing and Fulmer's hiring, what was going on behind the scenes that you were aware of?

JIMMY HASLAM: Yeah, hey Tom, hold on one second.

MATTINGLY: Okay.

HASLAM: Let me just, and I don't…and if you say, "I don't want to do it this way…" Let me give you a little background because I think this is real helpful to understand…

We, of course, were involved in the hiring of Currie and really once John was hired I literally—because, between Pilot Flying J and the Browns and all the stuff we all have to do—I really was not, despite what everyone thinks, involved in either the university or the athletic program hardly at all. Currie was in New York in October and I was there for an NFL meeting and he was aware of it and we had lunch together. I never asked him about the coaching search and towards the end of the lunch—and Butch was still the head coach—he said, maybe he wasn't I can't remember, but he asked me a question. He said, "Didn't you interview Greg Schiano once upon a time for the Browns?"

And I said, "Yes, we did."

He said, "What did you think about him?"

I said, "He was highly successful at Rutgers and one of the McCourtys played for us and liked him a lot." You know, the two twins who play for New England a lot—and just said he'd done a tremendous job there. He failed at Tampa Bay in a terrible situation, obviously did well at Ohio State, and all I said was: "He's tough enough to handle the job, you should look at him."

That was it. And then the night before we hired him, Charlie Anderson called me. We were playing Cincinnati, and he said, "It's down to two guys, Mullen and Schiano."

And I said, "What direction is it going to go?"

And he said, "Well, I'm not sure."

And I said, "Okay, great."

The next morning I'm in a meeting in our hotel in Cincinnati before the game with some of our football people and Jimmy Sexton's number comes up three times. We all know how agents are. They only want to talk to you when they want something so I didn't answer the phone.

Finally Jimmy texted me: "Urgent. I need to talk to you about the Tennessee coaching situation."

So I called and back and I said, "What's going on?"

And he said, "Well, Currie has offered to Greg Schiano. There's a little hang up because of some past issues at Penn State that aren't true, but I need you to help with Raja Jubran."

Raja, of course, was chairman of the board at UT, great guy, great friend of ours and I called Raja and he said, "Well, some of the people are a little spooked out because of the situation at Penn State."

I said, "I don't know what you're talking about."

And he went back to the Sandusky...that stuff, and I said, "Well, Ohio State, Gene Smith, and those guys are pros. They wouldn't have hired this guy if they hadn't have checked him out, if there were any issues." I said, "Call your counterpart at the chairman of the board at Ohio state. Get the chief legal counsel at UT to do the same and just see if you can't get some references and if there's a problem—which I don't think there'll be because Ohio State wouldn't have hired him—then back off, and if there's not a problem then move forward."

I get a text from a text from Sexton that says, "Thanks for your help."

And that's all before one o'clock when our game starts. At halftime, Currie calls me and says, "Hey can we use one of y'all's planes to come get me and Schiano's family and bring them to Knoxville?"

And I said, "Sure."

Well, we ended up losing. We're not playing very well. I'm pissed off. We fly back to Cleveland and I thought: "Well, I probably ought to call Currie and congratulate him."

I called him. I said, "Hey, congratulations!"

He said, "I don't think it's going to happen."

And I said, "Why?"

And he said, "Well, we got all this uproar."

I said, "Uproar from who?"

And he said, "You know over this Sandusky thing… The social media is just going wild, we're getting killed."

And I said, "S**t, John! You gotta stand tough here."

And he said, "Well, I'm having trouble with some

people at the university."

Didn't say who.

And I said, "Well, listen, let me talk to Dad (James A. Haslam II) and Bill (William Haslam, Governor of Tennessee). Bill deals with this stuff all the time."

I call both of them. I also call another famous Tennessee person. All agree we should hold tough. But by the time we call John back, he decided to back off. So I just wanted to give you that background because I don't know...besides Dad, and Bill, and John Currie, nobody else knows that.

MATTINGLY: Given all that, what did you think about the uprising against that hire back in Knoxville? I didn't realize you were elsewhere but what did...?

HASLAM: Tom, don't quote me exactly like this, because I don't cuss in public, but I thought it was total BS. I've seen this before.

You cannot kowtow to the masses!

You gotta stand up and it was a gross failure of leadership by the top people at the university in not hanging tough there. I mean, you can't let the masses—and I'm not saying Schiano would have been a great coach—but you can't let the masses run programs! I mean, that's the problem with social media and today's world. You cannot let them do that.

And that's what happened in that. They caved, the politicians all jumped in, none of whom know anything about football, none of whom could tell you anything about Greg Schiano. And I'm not defending Schiano. It could have been Joe Smith and I would have said the same thing: you cannot let that happen.

I mean, it's a gross failure of leadership, in my opinion, and I would say that...I know I'm saying it publicly obviously because it's going to be in a book but you can't—and don't use the term b******t, please—but you can't let that happen. You just can't. I was totally dismayed.

MATTINGLY: There is an idea out there that the boosters are the ones that are calling all the shots with major hiring decisions, is that true?

HASLAM: You know, I can only speak for myself but I would say we're pretty prominent boosters. My total involvement in that search was the little bit I told Currie. It was probably a two-minute conversation at lunch and then when Jimmie Sexton asked me to help, I called Raja. That was my total involvement.

MATTINGLY: Or looking at it again, is it just some of the boosters or is all that completely false?

HASLAM: Tom, I don't know that, okay? I can only comment on one other booster, my Dad, and you all heard him. I don't think he was involved at all. I may be wrong. And I'm not saying there weren't others but I'd be hard pressed to think who they might be. I think John did this search on his own and I'm not faulting that.

MATTINGLY: So when you say 'on his own', that's literally on his own with no other input?

HASLAM: Well, listen, John's a smart guy, okay? And he might've got all kinds of references on people, I just know...I don't want to speak for anybody else. I don't think he involved Dad at all. You all talked to him and literally, there were...he talked to me for two minutes at the end of kind of an update on "here's what I'm doing in the athletic department, here's the progress we're making" just like he would do for any other booster who's invested in the athletic department of the university and that was it.

And I didn't recommend or not recommend Greg Schiano, I just said, "You should talk to him, he's a tough guy, he can handle the pressures of being a head coach at the University of Tennessee which we all know are not easy."

MATTINGLY: What has, in your opinion, been the primary obstacle to UT athletics success over the past ten years or so?

HASLAM: That's a good question. I think...Listen I can relate because we're struggling over here with the Browns. I think everything comes down to selecting the right person and for whatever reason, since Coach Fulmer left, we've been unable do that. Whether it was bad luck... it's way harder than...There's way more demand than there is supply of these good coaches. So that's an issue. Tennessee is a great job; it's probably not as great of a job as our boosters think so I think that's an issue and I think the selector, whoever that might have been, did not do as good a job as he should have.

MATTINGLY: Being a businessman and a philanthropist, you have to be on top of the changes in the world around you. What do you think about the power of the internet, or how has the power of the internet changed the way we do business now in college athletics and elsewhere? Has it really changed things for the good or the bad?

HASLAM: I would argue unbelievably for the bad and I think our example is a great example of it.

MATTINGLY: In what way?

HASLAM: I just think what, I mean, listen: if Ohio State University, okay, looked into his background and said there was no issue, then how can all these people who... You know, one person said that he might have known about it, and so we're not going to hire the guy because of that? You know what I mean?

I think the internet has, in social media, and most of these people that are big players in social media, I don't think they have jobs, Tom. You know, I don't think they're people who are productive in society, for the most part.

MATTINGLY: Do you have an opinion on why Ohio State didn't make him the interim coach over the Smith gentleman?

HASLAM: I'm sure it's because of this issue, right?

MATTINGLY: Mmhmm.

HASLAM: I mean, I don't know that, I've never talked to them, that's not our business but if you ask me what I think, I'm sure it's because they didn't need any more controversy.

MATTINGLY: So, looking at what happened, is it back to business as usual or did Tennessee fans create a blueprint for other fan bases to follow in this whole deal?

HASLAM: I don't know that, Tom. I'm not smart enough to answer that. I just think, not just in sports but in the world today. I mean: we had an issue where we didn't have a flag up on our flagpole at Amarillo at one of our—you know, we have 650 truck stops—and one guy came in, some disgruntled guy, and claimed we were anti-veteran. And before we know it, we have three, four million people on the email, you know, it's just...

And what happened? Once our flag was torn, we took it down and the new one hadn't come in yet. You know what I mean? Things get out of whack. And here's my problem, there's no accountability for those people, right?

MATTINGLY: If you were going to describe the leadership at UT, not individually but the philosophy of leadership the university has displayed, how would you institute changes based on your experience at Pilot Flying J, within your companies?

HASLAM: Well, I will say this—I gotta be really careful if this is gonna be in public. I think it's really important for leadership in any major university to either have a firm grasp and understanding of college athletics or to have somebody who does. We, fortunately, have that now in Coach Fulmer.

MATTINGLY: And how does that manifest itself?

HASLAM: Well, Coach Fulmer has been through it all, okay, so he understands it. So let's say Tom Mattingly is the president of the university and is a top-flight academian but is not familiar with college athletics. Well, because you have Coach Fulmer in there who has basically been in college athletics his whole life, you have somebody who knows their way around, who can handle the pressure, and can educate you, Tom Mattingly, and say, "Tom" or "Dr. Mattingly, this is how it works."

MATTINGLY: What did you think about the hiring of Jeremy Pruitt? Now, what, seven or eight games into his first year? What do you think about him?

HASLAM: I think it's a great hire. I think he's a great person, first of all. He's a real football guy, number two. I think he can recruit which you have to do at the University of Tennessee. When Coach Fulmer really had Tennessee going, he was recruiting nationally and getting great players. I was talking to one of our guys here at the Browns and they said, "Jimmy, good players make good coaches."

And that's right, you've got to have the talent. And our cupboard is bare. I mean, I see that when our scouts come back and I look on our board and there's three Tennessee guys on there and not thirteen and the three that are on there are four through seventh round guys and there are seven Alabama guys going to the first round. So it's all about getting the talent and I think Jeremy can recruit. I think he's put together a good staff. I think he's tough. I think the cupboard was bare there and it's going to take some time but I think he'll turn Tennessee around.

MATTINGLY: What did you think about the hiring of Randy Boyd as the interim president of the university?

HASLAM: Randy is one of my best friends and, remember? We sold our minor league baseball to him so starting with that I think it's a great move. I think with the...I'll just say the turmoil we've had at the university, I think, and here again, I'm partial, my brother made the pick, Tom, so let's be realistic. Bill did the same thing at Memphis, the University of Memphis. They had some struggles, they put Brad Martin in there for a year. Brad calmed things down. They ended up promoting someone internally who I've heard has done a really good job and I think the same thing will happen with Randy. Nobody will put more into it or work any harder than Randy Boyd, I know that, and I think he has the university's best interests at heart so I think it's a real home run.

I also think the smaller boards that Bill has created around the state...I think...I can't remember, Tom, if there's ten, eleven, or twelve, it's much more realistic than having twenty-six on the board. I mean, twenty-six people you can't get anything done. Having ten or twelve people there is much better and I think the quality of those individuals that Bill's put together are not good but outstanding.

MATTINGLY: Going back to the social media aspect for just a minute or two. Social media is with us probably to stay and the word *transparency* is banded about a lot these days. How critical is it to involve the fan base and the fans more transparently than might have been done in the past?

HASLAM: You gotta be practical, okay? I mean, I was involved in the search for a new athletic director and you have to be practical. Most of these really good athletic directors have a great job. They don't necessarily want their boss to know that they have an interest in going somewhere else. They don't want their coaches, their fan base to know so these searches have to be done by one, two, or three people, by a small number of people and they've got to be done very thoroughly but very quickly.

You can't involve the fan base, that's nuts! I mean, I love our fans. I love our Browns fans. Tennessee has some unbelievable fans but you can't involve them in the search, that's crazy!

MATTINGLY: Another question is how does UT address the turnover rate within the administration? There's, what, Twenty-eight million dollars of buyouts out there? How do you address that?

HASLAM: Make good hires. And hopefully going forward with Coach Fulmer in there and Jeremy. I seriously believe that Jeremy will be there for a long time. I believe Rick Barnes will be there for a long time. I mean, I think Rick is probably my age but I think he will be there for a considerable amount of time. Though it's all about hiring the right people which is not easy.

MATTINGLY: One last question: is there anything you want the Vol Nation to know about you that they might not know?

HASLAM: *Laughs* No! Only that we have Tennessee's best interests at heart and are not nearly as involved as everybody thinks.

MATTINGLY: What is it about the University of Tennessee that gives you a good feeling about the university, that makes you love the university, and makes you want to be involved? What are those factors that get your attention to make you and keep you a Vols fan?

HASLAM: Well, I mean, let's start, I mean, my dad went there, played there, was a long time trustee so, Tom, when I was ten-, eleven-, twelve-years old, I was going over to practice and watching practice with my Dad, you know what I mean? So he's been a trustee for a long time, our family has given a lot of money, we're heavily involved in the business school, obviously heavily involved in liberal arts and music, etc. So we have a huge interest in...

It's not just sports like everybody thinks. We've given way more to academics and the university catches a lot of grief, some of it deserved, a lot of it, not, okay? And, I mean, very few people know that our business school is a top twenty-five business school in the country of public universities? Did you know that? Does John know that? How many people know that? You know what I mean? So despite some of the...

They have more freshmen this year than they ever have with higher test scores. The university is doing a lot of good things, I know with the business school, we have great things happening. I think overall the university does. You know, in today's world I think it's easier if thirty people come out or fifty students come out and protest about a change in chancellorship, that means out of 25,000 people, you know, one one-hundreth percent came out and protested, what do you think they cover? That's just the news cycle we're living in today. I understand it, but the university has a lot of things going on and if it wasn't for the University of Tennessee—

Think about this, Tom. Jim Haslam would have been, you know...my dad thought about going three places, West Point, Duke, and UT. His mom wanted him to go to Duke; his dad wanted him to go to Duke; he came to UT. Would Knoxville have been different if he hadn't have come here?

Jim Clayton's from a small town in Western Tennessee. Would Knoxville have been different if he hadn't have come here?

Raja Jubran's from Lebanon, okay?

I can go on and on. Those people wouldn't be in Knoxville, wouldn't be in Tennessee, if it wasn't for the University of Tennessee. That's why we feel so strongly about the business school, because hopefully the next Jim Claytons, Raja Jubrans, Randy Boyds etc…

I mean, John Compton is from Greenville, Tennessee, okay? He comes to UT, goes to work for Frito-Lay, working at a Frito-Lay plant in middle Tennessee, rises up to be the set number two or three executive in all of PepsiCo, and now he's back as chairman of the board at UT. The university attracts tremendous talent to the state and particularly to East Tennessee and Knoxville. Most people don't think about that or appreciate the difference that those people then make in our community. I mean, not just because he's my dad, but think what Knoxville would be like without Jim Clayton and Jim Haslam! You know, it would be a different community.

MATTINGLY: Okay, do you think that the athletic department is now at a point of stability? What do you see in the future for them?

HASLAM: I do, listen, Coach Fulmer's…I'm sixty-four, I think Coach Fulmer is sixty-seven or sixty-eight but looks to be in good health and I think he's going to do that for a while. It's interesting that Coach Fulmer has come in there and not had a background in athletic administration, recognized that, and to his credit—I think I'm right about this, Tom, check the facts—he's retained all of John Currie's people. And Currie, of course, came up through the administrative side, the fundraising side, et cetera, I think, and put together a team and Phillip is smart enough to look at those and go: "Well, I'm not changing them out just because John hired them."

So I think you have a good blend of people over there. I think Coach Fulmer will be there for a while. I think he'll turn around football, turn around some of the other sports. It's my understanding that the baseball and tennis coaches Currie hired got off to a good start this season—a ways to go but made good progress, so I think we will get stability.

But let's face it: it all depends on how you do in football: I mean, can you tell me how Alabama does in any other sport? And the answer is—*you* might be able to because you're a sports guy—but most people can't. It all depends on how you do in football. So that's why hiring Jeremy and Jeremy turning around the program is so crucial because that's the reputation your athletic department has and that's what generates all the money.

MATTINGLY: Jimmy, I appreciate that. We've had a good interview here.

HASLAM: Great to talk to both of you guys.

JOHN "THUNDER" THORNTON, UT DONOR

"An Athletic Dictatorship"

John C. "Thunder" Thornton founded Thunder Enterprises, an investment and real estate development firm, and has been its CEO and Chairman since 1993. The Thornton Academic Student Life Center on the University of Tennessee campus in Knoxville bears his name. He was Chairman of the University of Tennessee Development Council, Chairman of the UTC Roundtable, past Co-Chairperson for the University of Tennessee Lady Vols Development Campaign, and is the past Chairman of the Chattanooga United Way's Alexis de Tocqueville Society. In 1999, he was also inducted into the University of Tennessee at Chattanooga's Entrepreneurial Hall of Fame.

CELINA SUMMERS: First off, just basic bio question: what's your association or connection with Tennessee?

JOE THORNTON: I grew up in Maryville, and

most everyone was a Tennessee fan in Blount County. I recall back as a teenager, I was out raking the leaves in the yard with my Dad and a transistor Panasonic radio cranked way up. We set it on the front porch and listened, and when an exciting play would come, I'd stop that rake momentarily just so the rustle of the leaves didn't overtake John Ward and Billy Anderson's commentary. That was exciting then and exciting ever since.

SUMMERS: That's actually pretty much one hundred percent the story I tell too. We'd be sitting around in my grandparents' living room and they had a big radio up on the TV and the TV would be turned off because, you know, Vols games weren't on the TV back in the day. And we would all just sit there and stare at the radio. Now when I watch a Vols game, I hear John Ward's voice in my head calling the game. So you grew up in Tennessee and so because everybody around you was a Tennessee fan, that's what engendered your love for the university?

THORNTON: That's correct.

SUMMERS: What in your opinion has been the primary obstacle involving the Tennessee Athletic Department in the last fifteen years?

THORNTON: Leadership.

SUMMERS: Leadership? We're going to get into that a little bit deeper as we go on. What specifically with the leadership? Meaning...

THORNTON: There was so much turnover and bad selections actually for president of the university. And it...Joe Johnson (former UT President and President Emeritus) was just the greatest leader of the university, that we had in that role in my opinion.

SUMMERS: We actually have an interview with him as well.

THORNTON: That's great. Give him my regards when you see him. Since he left, it's kind of gone downhill ever since.

SUMMERS: It really has. Did you see the documents that were released last year about the coaching search? The Freedom of Information Act documents?

THORNTON: I read *a lot* regarding that search because I was so interested in it and so I don't know if the specific documents you're referring to are the ones I read. More than likely I did.

SUMMERS: In the document drop it seemed pretty apparent that the boosters were kept out of the loop. Would that be an accurate assessment of what was going on?

THORNTON: I think the Athletic board was kept out of the loop! Some on the search committee were kept out of the loop. *laughter* And not only the boosters but that's my understanding. I was not on either the athletic board or part of the search committee. But it was…I think arrogance played a role in that.

SUMMERS: Yeah. I mean Charlie Anderson was the head of the athletic committee on the Board of Trustees. He called up and asked about the coaching search and the athletic department basically told him, "You don't need to know."

THORNTON: That was my understanding. Not

very smart.

SUMMERS: No. Not at all. There were also no communications in those documents—and I went through every single one—with any coaches or applicants about the coaching position at all. Does that surprise you?

THORNTON: I didn't understand that, would you repeat that, Celina?

SUMMERS: There were no conversations, no emails, or phone calls or texts with any other coaches for this job. It's like they didn't talk to anybody, didn't interview anybody. Does it surprise you that they were that zeroed in on (Ohio State Assistant Coach Greg) Schiano?

THORNTON: For the most recent coach that (Tennessee Athletic Director) Currie was looking for?

SUMMERS: Right. The Greg Schiano hire is basically what I'm talking about.

THORNTON: Nothing that would indicate ineptitude would surprise me with the findings of that search. I wasn't aware of that but like I said it doesn't really surprise me.

SUMMERS: In the weeks between the failed Schiano hire and Currie's firing, what was going on—because the boosters aren't in the public eye with talking about what's going on at Tennessee—what was going on within the boosters and how you felt about that hire?

THORNTON: Well, I can't speak for all boosters. I know what I felt and some of my close friends. We would get on the phone and text back and forth and communicate.

We were really concerned. To me, it was just going to be another hire outside of the SEC conference, no connection to Tennessee, whoever the new coach would be. We've got to play Alabama every year with (a coach) with no appreciation for our history or tradition, what Tennessee stood for. And the fact that we could empower one guy who really shoved the chairman of the athletics board aside and didn't invite his input...not only that but didn't want to share with him any updates. Why do you even have an athletic board? I mean that's just an athletic dictatorship and so I think that was wrong and to allow that situation to exist with his superiors.

I mean, the chancellor (Beverly Davenport) and the president of the university (Joe DiPietro) I think also have to bear responsibility and I think the chancellor did. She (Davenport) saw it running out of control, brought him (Currie) in, and fired him. My hat's off to her. I think she did the university—and the athletic department certainly—but the entire university a great favor.

SUMMERS: Following up on that, when she was terminated, did you see DiPietro's termination letter to her?

THORNTON: Yes, I did.

SUMMERS: What did you think about that?

THORNTON: Well, he didn't write it. Lawyer wrote it. My opinion. I'm sure the legal department wrote it in an effort to put in points that only the president of the university knows that were critical of Chancellor Davenport. Such as "you didn't communicate with me." Well who on the outside can argue that, you know, other than Chancellor Davenport? And so there were a lot of these things and I think that was all done to temper any outrage from the fan base.

SUMMERS: Yeah, well that failed miserably didn't it?

THORNTON: Yeah it did. Look, Chancellor Davenport didn't make the right selection the first time for athletic director. What? She'd been on the job for a week? So I don't really think it was her decision in the first place.

SUMMERS: Whose decision do you think it was?

THORNTON: I'm not going to go there.

SUMMERS: Okay, no problem. Why do college football fans have the idea that boosters are the ones calling all the shots? With major hiring decisions and such? This isn't just the Tennessee fan base but every fan base. Do you think that's accurate?

THORNTON: Probably is in a lot of universities. I don't think any booster has the right to fire any administrator of the university. It's not the way it should work and certainly not just *one* booster. Other SEC schools have had that problem and some of them still have it today but it's not right. It's certainly not right for me to have that influence or anyone else, regardless of how much money they give.

The board hires the president. And the board should as a group evaluate that president's performance. Either retain him or fire him and then it works right down the line. The president hires the chancellor, the chancellor hires the athletic director and all of these...I don't think there's ever been a significant hire at the university where a search committee hasn't been involved or at least the chairman of the athletic board for a coach.

Like I know when Phillip (Fulmer) recently hired a golf coach, he solicited opinions from a lot of people that were much more knowledgeable about college golf than he was at the time. Philip had been on the job about six months when he made the decision on the golf coach but he sought input from a lot of different angles and look— he ended up making a great decision. I was for another guy! And he and I fished up in Alaska while he was up there making this decision and I said, "Well, you know, the assistant would be terrific. Sean Pacetti, I think he'd be great."

But he listened to a lot of people that know a lot more about golf than I do. I just gave him my opinion. And I said, "But there might be others out there."

And what does he do? He ends up hiring a young man from MTSU and a couple of months later he's got the number one golf team in the country.

SUMMERS: It's hard to argue with the effectiveness of that hire isn't it?

THORNTON: Oh sure.

SUMMERS: And that's a significant shift in leadership style within the athletic department.

THORNTON: Absolutely.

SUMMERS: Has the athletic department...In my opinion the athletic department has had issues since

Dickey retired (in 2003). Do you think that's an accurate thing to say?

THORNTON: Yes, I would agree but I liked Dave Hart. I thought Dave did some really positive things for the athletic department. No question he did. I mean he probably salvaged the solvency of the athletic department. And he got chancellor, he brought Chancellor Cheek along, to show the chancellor how important it was for the school. The athletic department was generating much of the funds. For them to keep those funds within the athletic department and still contribute heavily to the university's overall campus but (there were) certain things that the athletic department needed to continue to do and they needed the funds to be able to do it.

So Dave did, I think, overall a great job. Look, he probably had big decisions he'd like to make over again— probably the Lady Vols trademark—but I like Dave. I thought Dave did overall a great job.

Matter of fact, we were sitting at Cherokee Country Club, my wife and I, at a farewell dinner that was attended by most of the boosters and it was just one congratulations after another, lauding Dave's accomplishments and outlining them over his tenure there at UT. And my wife, who's not as involved in following the UT athletic department as I am, leans over and says, "Gosh, just one guy after another is saying what a great job he did. Wonder why they fired him?"

And I thought that was a pretty good question.

SUMMERS: Oh man! That actually is a good question. Do you think Donnie Tyndall had a lot to do with turning the opinion against Mr. Hart?

THORNTON: I guess he did. I don't know. Donnie was a good coach. I guess he just wasn't appropriately vetted and I guess that falls on Dave's lap. I'm sure that's another decision he would like to make over again. But at the same time, Dave Hart got Rick Barnes. He kidnapped Rick Barnes when Rick was on the outs with Texas—which I never understood. I mean what a great man! What a great coach, fabulous guy—and Dave did the right thing. He brought him to Knoxville, and basically quarantined him until Rick said yes. He did a lot of great things for the university.

SUMMERS: He really did. Coach Barnes is just… nobody could have expected how successful and in how short of a time that Coach Barnes would be with the basketball program. How do you think that the power of the internet, has it changed the way business is done in particular with college athletics?

THORNTON: No question it has. It has. It was proven that Sunday afternoon.

SUMMERS: What did you think of the uprising?

THORNTON: Well, I'd never seen anything like it, just the fast, broad communications. The fan base was outraged and it was like here we go again, getting a guy from Penn State and… Look, I don't know Schiano. I feel sorry for him if he was falsely accused. It's a horrible thing. Brett Kavanaugh would tell you the same thing.

However, it was out there and what do you think that the recruiting staff of Georgia, Florida, Alabama or Auburn are going to say when they're in the driveway of a recruit, and Schiano leaves the living room of that recruit? I mean it's baggage whether it's rightfully placed on him or not. It is something that he will have to fight through and puts his university and his athletic department if he had been head coach at a real disadvantage.

And it was a shame, like I say, if the man was falsely accused. I hate that, I hate that for him. Nonetheless you know you have to do what's in the best interest of the university and the people around there that don't walk into a living room on the defensive right off the bat. So I just thought that it was a poor choice to begin with and, you know, the fact that he had no SEC experience. And no appreciation for the tradition of Tennessee and the rivalries of the conference so I just...it was crazy.

SUMMERS: What did you think when the whole Urban Meyer debacle went down at the beginning of the football season and Ohio State didn't name their number two guy Schiano as the interim coach? Was that significant to you in any way?

THORNTON: No, it wasn't significant to me one way or the other. I don't follow Ohio State anywhere near as much as I would Mississippi State or...

SUMMERS: Unfortunately, I do. So how much did you know about Greg Schiano before that Sunday?

THORNTON: I didn't know him at all.

SUMMERS: Didn't know anything about him?

THORNTON: No.

SUMMERS: If you had known some of the stuff that has come out since like how all of the players he was coaching at Tampa Bay absolutely hated him and said it was like living in Cuba or some of his abusive coaching practices or...

THORNTON: I had heard that. I'd heard that he was not well liked by the players but I'm just glad for that uprising and the fact that...

You know, I think Currie wanted to turn this search into just a dictatorship, it was just who *he* was going to pick and that was it. And then the power of the internet kind of overtook that and created so much heat for him that he had to abandon that choice. Thank goodness for the internet that day.

SUMMERS: And were you surprised how quickly and how angrily Vols fans responded?

THORNTON: I was. The whole time I'm sitting in a deer blind on top of Jasper Island, a residential development up there, and my daughter was with me up there and my phone was just blowing up and I gave up the idea of the deer. Because I was on the phone texting back and forth with a lot of buddies. One who you'll interview later today, I think. (ALLAN JONES) You'll have fun with that. He's a great guy, a great friend of mine.

JOE MCCAMISH (This book's publisher was also present): So you were right in the mix of it.

THORNTON: Well I don't know about that.

MCCAMISH: No, but you were watching it in real time.

THORNTON: Yeah. Thank God I took my phone deer hunting! Yeah, I was kind of watching the whole thing implode and I hated...You know, in one sense after I'd heard several of the negatives on Schiano and I didn't think he was the right choice. With his coaching, he might be a great coach, I don't know, but I don't think he was the right fit for the University of Tennessee. He didn't have any SEC experience so I was glad that he wasn't named our head coach but I wasn't so happy for how it made Tennessee look. We took a lot of hits. Our stature, our image nationwide depreciated during that fateful week. All because of leadership, or lack of it.

SUMMERS: I one hundred percent agree. When you look at that week, and all of the agitation for the first time really in college football history, you look at a fan base that are demanding their voice and opinions be heard. Do you think that changed not only just Tennessee but how other universities are going to approach major coaching hires in the future?

THORNTON: No question that it did. No question. And I think that's scary for a lot of university administrators, not just Tennessee but all across the country. I think all of the athletic directors and presidents across the country, chancellors, they said, "Man, it's a new ball game now. Things have changed."

And I really do think that that was a moment in time that certainly signifies a new concern that athletic directors and chancellors will have in making key appointments that fan bases are really interested in and passionate about, care so much about them.

I had a conversation about just that with another very high profile AD in the SEC and he said it's changed. He was really shocked by the furor, the passion and the success really of the fan base so I really do think it's changed.

SUMMERS: I would agree. I also think that there isn't another fan base in the country that could have pulled it off the same way that Tennessee did because of just the perfect storm of events. The internet has a lot to do with that because the average fan is a lot more informed than they ever have been. I mean it's instantaneous.

THORNTON: Well, it gave (Clay) Travis a lot of credit. A lot of people hate him. I love him. I think he's a very entertaining guy. I like Clay and he's got his opinions and he weighed in pretty heavily that Sunday afternoon, that week. A lot of people in Tennessee listen to him.

SUMMERS: Tony Basilio was on the air for eleven hours straight on Schiano Sunday. What did you think about the way the national media was portraying not just the university but the fans of the university?

THORNTON: Yeah well, they…I can't say I didn't care. I did care about how the national media portrayed our fan base and our university and our administration but we brought that on ourselves with the hire of Currie.

SUMMERS: There was a text exchange between John Currie and Dan Wolken, a writer from USA Today, and the athletic director of Tennessee is asking a high profile journalist to help him spin the PR for the Schiano hire because, and I quote, 'our fans are wackos'. Is that the way the business is done when it comes to a program? Have you ever heard of any athletic director doing that kind of thing before?

THORNTON: Of course not. Like I said before,

(UT) brought it on themselves by hiring Currie in the first place. And regarding that: I couldn't believe that Currie was hired when he was. If you think about it—and I certainly hope that the boosters and the people that advocated for Phillip Fulmer's firing in 2008 don't miss the irony—the University of Tennessee's athletic department's problems started when Fulmer was fired in 2008 and they really didn't begin to be repaired and come back as a family and unite as a family—administrators, coaches, the whole family—until Fulmer was named the new athletic director a decade later in 2017. What irony!

And I often wonder if those boosters and board members that were cheering to get rid of Fulmer in 2008 were... how do they feel now? And will they admit it?

I knew it was a mistake then. I'm very close to Philip and he's my best friend. He's a great guy; he's a stand up guy. Through all of that decade I never heard him say one bitter, negative word about the university. His love of the university trumped any disappointment that he had for getting canned or that season.

And not only that, the hiring of Currie was not only stupid, it was mean! Currie was on the team that fired Phillip. He was the hatchet man for Hamilton. And I *never* understood that. I just said, "Oh my God, I can't even believe he would be considered (for athletic director)."

SUMMERS: Do you think the way that Coach Fulmer was fired mid-season after UT had been in the SEC championship the year before, do you think that prevented UT from being able to make a top tier coach hire? Over the next three coaches?

THORNTON: I think probably Hamilton was a bigger obstacle to being able to recruit a top tier coach than anything else. I mean who wants to put their career in this guy's hands?

SUMMERS: On October 29th, two and a half weeks before Butch Jones was fired, John Currie got a phone call from (Washington State head coach) Mike Leach and the message was: "Mike Leach wants to talk to you about coaching the Vols." The fact that Currie didn't respond to Mike Leach—and this has nothing to do with whether he would have been a good fit at Tennessee or not—but this is a high profile football coach and Currie didn't even respond to him at all. Do you think that means Schiano was always the guy, that that was the plan to bring him in?

THORNTON: Who knows? I really don't know. But once again the genesis of the problem that existed was Currie becoming athletic director in the first place. I mean all you had to do was check the two high profile coaches at Kansas State that worked for him—Frank Martin and Bill Snyder. See what their relationship was with that guy. Frank Martin, he was doing great at K-State and he leaves there, gets out from under the control of Currie, goes to South Carolina, and immediately puts them in the Final Four.

SUMMERS: That's really telling isn't it? If you were going to describe the leadership at UT, not the people, but the leadership philosophy over the past two decades, and you had the ability to make changes, like in a company that you own, what changes would you make?

THORNTON: Well, I think that...We just hired a guy (Randy Boyd) as interim president that I think will be great. Randy loves the university. Randy did not come from the academic side of hiring education; he's a brilliant businessman and he's proven that. He's a great communicator, he loves the university, he's an alum of the university.

I think one of the problems was the prerequisite for most of the search committees was that they (candidates) gotta be a sitting president, a university president, they have to have a doctorate level degree, I think that's...Look, I don't think that Jack Welch had a PhD before he was pegged to run GE and he did a pretty damn good job. It's a huge management job, billions of dollars budget and it's important that you get a great manager that understands the culture. No different really from the head football coach understanding the conference, the SEC, and the people. We were forced to pick in one president's race: the two finalists were a guy from Utah and another guy from Connecticut. Ended up with the guy from Connecticut. John Peterson. Which was a big mistake in my opinion.

I called John that Sunday afternoon right after Philip was fired and right after Philip called me and said, "Well, they finally did it."

I called John and I said, "John how could you allow this to happen? How could you fire a national championship coach who gave his all to Tennessee every day, who loved it, one of the winningest college coaches ever, 152 wins? I don't understand how you could allow this to happen! How you could allow Hamilton to fire him?"

And his response to me was, "Thunder, I don't micromanage my department heads."

I said, "Micro-fucking-manage the department heads? John, I'm not talking about what price we sell Coca-Cola at Lady Vols basketball games! I'm talking about who leads the entire revenue stream of the University of Tennessee's athletic department! How could you sit this out? This is such bullshit and lack of leadership!"

Haven't spoken with John Peterson since.

SUMMERS: I think a lot of people would agree with you on that. I know I do.

THORNTON: Horrible decision. And when you appoint one person in there like they did with Currie, shut out Charlie Anderson and many others, didn't invite...It's just wrong.

SUMMERS: Do you think that this problem is now starting to be addressed at UT with bringing back Coach Fulmer as AD, with bringing Mr. Boyd in as president? Do you think we're turning on the right track with these issues?

THORNTON: I do. I really do. I've got more confidence now in the leadership at the university than I've had in the last two decades.

SUMMERS: What strengths do you think that Coach Fulmer brings to being the AD?

THORNTON: Well number one, he's smart. He's a great manager—he understands people. He is a sensitive guy, he's extremely considerate. And he loves the university and will only make decisions that he feels are in the best interests of the university. And he...look people love him. When I've I was with him...oh, not too long back when we were walking over from Anderson Training Center to the baseball field. It was also the Spring game, Orange and White game. We were going from our East skybox to the West skybox. That should have taken about ten minutes. Took an hour and ten minutes to get over there. I mean everybody...The fan base just adores Phillip Fulmer. Rightfully so. He's just one of the greatest guys I've ever had the privilege to know. I mean—he never let bitterness, his own disappointment overrule his love of the university and his affection and his passion for what was best for the university.

SUMMERS: I would agree with that too. I was watching his farewell press conference, and he said, "Our fans at Tennessee and our boosters and administration are all divided as to what path we need to take. And I love Tennessee too much to be divisive." I'm paraphrasing it. And actually what makes it so brilliant is that it perfectly encapsulated what happened during the uprising that actually brought him back to Tennessee. Now I'm a novelist by trade, if you're going to write a story about vindication, you fire a national championship winning coach mid-season and then nine years almost to the day you bring him back to save the athletic department that fired him. I write fiction and I couldn't make that stuff up. But one thing that I noticed, I don't know if you did or not, as soon as he was announced as athletic director, all the agitation in the fan base stopped.

THORNTON: That's right.

SUMMERS: Stopped cold. And I think that was a sense of completion and, in a way. fair play. I think that bringing Fulmer back, in a way the fans are like: "You know what? That should have happened last spring!"

But they hired Currie instead and they've done Fulmer wrong for ten years—he never coached again after he left Tennessee, you know, he stayed loyal to the school that he loved.

THORNTON: Right.

SUMMERS: And to me that was initially his biggest asset to the program. Now with the hiring of Jeremy Pruitt, it's like the fans are looking at it this way, it's like he finally got to hand pick his successor, and he did a proper coaching search, interviewed multiple candidates, selected the right one in a very calm manner. Six days. A week and done. What did you think of the Jeremy Pruitt hire?

THORNTON: Well, I thought it was brilliant. I talked to Phillip about it after he had decided of course who he was going to hire. And he talked to me about people he had spoken with. About Jeremy Pruitt and his background. He did an exhaustive vetting of Jeremy. And he really identified with Jeremy. I mean they really...they grew up not too far apart and he really felt so confident in the hire and he was excited about it.

So when we went to Alaska fishing back in June this year he said, "Now look, I loved the guy in December when he came in, and I love him even more today. He is the right guy to lead our football program, I am absolutely confident of that."

Phillip's words to me. And it is really interesting Phillip told me that they made the announcement that afternoon in the Anderson training center and then at seven-thirty the next morning, Friday morning, there are seven assistant coaches walking out of the training center—Butch's staff that have been dismissed—and seven new ones coming in. They had jets flying all over the country picking these guys up *that night,* and bringing them in, and he had his staff already assembled, in they walk.

And that tells you something about the commitment of Jeremy Pruitt and the fact that Phillip made the right call—his staff is terrific. You wait and see. They are great recruiters, they are great developers of talent, as Jeremy is and I just think we are in for great things. It can't happen just overnight. The fan base has got to be patient, it takes a while. I mean it takes recruiting classes. And I'm not saying the cupboard was totally bare but out of eighty-five scholarship players I wonder how many of them could play on another SEC team or were recruited?

But Jeremy will fix that. He's already off to a great start with the people he brought in and the very short time frame he had to sign them up.

SUMMERS: What did you...we talked a little bit about the hiring of Randy Boyd as the interim president. We've had a lot of interims, chancellors, directors, Ads... do you think it makes it more difficult to establish a leadership culture at UT? What can we do to address that?

THORNTON: You know, I think it was the appropriate thing for the board of UT to do to hire an interim president. In higher education for some reason, they think it takes a year to hire a president. I've always thought that's crazy. Boeing could probably hire a new CEO in ten days, two weeks, but the University of

Tennessee and every other higher education institution thinks, "Oh well. It's July now so we won't be able to hire anyone until the start of the new academic year which would be July of *next* year so let's get forty people on a search committee and another forty people on an advisory search committee, and pass it by everyone that feels they have a vote on it…"

It's really crazy. Business ain't run that way. But I think the immediate appointment of Randy was fabulous. I think the immediate appointment of Wayne Davis was great. I mean here's a guy that's been there forty years and he understands the university and he's a smart guy and great leader and Randy will prove to the faculty and to the administration of UT that he's a great leader as well. So I think that doesn't hurt us, gives us time to maybe reflect and think about what should be the criteria for our president to lead the university.

SUMMERS: We are actually…that's pretty much all I had. We covered what I wanted to cover. Joe did you have anything you wanted to follow up with?

MCCAMISH: What do you think about the idea of the athletic director having to report to the chancellor?

SUMMERS: That's a good question.

THORNTON: It is a good question. I think it's a big mistake. I felt that way, I was on the board, 2000-2006, and I think was changed 2007 or 2008. The athletic department is such a high-profile department and it deserves in my opinion a more direct reporting status to the president of the system. It worked great when Doug Dickey reported to Joe Johnson for many years and I don't…

Other than the way it looks on a beautiful organizational chart, I don't know what other reason there was for changing it. I thought it was a mistake. You're just putting another layer of management on an authority process. And I do think this, you know: right after that was changed and the chancellor had a cabinet meeting, enter fifteen or so department heads, History and English and Math and Engineering, the Athletic Director, they're all sitting there, and look…

A lot of those department heads may not have really appreciated the athletic department and really how the athletic department recruited great engineering students or English majors or others. A high school kid's first introduction to the University of Tennessee was going to football games and being able to cheer for them. And so there may have been some animosity. I'm not saying that there was; I don't know if there was. I wasn't sitting in the cabinet meetings but I just see how it's a breeding ground for that and so now all of a sudden, they're on the same plane as the athletic department. I thought it was a mistake.

To me the athletic director should report directly to the university president. I think we had an interim chancellor who got upset with it or something. He had never had any involvement in athletics before; neither did Jimmy Cheek when he came in. Athletics was not in his resume when he came here from Florida.

SUMMERS: I think that became obvious really quickly.

MCCAMISH: Well Joe Johnson told us that he wouldn't even walk across the street to meet the coaches.

He had no interest in the athletic department. You think it could possibly go back to the Doug Dickey days, where the chancellor reported to the…?

THORNTON: I got a lot of confidence in John Compton. He'll be a fabulous chairman of the UT board, and I think the new board size is terrific. I think it's good. There are smart people there and I hope it never goes back and, but it'll…you know, it'll be that board's decision.

SUMMERS: I think we're good. Thank you.

LARRY PRATT, UT DONOR

"I Liked the Passion the Fans Showed"

Larry Pratt is a native of Athens, Tennessee and is a 1973 graduate of the University of Tennessee, Knoxville. His primary career has been as a mortgage banker. He founded First Savings Mortgage Corporation in McLean, Va., in 1989. The firm has grown to be the largest privately owned mortgage lender in the Washington D.C. metropolitan area, where Larry is Chairman and CEO. His support of the University of Tennessee has encompassed over twenty years. He has established endowments for athletics and students alike, such as the Pratt Pavilion, commitments to Neyland Stadium renovations, and, most recently, the lead on the Larry Pratt basketball locker rooms are some of the projects for which he has earmarked donations.

TOM MATTINGLY: According to the UT document drop, it seems apparent the boosters were kept out of the loop. Has that been the case over the past ten years?

LARRY PRATT: I think it probably varies a bit, think it probably depends on the boosters, and that depends on the search and who's conducting it. You're referring to the most recent football search, right?

MATTINGLY: Right.

PRATT: Yeah. That one was a little different because there wasn't a search committee and Mr. Currie wanted to keep that totally secret.

MATTINGLY: Well, that's my next question: did it surprise you that there was really no communication with coaches about the positions at all? Currie kind of had his own ideas about what to do and didn't communicate really with anybody. Did that surprise you?

PRATT: Well… Yes, it was surprising as I told him face to face in the Bahamas when the basketball team was in a tournament about a year ago. I said, "I feel like my neighbor knows about as much of what's going on at Tennessee as I do, and he went to Florida State."

MATTINGLY: Did it surprise you that Currie went to the Bahamas in the midst of a coaching search?

PRATT: No that didn't really surprise me. I knew his family and they were planning on going. So for him to make a quick appearance, that was not a factor to me.

MATTINGLY: In the week between the Schiano hire that failed and Currie's firing, was there anything going on behind the scenes that you were aware of?

PRATT: Just the rumors, because I wasn't aware of anything. I had no direct knowledge of anything. Basically no one did.

MATTINGLY: Fans have the idea that the boosters are the ones calling all the shots with major hiring decisions—is that true or is it just some of the boosters? Or is that completely false?

PRATT: Some boosters have a little more influence than others.

long pause

MATTINGLY: Do you think...let me...do you think...

Can you mention any of the boosters that might have been involved more than others?

PRATT: No I...It would just be conjecture. And it varies. But it probably should. I would think those that give a little more probably have a little louder voice.

MATTINGLY: What do you think about the power of the internet? Like the way that the Vols fans rose up against the Schiano hire? How has that changed the way how colleges do business including college athletics? What are the changes the internet has brought about?

PRATT: Well, at this time that is a good question. It's just not college athletics. I think it's just the way our life is now. Everything is much more open, much more transparent. Much more susceptible to criticism, just because it's put out front so much. So, you have to be conscious of that in anything you do. If you're making, in this case, coaching hires and so on.

MATTINGLY: How much information did you have about the intention to hire Schiano?

PRATT: Zero.

MATTINGLY: What did you think of Schiano as you looked at him? For whatever you knew about him... What did you think of him as a candidate?

PRATT: My only concern was the lack of SEC experience. But beyond that, I didn't know enough to make a judgement.

MATTINGLY: What was your opinion of the uprising, the furor that came after they announced that they were going to hire Schiano?

PRATT: That surprised me but really, I believe that was probably the frustration that had been built up over the years and that was one way to vent it. I think a combination of things, starting with, as I mentioned earlier the fractionalization at the school. Because we were going through a period where we needed to get to the fiscal house in the athletic department more in order. So that meant consolidating some things. As any business would do, we were running with many overlapping departments. Dual marketing, dual operational department from the Lady Vols to the Vols.

So, you had some of that going on...so that raised some sensitivities with some people because it was a change. And then you had the lack of success that we had been experiencing in a number of our sports. All of a sudden, that arose so I think everyone was much more sensitive and when this came there were some issues and obviously, he was made an easy target, but I think he just happened to be the easy subject at that time.

MATTINGLY: Do you think it was a good thing

the way the fans forced Tennessee to not only to step back from Schiano but also called them to account the way they were hiring the highest paid and the most visible employee in the state—was that a good thing to happen with the ReVOLution?

PRATT: What I did like was I liked the passion that the fans showed. I didn't like the way it was handled. I didn't care for our legislators to get involved. I think some people went too far over the line. There's ways to approach any type of movement, but you know it showed a lot of passion so that part I do appreciate. I hate when it goes after one individual when really that may not really be the real root of the issues.

MATTINGLY: So, is it back to business as usual in athletics or did Tennessee fans create a blueprint for other fan bases to follow?

PRATT: Well, I think other fan bases will do this regardless of what Tennessee did just because of the access of social media. So whether it's sports or politics or anything, now people obviously can get their sentiment and their demonstrations out there more easily. For Tennessee, things have really calmed down this year. I know this for a fact. I am involved. It was a good move to put Philip (Fulmer) in there as athletic director from the standpoint that it brought credibility and it calmed virtually all aspects of the fractionalization. And since then we've been on a quick healing process and I'm real pleased with where we have come to at this point.

MATTINGLY: Thinking about the UT overall leadership, the leadership philosophy the university has displayed, would you institute any changes based on your expertise and leadership within your company?

PRATT: Give me that again, Tom.

MATTINGLY: I'm sorry—if you were going to describe the leadership at Tennessee, not individual people, but the philosophy the university has displayed over the years, would you institute changes based on your expertise and leadership within your company?

PRATT: Oh, I would have made some changes a long time ago, yes. If I had seen…If I had experienced this at my company no question. Here's some things from my perspective and others may not agree with that.

If you go back and look at the way the trustees were formed. We had I think twenty-seven trustees, running the state, and really making some of the big hires and a lot of direction. The thing is, the school reaches out to many of us, and I've contributed significantly to the school. But I'm not a Tennessee resident so they reach out to me a lot for financial support. But the bylaw stated that you can only be a trustee if you're a Tennessee resident so there are a number of successful alums that are throughout the country with Tennessee degrees that would love to help and support and the only thing we've been able to do is write checks.

And I just think that philosophy right off the bat when you could be bringing other people in with great experiences across the country that could be involved. So hopefully now with the change of the structure…so now it's gone and now that is somewhat permitted with the new governorship, I would hope that we see better decision making, crisper decision making and that we all benefit from that.

MATTINGLY: What strengths do you think that Philip brings to being athletic director from his time being a player, a coach, and his experiences between the time he left and the time he came back, what are his real strengths as an athletic director?

PRATT: I think number one, obviously, we know his successes as a coach. I think number one when he was successful, a big part of it was because the support he had from the academic side, and he understood how important that was—watching the athletic director and the president at that time. I know that is something that is real important to him because he knows we need to have that to be successful. And I think that experience, what he learned and benefitted from is a key element that will help us going forward.

MATTINGLY: What did you think of Philip's hiring of Jeremy Pruitt?

PRATT: From that point in time, I thought it was a good hire, I've got to know Jeremy since then and that has reinforced that decision. And then I looked at the staff that Jeremy put together and its incredible background and the resumes. I've attended practices. I really notice what I see on the field. There's a lot of teaching, just like Rick Barnes and his staff they do at their practices and so I'm extremely positive about what we have there.

MATTINGLY: What did you think about the hiring of Randy Boyd as president? We've had several of those over the last few years. What does Randy Boyd bring to the table as an interim president?

PRATT: I was happy to see that and I told Randy that myself and he was a successful businessman, education is important to him as we know. He's a Tennessee guy and he loves sports, he's well rounded, he's got great integrity, he's a good listener and he's a good thinker.

MATTINGLY: Thinking about the turnover that's happened over the last few years, the hiring, firing, payouts of I think in the millions of dollars, how should UT address that in the future?

PRATT: Yeah, that's really been a concern of mine. I've given a substantial amount of money and as I was telling one of our highly regarded alums just recently, I said, "We can put our money together and it barely covers the buyouts."

That doesn't seem like a good formula. You know I wish...and I had conveyed this to a prior athletic director, I said it's gone too far one side. If I'm hiring a business person and I want them to excel, I give them great incentives to *perform*. Not a great incentive *not* to perform. And that's what's happened now if you look at the buyouts. If they don't perform, we terminate, and they walk away with a tremendous walking away package and we suffer.

I'd rather give a tremendous amount of upside winning the SEC, getting into the tournament, winning a national championship, SEC and all the championships. And instead of giving them $50,000, give a significant number when they hit those benchmarks. Don't move the money to the back end. The agents that have negotiated this and we have all fallen into the trap for it. So, I think we need to stop it. It's ridiculous how it's gone. It's not healthy for the schools, it's not fair for other coaches and it's just not good business practice.

MATTINGLY: What about the Tennessee football program ambience generally makes you love the university?

PRATT: Well for me, Tom, it was a family bond. And as my son has told me now, who is forty-five today, and I took him when he was young, so just like my father did. And that for us has been a family bond. As my son says there were a lot of times where I didn't know what to say to you and I knew I could say something about Tennessee athletics. So that's important to our family.

MATTINGLY: What do you see in UT's immediate future in the athletic department? Are we in the right direction, headed the right way?

PRATT: Yeah, I really feel we are. We've made good financial strides and I want to give credit to Dave Hart who really made significant changes financially—who addressed the shortfall. We were in a dire financial position in our athletic department. And he made some substantive changes and headed in the right direction. Philip's aware of that and we've had meetings on that and I really like where we're headed. I want us to win in every sport not just the bellwethers—football and basketball—every sport. He's made a couple of changes in some of our minor sports. We're seeing improvements that way and I really like where we're headed, and he's done a great job in just ten months on the job.

MATTINGLY: Just a couple more questions. What percentage of your colleagues in the donor category share these opinions with you? Is there a split of—I don't know how to approach this or are the donors pretty much on the same path? How would you assess that?

PRATT: As to what direction, Tom?

MATTINGLY: As to the problems within athletics and to where we're headed?

PRATT: I think the majority share the sentiment. Opinions vary on some particular items but I think the great majority, we share the same sentiment.

MATTINGLY: What is your opinion on the new trustees and that system?

PRATT: I don't know who they all are and I believe Kara Lawson is one but beyond that I don't know who they are.

MATTINGLY: Is it good to downsize that board to a more manageable level as the governor said or—?

PRATT: I think it's a great business practice to have a smaller committee, smaller boards, in any type of organization. I always like to see something less than double digits. So nine, seven, five, something like that I think is always healthier. Otherwise it gets too politicized, too lethargic, too slow to move and so I think that's exactly the way to do it.

MATTINGLY: One more question and then a couple of really minor questions. What did you think about the transfer oversight of athletics from the president to the chancellor? Has that worked in your opinion?

PRATT: It works better back to the president. Knoxville is the flagship. That should go directly to the president in my opinion. I'm for horizontal leadership not vertical. Less people making decisions, less people in the chain the better. Athletics is what? A 140,000,000 dollar budget? Should be the president of the university. It's too critical for the whole system.

JAMES ARTHUR HASLAM II, UT DONOR

"A Whole Lot of Churning Going On"

James Arthur Haslam II is a Knoxville business leader and philanthropist, best known as the founder of Pilot Corporation, which operates a chain of convenience stores and travel centers throughout the United States and Canada and is one of the largest privately owned companies in the United States. The University of Tennessee has benefited from his service as a trustee and donor to both academics and athletics. Schools, museums, theaters, churches, homeless shelters, the zoo, the United Way, the Foothills Land Conservancy, the Urban League and countless other civic bodies have also benefited from Haslam largess. Haslam's son, Jimmy, owns the Cleveland Browns, and his other son, Bill, is Governor of Tennessee. He was captain of the 1952 Tennessee football team.

CELIMA SUMMERS: Are you ready to go, sir?

JIM HASLAM: I'm ready to go.

TOM MATTINGLY: When we talked the other

day about setting up this interview, you said something about wanting to clear out misconceptions about the Haslam family and you touched on that a little bit. Can you expand on that?

HASLAM: Well none of us have ever tried... The university needs to be run by the university administration, the athletic department needs to be run by the athletic director. I was a trustee at the university from 1980 to 2007 and when I was on the board, we always let the president run the university and then the athletic director run the athletic department. I was chairman of the athletic committee for a while but, you know, we always took the direction from the athletic director. Now one of the things we all, and you said twenty years. I'll go back ten years to when all of our...

Phillip was, you know, in 2008 we were 5-7—I'm going by memory, you can check on this—then Lane came and we were 7-6. Lane was a good football coach. I mean, we all, nobody doubted that. And then he leaves, they get Derek. Derek had an unfortunate time here, he was... First year we went and played the Music City Bowl. I think we were 6-7 and he had two 5-7 records. Then we got Butch. And what we forget about Butch is that, I think he was 5-7 and then maybe he was...well then, he was 7-6, and then he went to the Jacksonville bowl and then he was 9-4 two years in a row.

SUMMERS: Yes sir.

HASLAM: And everybody was worried about him going to Michigan *laughs* if you remember. And then he...They had that disastrous season last year so in the last ten years it's not been *all* negative. Now the ten years before that when Phillip was coach and won a national championship, and was it 2003 we lost to LSU?

MATTINGLY: 2001.

HASLAM: Because we were going to the Rose Bowl?

MATTINGLY: Right.

HASLAM: And so that was a good thing. And one thing, it's interesting...the guy who's director of athletics at Oklahoma named Joe Castiglione. You remember him?

MATTINGLY: Yeah.

HASLAM: He's kind of the gold standard for athletic directors. Now Stoops left last year but he told me that David Boren, who was the president of the university who had been there twenty-six years, he (Castiglione) had been there twenty-two and Stoops had been there nineteen. That's not what we've had at Tennessee. In the last ten years, you've had, well you've had Phillip (Fulmer), Lane (Kiffin), Derek (Dooley), Butch (Jones), and now Jeremy (Pruitt). Five football coaches. We've had Mike (Hamilton), Dave (Hart), John Currie, and now Phillip (Fulmer). We've had four athletic directors.

MATTINGLY: And Joan Cronan.

HASLAM: Yeah well that'd be just a... yeah but that was kind of a...but yeah, you oughta... I mean it was a three to six month interval. You know what I mean?

SUMMERS: Yes.

HASLAM: So, you know, we've had a lot of churning going on and that has not helped the program. And what we need to get is...Now something else to remember is that...and you'll have to look this up, but the athletic department used to report to the president and when Dr. DiPietro and Dr. Cheek came, they shuffled around who reported to the chancellor. And so the chancellor for the first time had...they sort of wanted the things that he or she controlled.

During that time you had Jimmy Cheek, Beverly Davenport, and now Wayne Davis. So what I'm saying is, we've had all these things churning up and that's been a big factor.

Now let me talk again about the Haslam influence. We've...when I was on the Board of Trustees you made decisions as to who the president was going to be, but I never and, certainly when Bill's (Bill Haslam, Jim Haslam's son and Governor of Tennessee) been governor, he has never, and Jimmy ("Little Jim" James Haslam, Jim Haslam's son and current CEO of Pilot Flying J) despite some of the things that were said in this last go-round didn't...you know what I mean? And I want to get another thing straight on Jimmy and this last thing. The *only* involvement any Haslam had in the whole thing was early on in the process. John Currie called Jimmy, and when the Browns were looking for a coach, I forget the guy who was the search guy, but he mentioned...what's his name... Shirano?

SUMMERS: Schiano.

HASLAM: Schiano. And I think they interviewed him and they were impressed with him but they hired somebody else. And John asked Jimmy about that and Jimmy told him that. But Jimmy *never* once said he's the guy you ought to hire. And of course John looked at a whole bunch of guys and got turned down by a bunch of guys before he talked to Schiano. So anyhow that's the only sense of involvement any Haslam has had, and you know, it's kind of like I said, if you had called me and asked about something, it was not initiated by a Haslam family member. It was initiated by John Currie.

MATTINGLY: Can I ask one question going back just a second? Is it a good deal or a bad deal to have the chancellor over athletics from your perspective?

HASLAM: I think it's a good deal for this reason: the…A big thing on athletics—and Phillip will tell you this, Jeremy will tell you this, any coach will tell you, Rick Barnes will tell you—the big thing is academics. You have to get the athlete admitted, then he or she has to stay in school. The chancellor and the provost control that. The president of the university has all these other campuses so in my opinion you're better off with a chancellor who is close to all of these things. You understand where I'm coming from?

SUMMERS: Yes sir.

HASLAM: Than the president. And you know, the whole structure of the university, you know this, the president used to be, kind of the king of everything. Well, now the chancellor is so much more visible and he or she is so much more involved that I personally think it's good for the chancellor to be head of it.

MATTINGLY: Okay.

HASLAM: Now some people would disagree with that but I think it is.

MATTINGLY: And it's worked?

HASLAM: Yeah, I think for the most part it's worked. It's really working now. Phillip will tell you he and Wayne are getting along fine. The chancellor has now...and I think... actually, I think Jimmy Cheek started this with Dave Hart: the athletic director is part of the chancellor's cabinet and he or she sits in on all the meetings. I think they meet every Monday.

MATTINGLY: He's a vice chancellor.

HASLAM: He's a vice chancellor for athletics. And I think it's good. Now some people would think differently.

MATTINGLY: So, you said you'd never done anything the university didn't ask you to.

HASLAM: Mhm.

MATTINGLY: And...

HASLAM: That includes giving money! *laughter*

MATTINGLY: I understand!

SUMMERS: I'm sure they ask you that quite a bit.

HASLAM: Yeah!

MATTINGLY: Why have the past twenty years been so tumultuous? Why has it been such a problem to make the university run the right way over the past twenty years? There's been changes in administration, there's been changes in coaches...

HASLAM: Well, I think...Until ten years ago, in athletics we were doing fine. Now you had a lotta... and then the president was responsible for athletics but after Joe Johnson retired you had three or four different presidents and, you know, I think it's well documented how they worked out. *laughs* I won't even comment on that!

So I think that added to the turmoil but I think it all goes back to...If you could have the same, in this case same chancellor, the same athletic director, you know, and the same—and we're talking about football, the same football coach, you know—you're gonna have...I mean, it lends stability. Everybody can read each other and, you know, in the first—and Phillip will tell you this—when Phillip first became coach, Doug (Dickey) was athletic director and Joe Johnson was president and the three of them worked together great. And they stayed there until Joe retired, you know what I mean? And then you can trace a lot of this chaos, quite frankly, to when Doug retired. Because it was...you knew Doug (to Tom). Did you know Doug(to Celina)?

SUMMERS: No sir.

HASLAM: Dickey is a very strong guy.

SUMMERS: Yes, he has a very strong personality.

HASLAM: And Dickey would knock you over but Doug would always pick you up. And Doug was a really, you have to understand Doug—his father was a speech professor, Doug was born on the campus at South Dakota in whatever town he was born in.

MATTINGLY: Vermillion.

HASLAM: Okay, it was a campus...was it North or South Dakota?

MATTINGLY: South.

HASLAM: South Dakota. Okay.

SUMMERS: You just know everything, Tom.

HASLAM: Yeah, he does. And then his dad went to LSU and Florida. Doug…when he came up, when he became athletic director—except for the two years he was in the army and the one year when he was working for a Florida tile company after he'd left Colorado—had always been on a college campus.

But that gives you an idea of the kind of personality Doug had and you know, of course Phillip was his protégé and Joe Johnson, to his credit, let Doug run the athletic department and things went well.

SUMMERS: Would it be safe to say then, that in your opinion, the real changes began when Phillip Fulmer was fired in 2008?

HASLAM: Mhm yeah you…well, I think they almost began when Doug left.

MATTINGLY: In '03.

HASLAM: Yeah, I think that's when you started… the churning and everything and, you know, if you look at the history of coaches or anybody, it's hard, you know.

points to picture of General Robert Neyland hanging on his office wall

There's *my* hero up there. Harvey Robinson followed him and had two losing seasons, you know what I mean? You don't want to be the guy or gal who follows the strong person, you want to be the next one, and so, you know, Mike was at a little bit of a disadvantage in following him. But I think that you could say that that's where.

MATTINGLY: During the coaching search, it appeared that the boosters were kept out of the loop a little bit. Is that a reality—were they?

HASLAM: Yes, they were and I think they should be. I think, as I said, the only time somebody...The only time you should talk to any donor, booster, whatever you want to call it is when they ask you to do it and everything. And I think they were left out of the loop and that was a—well, of course they're both gone—but you had a chancellor who had been there six months.

SUMMERS: Right.

MATTINGLY: Mhm.

HASLAM: And you had an athletic director...They both came at the same time and they were both new in the search and I think that people have never brought that out as one of the reasons but it is one of the reasons. And there was very little communication between the two of them and...or anybody else.

MATTINGLY: After Butch left, after Butch was fired, it appears there was no communication with any other coaches, is that...Did that surprise you?

HASLAM: With any other...?

MATTINGLY: Coaching prospects.

HASLAM: Yeah, you know, everybody does searches a different way and John wanted to be a lone wolf on the search and that was his way of doing it and he did it that way. You know, Doug did it a certain way, Dave Hart did it a certain way, you know what I mean? Everybody does it a certain way but that was John's way of doing it and I...Now, be careful how you write this down but I watched Dave Hart do the search for...when they hired Butch and when he hired Rick Barnes and he kept Jimmy Cheek in the loop all the way. Now be careful how you write this, because I don't wanna involve...but I don't think John and Beverly were on the same page. Now that's my...and I have no reason to say this but from afar that's how it looks.

MATTINGLY: When Schiano Sunday came and there was that seven or eight day period when Currie was let go and Fulmer was hired, was there anything going on behind the scenes that you're aware of that was important?

HASLAM: You know, it's funny. The Browns were playing somebody and when I got off the plane *laughs* my cell phone was lit up about Schiano! That was the first I knew about it. I got calls from political people, everybody just left me messages about it and then when did... when was Currie...

SUMMERS: The following Friday.

HASLAM: It was Friday...

SUMMERS: Friday was when he was fired, Thursday was when he disappeared on the west coast.

MATTINGLY: And then she called him home and fired him in like nine minutes.

HASLAM: Yeah. I think there was...there might

have been behind the scenes discussion but I think some members of the Board of Trustees, as they should be, were involved with Dr DiPietro and Dr Davenport. But I, you know, I was not involved in any way and I'm not sure any—whatever you want to call it—boosters that said they were. It was kind of a…What in the world is going on? I don't know how many…well, he offered it to the guy at Purdue (Jeff Brohm) Saturday and the Oklahoma State guy (Mike) Gundy. First of all, Mullen turned him down. And then did he go to Schiano or did the Purdue guy turn him down first?

MATTINGLY: Well there's some debate about whether he (Brohm) really actually turned him down.

SUMMERS: Jeff Brohm is the coach from Purdue and he said that Tennessee never approached him and that there was never a deal.

HASLAM: Now I don't know. I just heard that he talked to…Mullen turned him down and I don't know if he talked to Gundy and Schiano but, and you know, the reason he went to the west coast was to talk to the pirate there. Mike Leach.

MATTINGLY: Yeah, Mike Leach. Then there was the guy from North Carolina State that…

SUMMERS: Doeren.

MATTINGLY: I'm not sure they really offered him because there was some push back against him.

HASLAM: Yeah, yeah. Yeah.

SUMMERS: They did offer it to him and he was considering it and then (UT) fans got all riled up and started tweeting him that he didn't want to come to Knoxville.

HASLAM: And then you had the mysterious flight when Currie went to the west coast.

SUMMERS: Right. The only flight in the country where wifi wasn't working in first class.

MATTINGLY: And do you remember seeing anything like that happen in UT athletics?

HASLAM: I've never seen anything in my life that approached all of this happening.

SUMMERS: Now, I'm sorry I didn't mean to cut you off but wasn't there a similar situation in 1963 where there was a lot of discussion or debate over who to hire as athletic director?

HASLAM: Now let me tell you what happened in 1963. It was pretty simple. Bowden White had some alcohol issues, okay? There was a discussion as to what to do and it was in the summer before football started. There were two candidates. There was Bob Woodruff who'd been the football coach of Florida and I guess you'd call it the line coach and then Jim McDonald who was a former Ohio State player who was also on the coaching staff and which one to take? And Dr Andy Holt—and if you knew Holt, this was a typical deal—he had great wisdom and he made Woodruff athletic director and then they gave McDonald a one-year thing as the coach and Jim McDonald coached for one year and then Coach Woodruff hired Coach Dickey.

SUMMERS: That's fascinating.

MATTINGLY: Yeah it is.

SUMMERS: A one-year contract is something that nobody...

HASLAM: Well I take that back, I'm not sure they had contracts then.

SUMMERS: That's true too.

MATTINGLY: They hired McDonald in June.

HASLAM: Yeah, well, that's what Bowden, you know, had his problems.

MATTINGLY: He pushed a writer—

HASLAM: —in the swimming pool.

laughter

HASLAM: Yeah.

MATTINGLY: And McDonald got the deal to be the head coach and then they negotiated a deal with McDonald to be an assistant AD and Dickey would be head football coach.

HASLAM: After the season.

MATTINGLY: After the season.

HASLAM: But McDonald didn't like that at all. He was very unhappy. He thought he'd done a decent job in the season, and at the end of the season Coach Woodruff got Dickey because Dickie had played quarterback for Coach Woodruff at Florida. In fact, Dickey played quarterback here against us when we were playing...What time do I need to leave?

Haslam's Assistant: You need to leave here in about five minutes.

HASLAM: Give me ten. James is gonna take me?

Haslam's Assistant: Yeah, James is taking you so we'll break the speed limit.

MATTINGLY: We'll do it.

HASLAM: Okay. I apologize I've got to be somewhere.

SUMMERS: It's okay.

MATTINGLY: Is there anything more you want to say about Woodruff and Dickey?

HASLAM: Woodruff, you know, Coach Woodruff was... *laughter* He is one of the smartest guys I've ever known but he didn't come across that way. He was as smart as could be but he was a very poor communicator. But he couldn't...In that world, he was one of the smartest guys and he did everything really well at the athletic department. I mean he's the one who started all the expansion of the stadiums and everything, got Coach Dickey. Now you know, people criticize him for getting (Coach Bill) Battle but, you know, he just wanted to do that and then he got Johnny Majors so he did a good job.

And basketball—of course, when he was here, Ray Mears was here. Then Mearrs left and he got DeVoe and DeVoe was a good basketball coach so you can't... Woodruff's stewardship of the athletic department was very good. He got Penn State to come down here; he put in lights so they could play at night. You could go on and on about Woodruff. He was a really good athletic director.

MATTINGLY: What do you think about the power of the internet and the way it led to the uprising and has it changed the way you do business in college athletics?

HASLAM: Well, I think people, you know, I think it's unfortunate that you have the internet because... You are a writer—you are a writer, you have an editor and the editor can, you know, if there's something that is incorrect, the editor is a filter. On the internet, there are no filters and somebody can say anything they want to and it can't be, you know, you can't say, "Ooh, that's not right." You understand what I mean? So, you know, in that thing I think it's wrong. Now, letting people voice *legitimate* things, you know, I think it's okay. But a lot of stuff on the internet is not factual.

MATTINGLY: And you said you were in Cleveland that day when...at a game when it (news of the Schiano hire) broke?

HASLAM: Well, I think we were in Detroit. I think the Browns were playing somebody and it was a one o'clock game and we got off the plane and were riding to the stadium and all of a sudden, I look and *laughs* my thing (cell phone) is all lit up and everything. What time did they announce it?

SUMMERS: Well the rumors started to break right, a little bit...well, some people heard Saturday night and then the rumors started Sunday morning about eleven o'clock.

HASLAM: Okay, well this was twelve o'clock. You know, and I got all kinds of texts and emails from everybody.

SUMMERS: Oh, I bet. Well, I know I did. I know I did.

MATTINGLY: Was the ReVOLution as we call it, was the ReVOLution a good thing in making athletics more transparent? Was that something that...

HASLAM: I think in today's world everything has to be transparent and so I think in that case it was, you know, it was good. I don't think, you know, obviously the...Currie and Beverly and Davenport didn't do enough homework on Schiano. I mean, I had heard of Schiano because he coached Tampa Bay and Jimmy said they'd interviewed him. I had no idea of his involvement in Penn State. Now I will say this: a guy I know who's a big Penn State booster, after all this happened said, "Hey, the guy is completely innocent, he wasn't involved at all." So, but, you know, it was obviously out there.

MATTINGLY: Right now, I think we're paying out $28,000,000 in buyouts...

HASLAM: I don't think it's that much.

MATTINGLY: Is there a way around that?

HASLAM: Well, in today's world...You see what's happening at Auburn is—of course he (Auburn football coach Guz Malzahn) won Saturday but he signed a seven-year, seven million dollars, forty-nine million. If he wanted to leave, I think it was thirty-five million to buy him out. I think if the marketplace is dictating that this is what a coach has to get, you know, to get the coach then the marketplace is going to dictate some of this stuff. I don't think it's, you know, I'll put it this way: CEOs in business don't have the same kind of contracts that they have in athletics now and, you know, you can make your case for these coaches any way you want to but Nick Saban is the biggest bargain in the world right now.

SUMMERS: He is actually.

HASLAM: I mean the...Since he went there (University of Alabama), enrollment's up fifty percent. They're all out of state, paying higher tuitions. I mean it's a bargain if you get a good coach but I think... and I think all the athletic directors are taking a second look and saying "Hey, do we have to do it this long?" and everything. And I know it's a big source of concern but, you know, some of that total, what is Butch's (buyout)? Nine million?

SUMMERS: Yes sir.

HASLAM: Okay but the assistants have mitigation so you won't have much to pay the assistants and then you gotta pay John (Currie), which was—?

SUMMERS: 2.2 Million.

HASLAM: So that's 11.2. Who else you paying?

SUMMERS: Beverly Davenport, I believe, settled for $500,000.

HASLAM: Of course that's not athletic—

SUMMERS: Right. The buyout number we quoted was for athletic directors, coaches, chancellors—

HASLAM: Right. Dave Hart is...That was a small, just a payment for one year wasn't it?

MATTINGLY: I think so.

HASLAM: Yeah, that was a small amount. No

basketball coaches so yeah, it's…

MATTINGLY: Well we did pay Fulmer but he's out of the loop on that now.

SUMMERS: Oh yeah.

HASLAM: Oh yeah, that's long gone.

SUMMERS: What did you think of the Fulmer hire as AD?

HASLAM: I think it was the…I think Phillip has done a great job of uniting the university behind him and I think Phillip is a quick study. He's quick at studying things, he's got his arms around what's going on over there, and the interesting thing is that his key people are people who John (Currie) brought in, Reid (Sigmon) is his number one guy, Kurt (Gulbrand), what's his name, is the fundraiser and Janeen (Lalik) is the marketing person. They would be his top two or three people and they were all John's people so I think that is a credit to what Phillip is doing. And a lot of people would go in there and say, "I want my people."

So I think he's off to a good start. I think Jeremy is a good hire and, you know, I think… and Phillip has negotiated a new contract with Rick Barnes, he did a good job on that and they got a new golf coach. Golf is doing well and so I think Phillip is doing…

MATTINGLY: Was Wayne Davis a good hire?

HASLAM: Oh yeah, really good. See, Wayne has been there forever and he knows what's going on, he's been at the university for forty years, he understands everything…I hate to cut this off but I got to be some… is there anything else?

SUMMERS: I have one more question.

HASLAM: Yes ma'am.

SUMMERS: If General Neyland had seen what happened last year, what do you think his reaction would have been?

HASLAM: *laughter*

SUMMERS: I think every Tennessee fan would want to know the answer to that question.

HASLAM: Well General Neyland would have... Put it this way, he was always in control of everything. So he wouldn't have let the situation get out of control, you understand where I'm coming from?

SUMMERS: Yes sir.

HASLAM: So I mean the one thing I would've loved to have seen is at halftime when the sideline reporter came out to *laughter* (interview General Neyland)—

SUMMERS: That might have been very interesting.

HASLAM: That might have been very interesting!

MATTINGLY: I just can't imagine him having a microphone stuck in his face.

HASLAM: Oh no, he wouldn't like that at all. He was...but General Neyland—whatever modicum of success we've achieved here is all due to him and teaching us about... So believe me, and we (Haslam family) don't want to control anything at the university. All we want is for the university to do well, the business school to do well, the whole athletic department to do well and that's it. And you know, administrators administrate, coaches coach, players play, and fans go to the games.

SUMMERS: So it's simple common sense.

HASLAM: It is. And you know, I think all the Vol ReVOLution and all this stuff, the internet has over-emphasized it, you know what I mean? I think the decision that was made to hire Phillip was a very, very good decision, I think it's going to work out, the decision to hire Wayne was very good and you know, I think it's all going to work out.

MATTINGLY: Do they still call you Young'un?

HASLAM: Yeah. God, that's a long story. When I was a freshman, you know what they…They would list, they would have the heaviest guy on the team and the, you know, the one from farthest away, and then like I say, I was seventeen when I came up here and they said the youngest person—Jim Haslam.

SUMMERS: There you go! I really appreciate you taking the time to talk to us.

MATTINGLY: This has been really good.

SUMMERS: It really has.

HASLAM: And I hope you can understand where we're coming from and we don't want to control anything. All we want to do is have the university do well and win.

DR. JOE JOHNSON, EMERITUS PRESIDENT OF THE UNIVERSITY OF TENNESSEE

"The State Is Our Campus"

Dr. Joe Johnson has had a distinguished career at the University of Tennessee, since he arrived in 1963. He has served as Executive Assistant to the President (1963-1969), Vice President for Development (1969-1973), Chancellor-Center for the Health Sciences (1970-1973), Vice President for Development and Executive Vice President (1973-1990), President (1990-99), President Emeritus (1999-2003), Interim President (2003-2004), and again as President Emeritus (2004-Present). His primary assignments before becoming President were in alumni relations, public relations, fundraising, governmental relations, campus planning, capital construction, and liaison between President's office and intercollegiate athletics.

CELINA SUMMERS: All right, we are recording

your interview, Dr Johnson.

TOM MATTINGLY: What we're doing is: the people we're interviewing for this book, is giving them their own chapter that will have verbatim what you tell us today.

DR. JOE JOHNSON: I don't believe that.

SUMMERS: We actually are. We're writing them up in transcript form so literally say Tom Mattingly and then a question and then Dr Joe Johnson and the answer, no...

JOHNSON: What is this about? What is this book?

MATTINGLY: We are looking at the events of last November in the context of what happened during those five or six weeks where everything seemed to fall apart with the football program, with the demise of John Currie, the demise of Davenport, the hiring of Jeremy Pruitt, the ascension of Phillip Fulmer to the athletic director but in the context of a twenty or twenty-five year period where we've gone to the heights in 1998 winning the national championship and then began a rapid descent to where we went to 0-8 in the SEC and all those events I talked about happened. Celina has been very well wired into the Twittersphere?

SUMMERS: Social media.

MATTINGLY: Social media. And my role as a UT historian over the years and so we've talked to a number of different people about this and we wanted to get your gauge of how all this came about and so we have a few questions just to discuss with you. And I guess that personally, the university over the past few years has had an attrition in the administration from the president on down and we were interested in your opinion of how that happened, or was it just bad luck?

JOHNSON: *Laughter* Well we had a flat long period of stability in the...if you view it as—the president of the University of Tennessee. Andy Holt was here about ten years, Ed Boling was eighteen, I was nine, and then there was Lamar Alexander who was there for about two and a half years. And then we went through a period of—if you counted me twice—we had about six presidents in about a seven-year period and then we got stabilized a bit with John Peterson and then we've had DiPietro. In terms...

Tom, what I would say happened there was, part of that was bad luck because you had a process. People were interviewed, different people were considered, and then you went through that turnover with Gilley and Shumaker and Peterson here a little bit longer period of time, then Eli Fly was there, filled in for a year. I was filling in for a year and I would say that was just a matter of...Nobody intentionally decided to do that and sometimes when you hire people from afar...

I've hired people from afar, but when you do, quite often, you don't know what you've got until it's been a year or two. Even though you've done all your reference checks, all your checking out, all of that sort of thing, but you don't know what you've got until they've been here for a while. And how do they fit into this culture, this environment, and I know in my own case I once hired a chancellor for a campus—not this one—that I thought I'd made a good choice, but in about a year I found I hadn't made a good choice. Once hired a chief academic officer when I was chancellor at UT Memphis, thought I'd made a good choice, and within a year I knew I hadn't made a good choice. So that can happen.

I think what's unusual is you had two or three people in a row that you had to replace in a shorter period of time than you would like to. So, I don't think...it certainly wasn't intentional so don't...I think it was just a matter of choosing the wrong person but not intentionally choosing the wrong person, you would never do that. That just wouldn't...and I don't think our Board of Trustees would do that. I think there were some choices made that for a variety of reasons didn't work out.

MATTINGLY: We hear a lot of talk about culture at the university. What in your opinion is the culture of this university? That some of the presidents measured up to and some of them didn't?

JOHNSON: Well, I came into this culture in 1963 as an assistant to Dr Andy Holt. There was a lot of family orientation to it. And I worked for Andy for six years, he and Boling for eighteen. There was a real attachment to the university and to its various parts: Memphis department, Nashville, Chattanooga, Knoxville, whatever. And those people with whom I worked with, Andy and Ed, had a great commitment to the University of Tennessee. Now everybody forgets; they say Andy was an insider.

Well, Andy had no ties to the University of Tennessee until he became vice president and then became president but Andy had a great affection for the state of Tennessee, and Andy had been a part of it forever. And I guess when I became president, I'd been there twenty-eight years. And a part of that culture, I think, is understanding the different campuses, what they are, the role of agriculture, and understanding the role of the faculty senate, the faculty, having a way to attach yourself to faculty leadership, student leadership, and realizing there's something over there called the state legislature and governor that you have to get acquainted with and, in the case of Ed and me we worked in state government and I worked in the state government. And then, so that's a part of it. Andy and Ed operated immediate staff almost like family members and you spent a lot of time on each campus trying to get acquainted with people.

And it's not bad bringing people from outside but when you do, they have to figure out all those different parts and how they fit together, and I think for example, we had an outsider named Joe DiPietro. Florida, Illinois, and here for four or five years as vice principal of agriculture, but when he became president, he understood that culture and I think has adopted it very, very well. And so that's... and I think also a part of it is understanding, what is the role of athletics at Martin, Chattanooga and here? You have to understand...and for DiPietro that's a big enterprise and you have to spend a little time to understand it. So, I guess I'm saying culture—it's family oriented. You get to know all of the parts of the university, understand their roles and be supportive of all it.

MATTINGLY: When there is instability, how does that affect the university?

JOHNSON: Well in contrast, I worked four years in state government and worked thirty-eight here and during that time I really worked for three people. When you have a rapid change over in the president of University of Tennessee, it does create some instability because all those people who are on the campuses—faculty leadership, student leadership, chancellors, vice presidents—all of a sudden, you're changing your leader every two or three years and that creates some instability. It's inevitable that you have that.

You've got to learn, "I'm no longer working for Andy Holt or Ed Boling, I'm working for Wade Gilley or John Shumaker or Tom Peterson—" and you have to adjust to that for better or worse. We have different leadership styles, we approach things differently, we make decisions differently, and so inevitably it creates some instability.

Now sometimes instability is good. You can stick with the same people for year after year after year and you're in a rut, so I'm not saying I'm opposed to bringing people from outside. I did that on occasion. Ed did that on occasion. Andy did that on occasion. And bringing Herman Spivey from Kentucky by Andy to be chief academic officer was a heck of a decision. An excellent move, in fact. So, I'm not saying it's bad to bring in people from outside but when you're changing people from outside rapidly it creates—well how is this person going to operate? What's their decision-making style? And all of a sudden, all of them new, they got to learn the legislature, the governor, the board of trustees and how do you get along with the Tennessee farm bureau if you're the agricultural campus?

MATTINGLY: Is there anyone who should be held responsible for all the attrition that's happened or has it just happened?

JOHNSON: I... *laughter*

SUMMERS: Not necessarily just a single person. You know: is it the state government's responsibility? Should the Board of Trustees have some accountability for the rapid turnover?

JOHNSON: Well…if you're going to write a book, I'm not going to point a finger at anybody, so okay, I'll just make that point, that's not…I will not do that.

SUMMERS: Okay.

JOHNSON: I just, I will not do that. The responsibility for choosing the president of the University of Tennessee is a responsibility of the Board of Trustees. And because that's their choice and their choice only. And I think in most of these instances there was a search committee and that's run through that process. But ultimately the Board of Trustees decides who will be president…and each president that during that period of stability or instability, the Board made those choices. But as I inferred, the Board seeks to do…to pick the best person but regretfully, sometimes picking the person you think would be best doesn't end up being what you thought they would do. But the Board selects the president. Now in the case of chancellors, that's the president's responsibility. Now it has to be concurred on by the board, by chancellors and vice presidents. If I pick the wrong person, that was my responsibility.

SUMMERS: And so the athletic director is the chancellor's responsibility then?

JOHNSON: Correct.

SUMMERS: So it's like a trickle-down tiered effect then?

JOHNSON: And in recent years when the University of Tennessee system was formed, we have three campuses that have athletic programs—Martin, Chattanooga, and Knoxville—and in the original arrangement, the athletics director reported to the chancellor. Because the students on this campus, they're Knoxville campus students, the faculty are Knoxville campus faculty and so when we created that, we said the athletics director should report to the chancellor and then along the way that was switched when Charlie Weaver was chancellor here, the first one. It came time that he had to fire Bill Battle and he couldn't do that and the trustees said, "Mr. President Boling, it's your responsibility." So for a number of years, the athletics director reported to the president.

Interestingly, the women's athletics director reported to the chancellor and then we changed that while I was president. That was changed then a few years ago, the move went back to athletics director reports to the chancellor. That was discussed with me and I said that is logically the way it ought to be.

But I also made a point that when the chancellor and the president have to be in sync and well informed about what goes on in athletics here because it is a big enterprise and if it goes well a lot of people get praised and if it doesn't a lot of people get chewed up and spit out. And while Ed Boling was responsible for athletics, he and Jack Rees; when I was responsible, Bill Snyder and I were pretty well in sync with athletics and I think it can work well the way it is now. But the chancellor and the president have to be in sync because if something blows up in athletics both of them are going to be in the middle of it.

MATTINGLY: Well that brings up the idea that UT is paying an enormous amount of money for buyouts for coaches, chancellors, and other people. Why is that the case and what can be done about it?

JOHNSON: *laughter* Well, what you could do is what went on way back in the day which is why when I was here the only person that had a contract in athletics was the head coach...the head football coach. Nobody else had one. If you do away with contracts, you'd do away with all of that. And certainly, presidents and chancellors did not have contracts. So, if you did away with that...

But I don't think it's going to go back that way. Not only do coaches have agents, athletic directors have agents, and when you hire a new chancellor or new president there's a very elaborate process. And I'm not opposed... that's okay.

I never had one. My employment was day to day, and if I got fired for not doing well—tough, I got fired. But today it's a different world and people have agreements and contracts and all sorts of things.

The other side of that is we have contracts with all sorts of expectations, evaluation points, I didn't have those. Ed didn't have those, Andy didn't have those, and if we got fired— bye, it's been nice having you guys.

SUMMERS: So you do have an evaluation procedure that you use with athletic directors and coaches and things like that?

JOHNSON: There is now. You look at these contracts for arrangements for the president, the chancellor, athletics director, coaches, you got all these factors, graduation rates, retention rates, discipline rates, and all of these things. And if you graduate more students if you're a coach you get extra pay. That's all new. That happened after I retired. We just didn't do things that way. And in some ways, it has a lot of plusses. But Tom's question was: "How do you get rid of paying people when you fire them, whether they be administrators or...?"

Quit having contracts. But that's not going to happen.

SUMMERS: No, it isn't.

JOHNSON: That's not going to happen because that's the way it is and if a fellow is president or executive vice president of Illinois, you try to hire him or her here, they want all this written down. And the world's changed. I've been retired since 1999 and Ed Boling didn't have a contract, Andy Holt didn't have one, Doug Dickey didn't have one. I mean: the world has changed. A lot. And therefore you have a contract and if you fire somebody it says you'll pay them, you have a buyout. Somebody was telling me what is it? The buyout for (head football coach Gus) Malzahn at Auburn is thirty-two—

SUMMERS: Thirty-two million dollars.

JOHNSON: That's unbelievable!

SUMMERS: A forty-nine million-dollar contract not including bonuses for seven years—that'd be a Jimmy Sexton negotiated contract.

JOHNSON: Well, he's one of our graduates.

SUMMERS: Yes, he is.

JOHNSON: His father was a dental graduate.

MATTINGLY: He learned his lessons pretty good.

SUMMERS: He did.

JOHNSON: And also, I had never dealt with an agent. When I retired in 1999, I'd never dealt with an agent. When I came back in 2003 and 2004, I was told we needed to deal with Phillip Fulmer's agent.

And I said, "Do tell."

SUMMERS: *laughter*

MATTINGLY: You were surprised, right?

JOHNSON: Yeah and...I didn't deal with him. I told Mike Hamilton to come over to my office and we'd work it out and we did. But that's changed, and if you want to get out of paying people off, eliminate contracts and then you don't pay them if you fire them. But that's not going to happen.

SUMMERS: Let me—could you give me one more?

MATTINGLY: Okay.

SUMMERS: We actually had this later in the interview. I'm just bumping it up. Firing a coach or an athletic director with cause—could you explain that so like a normal person like me could understand what "with cause" means?

JOHNSON: Well, what you—and today you put into the contract—reasons for which you may be fired for cause and we don't owe you a dime. If you violate NCAA rules, you sexually abuse somebody and those...and most of those are spelled out in these contracts now. But "for cause" means you have done something really bad and we can fire you without paying you a dime.

SUMMERS: And...

JOHNSON: That's my amateur definition. You're fired for cause, which means you have done something that is contrary to law, ethical standards, NCAA standards or whatever.

MATTINGLY: But that seems to be the exception rather than the rule. It seems they go to the point of trying to avoid firing for cause for whatever reason, whatever legal reasons, they don't want to appear in front of a court—

JOHNSON: Well, sometimes if you do that and the coach says, "Well, I'm going to sue you!" and you got to go to court and sometimes you pay people. You settle rather than going through court and anyway...Cause is you spell out: we can fire you for these reasons and they are legitimate reasons for firing you.

SUMMERS: So John Currie's coaching search and his behavior after Schiano Sunday, you know, didn't interview a single candidate—I'm just going off the Freedom of Information Act document drop—didn't interview anybody before Schiano was announced and then that week traveled all over the country and basically, what it appeared to us on the outside was he was just offering the position to anyone he talked to, and then going AWOL for a whole day and being told to come back to Knoxville, wouldn't that constitute "with cause"?

JOHNSON: That would depend on who hired him whether it was cause. I don't know.

SUMMERS: To me, logically, it would seem like that kind of behavior would qualify as with cause.

JOHNSON: Yeah, well, that would depend on what his contract said.

SUMMERS: That's true too.

JOHNSON: And I wasn't in a role to do that.

MATTINGLY: That was a really tumultuous period. What were your thoughts as you lived through that period on how we got to that point?

JOHNSON: Well…

MATTINGLY: I mean that was a national embarrassment.

SUMMERS: Yeah.

JOHNSON: Well, anything you do in athletics gets more attention than anything else you do. You can fire a dean of business and no one gives a rat's ear. But if you fire an AD or a coach, it's nationwide. If a student gets arrested on Cumberland Avenue, nobody cares except the parents, the police, student affairs. But if it's an athlete, it's on ESPN and it's national news.

I was sorry that went on. I worked with John here and what happened there—I don't know; I'm retired. It would appear that part of what was going on was the right hand didn't know what the left hand was doing.

MATTINGLY: So, Dr Davenport was ostensibly responsible for what Currie was doing, is that right?

JOHNSON: Well, he worked for her. So if he wasn't

doing what she had told him to do, what they had agreed to do, that's John's problem that she had to deal with.

MATTINGLY: These coaching searches—is it possible to hire a coach when no one else is interviewed, does that make sense?

JOHNSON: Yeah, we've hired coaches without interviewing anybody.

SUMMERS: But until we hired Lane Kiffin, every football coach, for example, had Tennessee ties and once Fulmer was terminated then we started bringing in coaches that didn't necessarily know the culture down south or didn't necessarily understand how football works in this part of the country. Do you think that makes a difference?

JOHNSON: Mmm, could have. Those people could've worked it out. But they didn't. It's like hiring a person from outside. You really don't know what you've got until they get here. That's one of the risks you run. Doug Dickey and I hired a number of basketball coaches that didn't work out. And we didn't interview but one person, so the not interviewing somebody is not new. Doug and I had pretty good experience with football coaches but basketball coaches we had a lot of things that didn't work out.

MATTINGLY: They always said Coach Dickey could meet Bob Knight on Gay Street at high noon and not know who he was.

laughter

JOHNSON: Well, I made every trip with Doug when we hired a different basketball coach while I was president or executive VP and we had a few good choices but most of them didn't work out.

MATTINGLY: UT in last November—

JOHNSON: And back to your question, that was mine and Doug's responsibility.

SUMMERS: Okay, okay—

JOHNSON: And we had to fire them so…

MATTINGLY: UT really took a beating last November when the fans raised heck about the Schiano hire. What was your opinion of those seven or so days? Were you watching that closely?

JOHNSON: Well, since I spent thirty-nine years here, I sort of follow the news quite closely and it's one of those things you wish hadn't happened. In those cases, when you look at that, was Schiano being falsely accused? Was he somewhere where something awful went on? And he just happened to be on the staff? Was he guilty of anything? And obviously some people who observed that thought he was and that became a national issue with a number of people and, you know, from my point of view… When that blows up, what do you do?

Do Currie and Davenport stick with that choice or do they say, "Let's drop it?"

And that's a decision you've gotta make when things blow up with you and you get a lotta national publicity that says this guy was at Penn State and this…You have to make a judgment call in that case and one was made and some people agreed with it and some people didn't agree with it. But that's one of the responsibilities that an AD and a chancellor looking for a coach and when things like that happen you've got to make a judgment call and hope that you have a sound basis and you're right in doing it.

MATTINGLY: Will this November deal have a lasting impact on the university? Will it make the process more open or transparent?

JOHNSON: Which November deal?

MATTINGLY: Last November when the Schiano thing...

JOHNSON: Oh, I don't know. Phillip didn't seem to have a hard time finding Jeremy Pruitt.

MATTINGLY: What about other universities? Is this the model for other universities to follow, the way things developed?

JOHNSON: Well, other universities sometimes do things with which you don't agree. I couldn't evaluate or assess that. All that would say to me is when you're looking for a coach approach it cautiously, carefully and make sure all the people that are part of the process are together and understand what's going on.

SUMMERS: Common sense. I like it.

JOHNSON: Yeah, it is.

MATTINGLY: What does a president or a chancellor hear from the fan base when things like this are happening? Are there a lot of emails going in? Are there a lot of phone calls?

JOHNSON: We didn't have much emails when I retired in 1999. I think you have to be careful, you know, and particular all the talk shows and all the stuff that goes on these days. I think you have to be...If you're sitting as a responsible official, president, chancellor, AD, whatever, you have to do what you think is sound and solid and you can't be paying attention to the racket out there because you're going to have all kinds of things going on and all kinds of people observing things that don't know what's going on. But you need to stick to ethical, sound, fair processes and then be aware of how fans may feel because they buy the tickets but sometimes you can be misled by forty-two emails on a topic and you better make sure you're doing it the right way and what you do in the end you can justify doing it.

MATTINGLY: What did you think about the aftermath of that when Coach Fulmer was hired and Coach Fulmer hired Coach Pruitt? How good a response was that to all the criticisms that came—

JOHNSON: Well, Beverly Davenport hiring Coach Fulmer calmed things magnificently because I think they said, "We've got Phillip. He's been here, he's been our coach, and we have confidence he will do things in the right way."

And I thought it was an excellent move because it just—

Calmed. Things. Down.

MATTINGLY: And then the hire of Coach Pruitt. Did that impress you?

JOHNSON: Well, he and I are from Alabama. He's northeast, I'm northwest and I know what aight means.

SUMMERS: *laughter*

JOHNSON: That's A-I-G-H-T.

SUMMERS: Yes, it is. Aight.

JOHNSON: And I know a lot of…and it don't make no difference neither. So I don't understand that.

MATTINGLY: Well, we always say we didn't hire a coach for grammar; we hired a coach to coach.

JOHNSON: I had to tell some people it all—if he wins ball games it don't matter. No seriously, Phillip made a hire and I hope it works out. We'll know four years from now, or three years from now.

MATTINGLY: Have things really calmed down because of that?

JOHNSON: Well you've hired a coach, people feel pretty good about it. It will all, you know…who was it? Dave Hart hired Rick Barnes. Well Rick Barnes didn't do so good first year until—golly Moses, that was a fantastic hire! Phillip's hiring of Pruitt will be decided how he does two or three years from now. And I hope it goes well, I think he's got promise, but coaches are judged on what their win-loss record is.

MATTINGLY: But there is a honeymoon.

JOHNSON: And everything I've seen about him? I like the way he handles himself. I like the fact it's not a slogan of the week contest. He often says, "I didn't coach them very well." I like that. But the proof of the pudding is…and I think he'll do well, I hope he does well but that's all going to be determined two-three-four years down the road.

MATTINGLY: So we seem to be in a relative period of stability right now?

JOHNSON: Yeah, and you got Wayne Davis which was a great move that Joe DiPietro made. And that calmed things greatly.

MATTINGLY: Was Dr. Davis ever considered to be a chancellor before he got hired as an interim. Did they ever look at someone of his stature in the university? I always wondered why they didn't consider him before.

JOHNSON: Well, you'll have to remember, and I don't know this from memory, he'd been here forty years and he was ready to retire. I don't know whether... someone may have... I don't know, but he could have said, "I'm ready to retire."

MATTINGLY: Did they have to twist his arm to get him to make the decision?

JOHNSON: Ummm, I doubt that, twisting his arm. He's so dedicated to the university. Probably shared the feeling that: "If I can be helpful, I'll be glad to do it for a short period of time." But I thought that move was masterful on the part of DiPietro.

SUMMERS: So here we are and we have a new football coach, new athletic director, new chancellor, new president, completely new Board of Trustees that has been restructured and shrunk. Do you think this is the first step that the university needs to get itself back on track as far as leadership goes?

JOHNSON: Well the new Board of Trustees is in a

situation where it has to find a new president and has to find a new chancellor for this campus and those two choices are very important. The members of that board are solid people. I know most of them—some of them very well, some of them casually—and my view is they're excellent appointees to the board and I believe they will. The board members will devote themselves to finding a solid long-term president and find then a top notch chancellor for this campus.

MATTINGLY: What characteristics will that person have to be that long-term solution? What will be the job description that he has to meet?

JOHNSON: Oh good lord. *Laughs* Sometimes job descriptions are meaningless. If you're looking for a chancellor or president, you're looking for somebody that...Number one, you're looking for a leader. You're looking for a leader, that's the first thing. Is this person a leader? Dynamic, thoughtful, considerate. Secondly, does that person either have a knowledge and acquaintance with what a university is, what it's supposed to be doing, or surrounds him- or herself with people who can. Andy Holt had supervised *five* people when he became head of UT. He'd never been a dean; he'd never been a chancellor. But most people will say Andy Holt will go down as one of the best presidents we ever had. But he was a leader. He was dynamic. He could get people to rally, to do things and so...you're looking for leadership number one,

Number two, you're looking for someone who appreciates what a university is: its teaching mission, its research mission, its outreach mission. And has some understanding of the unique culture of a university and the role of a faculty in that process. I had never been... never had tenure. Ed Boling had never had tenure, never been a department head, never been a dean but he was a pretty darn good president for eighteen years. I'd never done any of those things. Whether that was good or not, I don't know, but I did it (UT President) for ten years.

MATTINGLY: What was the learning curve on that? When did you feel like you were really getting to understand what you were involved in?

JOHNSON: *Laughs* Well, I guess I had a quick learning curve because Ed Boling in 1970 sent me off to be chancellor of the UT science center with my degree in history and political science, and industrial management. And people thought I did well enough that they asked me to become a permanent chancellor rather than acting. But my learning curve was pretty steep in that case—but it did teach me the role of the faculty. It helped me learn to appreciate good quality deans and what they could do. So, it's a right complex organization and it's a public organization and the people that vote for governors quite often feel this is our university and you need to pay attention to us. "Us" being legislators who represent the people and governors who do and that's a very...You gotta deal with that element. It's very important, in addition to dealing with the faculty.

MATTINGLY: A long time ago, there was a phrase that said, "The state is our campus." I think they had a billboard that said, "The state is our campus." How long did it take you to get used to that?

JOHNSON: Well, I came here and I quickly realized we had a campus in Memphis, we had a campus in rural west Tennessee, Martin, we had a space institute in Tullahoma, we had a campus at that time in Nashville, and later got one in Chattanooga one year. We have three ag employees at least in each of the ninety-five counties. And we've got consultants and MTAS (Multiple Technical Advisory Service) and CTAS (County Technical Assistance Service) that consult with every city and county in the state. So in that sense, the state *is* our campus and he or she who sits as president needs to realize that.

MATTINGLY: Just for the record, he (Dr. Johnson) has a Master's degree in Public Administration right? And I have one. And you were the President of the University of Tennessee and I'm a sports writer. Just shows what can happen when you get an MBA.

JOHNSON: *Laughs*

SUMMERS: It could be worse.

JOHNSON: Well, I had that when I was hired by UT and then Andy Holt told me I needed to get a doctorate so...I got to tell you what Andy Holt...

When I was in Nashville, I went to work for Ed Boling in Nashville in 1960. Yeah, I'd been there a year and a half and I'd worked some with Governor Buford Ellington and...on budgets and Governor Ellington appointed his executive assistant Ross Dyer to the Supreme Court, and asked me to come down and be his executive assistant.

And I said, "Governor, I don't know anything about politics. I didn't even vote for you."

And he said, "That's all right, I'm a politician, I'm surrounded by...I need you to protect me from my *friends*."

And I worked for him for two years but also that first day he said, "Now sometimes, we got Don Binckley as our press secretary, but sometimes you'll have to be able to talk to media and I've got three pieces of advice for you. Number one, don't talk to them"—not good advice then or now but the next two, he said—"if you have to talk to them, say as little as you can, and before you say that visualize how it'll look in tomorrow's headlines."

The best PR advice I ever got In. My. Life.

SUMMERS: And you know what? That does lead me to an important question. It's not just Tennessee. I've been tracking—I do a lot of work about sexual assault, domestic violence, and a lot of major universities have had that problem: Baylor, Michigan State, Minnesota, Ohio State now. One thing I've noticed about all these schools and it's also very apparent with Tennessee last November is that there doesn't seem to be active crisis management or a PR department that can realistically try to manage these situations for the university. Is there not anything like that in place here?

JOHNSON: I think if you asked DiPietro or Davis they would say yes. They've got people in PR and also got people who devote themselves to Title IX and that sort of thing. But it's...Managing a crisis is a challenge. Tom will remember this—I got a call at four in the morning once and he said, "We've had an alleged gang rape in an athletics dorm." You remember that? "You better come down, the police are here."

You know, you gotta manage that. You gotta manage that. And it turned out it was not rape, it was consensual sex. Messy, lurid, awful. Delightful freshman who, a girl whose objective was to have sex with every athlete in Gibbs Hall.

MATTINGLY: She was ambitious to put it mildly.

JOHNSON: And one night it was about thirteen or fourteen.

SUMMERS: Good lord.

JOHNSON: And last time she was there she went back to the dorm crying and her roommate said, "What happened?" She said, "I was raped."

It was awful, absolutely terrible, but you know, and that's there and you gotta deal with it. And those people who sit in these roles, you have to anticipate that one day you may have a mess and you gotta deal with it. You gotta deal with it. And you don't like to think about it but sometimes they do happen and you need to know who's on first base, who's going to save what.

I've got to tell you the one time I did not follow that and these two people know it. When I came back as president, Wade Gilley had been fired for having an affair with his mistress. John Shumaker had a girlfriend in Birmingham and so when I was brought back after *he* was fired, a little fellow from Channel 10 was interviewing me and I violated Buford Ellington's rule.

But at some point, he said, "What do you bring to the job?"

I said, "No girlfriend, a wife, and my mistress is a black lab dog named Ebony Duchess the Sixth."

And that's all they covered. It went all over the

state. My daughter called from Nashville and said, "You really didn't say that?"

SUMMERS: *laughter*

JOHNSON: And I said, "Regretfully I did."

The part of the story nobody knows is that Pamela Reed (Gilley's mistress) wrote me a four-page letter demanding an apology that I'd referred to her as a mistress. I didn't answer.

I wanted to write her saying, "My dog's upset that I said my dog is my mistress."

laughter

MATTINGLY: You one time said that Andy Holt told you never to be three things. One of them was surprised, one of them was I don't remember...

JOHNSON: Shocked, one of them was shocked. Andy Holt was approached mid-sixties by some local ministers going to have Billy Graham come and do one of his revivals in Neyland Stadium. Neyland Stadium had never been used for anything except football and track. And I found Ed Boling and I said, "Well, if we do it for Billy Graham we can't turn down anybody else that wants to use it."

And he came. Everything was fine except Billy invited President Nixon to come and we had some students and faculty who got arrested protesting and Andy called a guy named Harris, a PR guy and he said, "Do me a press statement to release and show up in next morning's paper." and somewhere we said that Andy said, "I was *shocked*."

Well, Andy called me and said, "I've never been *shocked!*"

And I said, "Well, you approved the statement! And you might ought to have been *shocked!*"

But he said: don't be shocked or disappointed or whatever but he chewed on us a little bit for leading him into saying, "I was *shocked."*

SUMMERS: Oh man, so there really isn't then a specific section of the PR department that focuses on crisis management?

JOHNSON: Well, while I was president, we didn't have that. We assumed that my PR people, me and my staff ought to know how to deal with a crisis and whether we did or not, somebody would have to judge that.

SUMMERS: Well, it just seems like the university ignored what was going on last year. I mean we went several weeks and didn't hear anything from the university at all.

JOHNSON: Which university?

SUMMERS: Ours. This one.

MATTINGLY: About the coaching search.

SUMMERS: About the coaching search, about, it just was like radio silence.

JOHNSON: But just like I was saying—that was not a crisis.

SUMMERS: I am not shocked.

MATTINGLY: I always thought we were a little

reactive as opposed to proactive over next door. When crisis did arise, Coach Dickey had big shoulders and I wanted him next to me if there was a crisis.

JOHNSON: Yeah, well, he and I dealt with the alleged rape in Neyland Stadium and he and I dealt with the firing of John Majors which became a major issue. And...

MATTINGLY: Still is by the way.

SUMMERS: Yes.

JOHNSON: I guess it's...I was asked to be on a national ESPN interview and explain why I fired John Majors. And I was and he was on the same show later from his house here explaining his side of it. And I don't take pride in that but I did it and I knew it would be a flap and it was and I thought I'd made the right decision and John doesn't agree with that.

MATTINGLY: It doesn't take much to set him off about that either.

JOHNSON: Yeah? And I'm delighted my friend Phillip Fulmer has never reacted that way over being fired.

SUMMERS: How did he react?

JOHNSON: He's always been very polite, he's never said anything bad about this university. Made one statement one time somewhere. DiPietro said, "Could you help him not do it?"

All I ever said to Phillip was, "Don't ever say anything bad about your university even though you're disappointed you're fired."

One time I called him and he said, "I know why you're calling and it won't happen again."

And it hasn't. He has never been negative; John is very negative. And I understand it, you know? Would you tell somebody to be happy if you fired them? And I'm the guy that did that and I know he's unhappy and will always be unhappy and I'm sorry.

MATTINGLY: Phillip, only thing I remember Phillip saying remotely that way was: "It's not hard to love your university but it's hard for them to love you back." He said it's just bricks and mortar.

SUMMERS: Oh no—let's not bring up bricks or…

MATTINGLY: Sorry.

JOHNSON: No, and if anybody ever says, "I enjoy firing somebody." *they* oughta be fired. I didn't enjoy firing John Majors but I explained that on the ESPN and the national story went away. The local story never has, because John brings it up regularly. And I'm sorry.

MATTINGLY: We got it?

SUMMERS: I think so. Thank you so much for letting us do this.

JOHNSON: Well if it comes out before I get kicked, but I probably will die by the time this book is…

SUMMERS: Ahhh, this book is coming out November 21st.

JAYSON SWAIN, FORMER PLAYER/ALUMNI/MEDIA

"I Was Really Proud Of Our Fan Base"

Jayson Swain garnered rave reviews upon arriving at Tennessee in 2003. He was part of a heralded recruiting class with receivers Robert Meachem and Bret Smith. As a freshman, Jayson caught 21 passes for 285 yards and was on the Knoxville News Sentinel's All-SEC Freshman Team. Swain started five games in his sophomore and junior seasons, before becoming a full-time starter in the 2006 season. In that season, Swain had 49 catches and 688 yards receiving and six touchdowns. He is currently #6 all-time in UT history with 126 receptions and is also #13 in career receiving yards with 1,721. Swain was a co-captain of the 2006 Volunteer squad. He is the host of the "Swain Event", and Vol Nation affectionately calls him Swain.

CELINA SUMMERS: I think your insight on this is gonna be really beneficial to the book. You're one of the few people who has a foot in every camp in this story. You deal with the fans every day, you're a former player, alumni, and the media so thank you for doing this.

JAYSON SWAIN: Let's do it!

SUMMERS: Okay, so what do you think the situation was like at the beginning of the football season?

SWAIN: The beginning of the last football season?

SUMMERS: Yeah, you know, with like the fans and Butch Jones's tenure and stuff like that?

SWAIN: I mean, I've seen fans who're excited because it was football season like any other season but they had realized that, you know, we had missed our window of doing anything because we didn't take advantage of our talented team in 2016 and the team had kind of fell apart and there was a bunch of drama. But most were still excited about football and, you know, they went out there and they had a comeback from behind, winning against Georgia Tech, but that was probably the high point at the beginning of the season for sure. But everyone was just excited about football.

SUMMERS: Now do you think that Butch Jones got us in trouble before the season even started?

SWAIN: I thought he was in trouble after the Florida game in the second year. No one would probably say that you know, his job was in jeopardy but I didn't think he was built for the job. I didn't see it to be honest.

SUMMERS: That game was kind of like a dead giveaway.

SWAIN: Yeah I mean, you can just tell if a coach can handle a certain situation or if they were gonna be successful at a place depending on, you know, just one situation and there were several situations there in 2014 and 2015 where you're like: "Yeah, this guy's...you know, he's doing a pretty good job but he's not the guy. He's not gonna last long. It's not 'if' it's just 'when' he gets fired."

But that question is really hard to answer because I guess Currie would tell you, and we know that he was all about saying whatever sounded good but, you know, he'd mention all these nine wins, you know, the two nine-win seasons and was very complimentary of what he was able to do bringing the program back. But I just... I just don't... I just didn't see it. And you know, we're looking at it from February 2018 which I look back on, you know, what happened then so it's really hard to say, "Yeah, you know, 100% support!"

But I can hardly believe that those boosters after witnessing 2015 and 2016 had confidence that Butch Jones would be a long-term answer.

SUMMERS: When do you think that, like this season when people really got to the point where they said, "Okay, that's it"?

SWAIN: I think the Florida game was half of the people and I think the Georgia game was the rest of them.

SUMMERS: I agree.

SWAIN: And you also got to take into consideration you still got those blind, loyal folks that are still there to the end even if it's a losing season so...like Butch deserved to have a second chance! I'm not talking about realistic folks who think with their heads and not with their hearts so for the head thinkers? Georgia.

SUMMERS: Yeah, I think we were all there on that day. Okay, let me ask you this. I want to get really into the athletic department situation too because I think Georgia was the cut-off point for just about everybody. But then, nothing happened for like a month and a half. I mean, Currie didn't even mention what was going on. Do you think that like really affected the temperament of the fan base?

SWAIN: Oh, absolutely. It made it seem like that was okay that everything was going on and losing the way they were losing. Everyone was watching Currie, and Currie came across as being transparent with the letters and stuff and trying to update the fan base on what was going on with the athletic program but he never spoke on, you know, the chaos inside the football program and all the drama and then losing games. They were playing so poorly and Currie refused to really address that. So, I think everyone's frustration just festered and festered.

SUMMERS: The local media has been in-fighting for years and years but after the Georgia game they all came together and were pretty much on the same page, right?

SWAIN: I don't know if I would say "come together" because they're still at the end of the day competing against each other for information and so they, you know, would still backstab each other literally. So I wouldn't say come together.

I would say that the point where they did come together was when the national media were blasting Tennessee fans for getting involved with the Schiano stuff. I think the local media gave encouragement to the fan base.

SUMMERS: That makes sense.

SWAIN: Local media seemed like they were together because every other time? Man, they are stabbing each other in the back.

SUMMERS: So what did players think of what was going on with all of this before Schiano?

SWAIN: I don't really know. I don't talk to a lot of the players but I do just from people that I know who talk to the players, you know, I think they were just trying to play, you know, trying to go out there and pretend like it still didn't bother them but it did.

SUMMERS: Right.

SWAIN: So they're playing so bad and you had several guys that were trying to stay away from the program or, you know, not playing while being a little bit hurt because they just didn't feel right about the culture and stuff like that but I'm not real familiar with how the players felt. They were obviously not happy and down because they were losing games.

SUMMERS: Yeah. So after Butch Jones got fired and we had that ten-day period before Schiano Sunday, how long did it take for the natives to start getting restless?

SWAIN: It feels like it happened automatically the moment he was hired. It feels like people just started to revolt against the move. It didn't really hit me until, you know—that took me a while to process everything. It happened pretty fast. A firestorm happened really, really quick. And of course, you know, it wasn't just your normal fan, it was politicians, it was former players. I know for a fact that there were texts from Peyton Manning that went around trying to get guys to buy into the hire and he was assuring them that he had did his due diligence to talk to Bill Belichick and Urban Meyer and that it all checked out and even then, a lot of the guys were not on board with it. Didn't feel comfortable about it. So yeah, it took a life of its own pretty fast.

SUMMERS: What do you think everyone's expectations were with the coaching hire? I'm not necessarily getting into Jon Gruden here because I'm kind of torn on that but Greg Schiano wasn't the guy that we were promised when Butch got fired, was he? Opening up the checkbooks and all that—

SWAIN: No, well…They *did* open up the checkbook it was just forwarded to the wrong coach that they unfortunately felt would fit and—you know, with this community, with this fan base, with this program. But they did try and pay him a lot of money so I guess they answered that question about Tennessee being cheap. It was just to a guy that, you know, the fan base just didn't think was worth that money.

SUMMERS: Right.

SWAIN: I think the fan base, anytime there's a hire being made we are unrealistic and I'm not saying that because that's a *bad* thing. We just think more of our program than maybe…

SUMMERS: Than everyone else does.

SWAIN: Than we should! It's just we are very prideful in our tradition, we are very prideful in our resources, we're prideful in our fan base and we think, "Hey, why wouldn't anyone want to come and coach this place? Why wouldn't the fans want to come and be at Tennessee?" because we consider Tennessee to be one of the best programs in the country. But in actuality the best coaches out here, they're comfortable and they're not willing to move from a comfortable situation for an unknown—especially an unknown that has had so much turnover in leadership over the years and still has a questionable leadership.

So the fans became really confused, and the confusion turned into a little bit of anger because you're getting a bunch of noes.

SUMMERS: Right.

SWAIN: And so I think we've been through a couple of coaching searches to know that, you know, how we view our school is not how everyone else views our school. I mean, Jim Kelly told Florida no so...You know, Gary Patterson just told teams no. He's at TCU, we know there are a ton of programs out there that are better than TCU but he's comfortable there. He's good, you know. Mike Dunleavy's done the same thing, he's comfortable, he's good and people just don't want to move or change.

SUMMERS: Well, let me ask you this: do you think the way that Tennessee got rid of coach Fulmer back in 2008 kind of changed perception within college football that maybe this is a program you didn't want to work for?

SWAIN: Yeah, yeah, they got rid of him in 2008 and yeah absolutely. I mean, you have a guy that's won seventy percent of his games and he won a championship for you and if you don't want him that's fine, but I think there's a certain way you do it.

SUMMERS: Right.

SWAIN: You do it with a little bit more grace and you don't embarrass the guy. That's kind of what they did and if I want to coach anywhere and I get a phone call from Tennessee? "Golly if you're gonna treat one of your own like that who won a national championship for you, how are you gonna treat me—

SUMMERS: Exactly.

SWAIN: "—who's not one of your own? Do I gotta win *eighty* percent of my games to get better treatment?"

So, you know, absolutely, I think the treatment of Coach Fulmer really did hurt the perception of Tennessee, whether or not you believe that Coach Fulmer should have been replaced. That's a whole other topic, and I get why someone would feel that way. I mean, the program became stagnant, you know?

I understand that part, but there is a certain type of way you handle your own. Your own blood. And we didn't do a very good job of that.

SUMMERS: No, we didn't. I agree. Okay, take me through your Schiano Sunday. How did that go down for you?

SWAIN: I was...Literally at the time I had just became so like emotionally empty because of discovering everything that's happened over the last couple of years under Butch so I had to like...I had different things I did to disconnect and on Sunday is perfect for that. Sunday afternoon, so I was disconnecting, I was...I was raking leaves actually and I got a notification on my phone. I got several calls, text messages, like I felt my phone vibrating. I was so focused on the leaves I didn't even look at my phone. When I took a break and I saw people kinda going off about Schiano stuff, I had to stop and process it a lot. I got a buddy of mine I know who actually played for him at Rutgers and he's involved with a big-time D1 program, a top-tier program, he works in recruiting and so I reached out to him. He had nothing but good things to say about Schiano so I knew his first-hand account, but at the same time I didn't know what happened with his time at Tampa Bay and how he had leaked negative information about Josh Freeman. I heard things about Rutgers. I heard some good things about Eric LeGrand so I had some mixed reviews on him and then all of a sudden stuff about Penn State started to...

That's when it came up and I started thinking about that and regardless of what he saw or what he didn't see, him being attached to that would probably be a bad look for Tennessee and I just couldn't get on board with that hire. I mean, at first I was conflicted because I heard some good things, I heard some bad things, but at the end of the day no one else was talking to him, no one else wanted him, and where Tennessee was, just getting rid of Butch Jones—who had a toxic culture in the way he was treating people, you know—I heard some of the same things about Greg Schiano, even the Penn State stuff aside.

I didn't think it was a good fit because of the style of Schiano, you know: really abrasive, more like a dictatorship, some respect issues amongst players, things like that. I didn't think it was a good fit for Tennessee at the time.

SUMMERS: Yeah, I can agree with that too. All right, so how important do you think it was the way that everything came together on that Sunday to keep Schiano from being hired? Had you ever seen anything like that?

SWAIN: No, absolutely not. I've never seen fans petition a freakin'...I've never seen anything like it. Fans complain all the time about hires or what's happened and what didn't happen and so at first I was like, "Okay. Well, here's some fans complaining, you know, nothing's gonna really change, nothing's gonna happen, you know, and I guess we're gonna be stuck with Schiano—" But then I started to see some politicians starting to complain and you know, people going to the complex and—

Wooo! I was like, "Okay, maybe we might have something here." Then I started hearing reports of, you know, the deal's not gonna be done and I was like: "Wow, I can't believe this! I can't believe that they're really going to stop this hire!"

And I became really proud, you know? I was really proud of our fan base for stepping up and shutting that hire down because it probably would have been a disaster anyways.

SUMMERS: Oh yeah, it would. I actually have a long interview I did with a former football player under Butch and it really sounds like Schiano was basically Butch's clone.

SWAIN: Yep.

SUMMERS: In a lot of ways.

SWAIN: Yeah, pretty much.

SUMMERS: Okay, so then the week comes when John Currie is running around like a chicken with his head cut off. How realistic were any of those hires that week that he tried for? I mean I can't imagine Gundy was a realistic option?

SWAIN: No, I don't think Gundy was ever realistic because Gundy has done this before to Tennessee, he's done this before to other schools and he's comfortable. He's never really been outside of the state of Oklahoma for that long so I didn't see a scenario where he would leave. Now Mike Leach wanted to come to Tennessee, he couldn't wait—but I was kinda skeptical as to how he would fit in the SEC with his style of play. Of course, if you are Jeff Brohm you want to get back to Louisville at some time. But I thought that would probably happen with Brohm because he could always come here and treat us like crap so I thought Jeff Brohm was realistic. I don't know what the hell we were doing with Dave Doeren at NC State. That didn't make any damn sense.

SUMMERS: That was actually funny. NC State fans tried to give him away and our fans refused to take him.

SWAIN: Yeah, that should have been a red flag right there.

SUMMERS: Exactly.

SWAIN: Then you start hearing stuff about…This is after coach Fulmer took over. You know, Les Miles which was an easy choice but, you know, you wonder why he was unable to win more at LSU and then you dig a little bit, you know, you gotta find out why. And then Kevin

Steele being someone who knows this conference. Coach Fulmer is also somebody who knew the conference, that knew how to recruit at a higher level. Kevin Steele knew how to do that but he's a little older, didn't know how long he'd be in it. So yeah, I mean, a lot of names we're talking about, a lot of coaches that almost were the coach of Tennessee.

SUMMERS: I think we ended up a lot better off than we would have been but that's just me.

SWAIN: Oh yeah, I believe so too.

SUMMERS: I'm really impressed so far with what we're seeing. Ok, national media. Were you surprised by the backlash?

SWAIN: I was surprised that the national media made it seem like, it was like they were Greg Schiano's agent, like they were really bothered and hurt by it. Now there were some fans that really took it overboard, made it seem like he was a witness (to Sandusky) and, you know, that wasn't the case at all. But his name was connected to it and for me, that's just enough to say, "No, thank you." But you know, the national media really came hard to his defense.

SUMMERS: Yeah, they really did. I mean, have you ever seen that before? National media attacking a fan base with that much like, I don't know, poison, in a way?

SWAIN: Yeah, they did that with (former UT basketball coach) Cuonzo (Martin).

SUMMERS: Oh that's true too. You're right. They did. So it's just a Tennessee thing evidently...*laughs*

Sorry. Okay, what is it about Tennessee that you think makes the fan base different? Is it somehow unusual compared to other schools?

SWAIN: I don't think Tennessee fans are much different from any other passionate fan base that's had success in the last fifteen-twenty years. I mean, you look at Alabama's fan base, you look at Georgia, Florida, I mean, they all expect to win at a high level, they all have great resources, they've all experienced some success and they want more of it. I mean, as much as I want to sit here and say that Tennessee's fan base is so much different than everybody else's, I just don't...

I think the only thing that's different is we've been patient and we've watched so many leadership stumbles that we've just had enough. But as far as the characteristics of the football fan base, I think we possess the same characteristics as most big-time football program fan bases. I think they're pretty much on par with everyone else of a big-time, successful, traditional powerhouse.

SUMMERS: Do you think that what happened in Tennessee is going to shift the power base any or change the way that universities look at these coaching hires in the future?

SWAIN: Ooooh. Well, I think the early signing period is going to change that because you have this early time period in December and you can't wait forever if you're gonna fire a coach. You gotta do that earlier in the season so that way you can have a new coach in place so you can try to switch and recruit in your direction. I think as the money goes up, you gotta be really careful about the number of years that you guarantee a coaching staff because if you don't you'll be caught up paying the coaching staff millions of dollars over a long period of time which may affect you being able to hire the next coach. That's a tough question. Because again you see all these top coaches, these established coaches, they're not leaving anywhere. If you gonna get someone good, it's gonna be a coach maybe at a smaller school or a coordinator at a bigger school. That's kind of what you're seeing around the conference, around college football.

SUMMERS: Yeah, that's true, that's true. You know, my thing of it is, when you look at what happened I think that...I think that *somebody* in PR—who wasn't obviously available through any of this for Tennessee—somebody would step up and say, "We don't want to rock the boat and have a Tennessee situation happen here." You see what I'm saying? So they might not be as inclined to take a risk on a rehabilitated coach like Schiano may be now or Lane Kiffin, somebody who's had their reputation trashed for whatever reason and has to try to rebuild it and get back into the game so for me that's what I think, but I'm interested in what you think on that?

SWAIN: Yeah, I just... well, I think every school's situation is different. I think Tennessee's situation right now, they just...they couldn't attract a big time coach. They got a coach from a coordinator, real simple coordinator at a really successful program that's having success right now and you know, I think they weakened Alabama by taking probably one of their best assets. Alabama wasn't even in the top three in recruiting this year so I thought Tennessee did a really good job considering the circumstances of not having an AD at one point and having a fan base rebel against a hire.

SUMMERS: Wasn't it kind of like redemption for coach Fulmer to be named AD? Kind of like ending the Fulmer curse that people have been talking about since he got fired?

SWAIN: Oh yes, yes, yes, no doubt because Coach Fulmer all along just wanted to *help*. And we do this for some reason here, you have these people that are here, right here in your face and you kind of refuse to let them help. You'd rather do it yourself or do it your own way but you have someone that's proven in Coach Fulmer and you don't want his help? I mean—that's kind of how Butch was, that's kind of how some of the other people were, and you kind of send them out or whatever and you'll use them when you need something. And then with the AD hire this time last year you should have made him the AD then, but you found some excuse *not* to make him AD—citing experience which was ridiculous. But yeah, I mean, it was cool. It was cool to go for the (Fulmer announcement as AD) press conference, I went just to see all the people there...

NATHANAEL RUTHERFORD, MANAGING EDITOR ROCKY TOP INSIDER

"Oh my God! The Fans Just Saved Tennessee"

Nathanael Rutherford is the managing editor for Rocky Top Insider, a site that covers Tennessee athletics. He's a graduate of the University of Tennessee and has lived in Knoxville his entire life. He's covered the Vols since the spring of 2014. Rocky Top Insider brands itself as the "digital destination for Vol fans." RTI has weekly podcasts, weekly live shows, articles each day, and has big social media followings on Twitter, Facebook, and Instagram. Nathanael is one of the most visible Knoxville journalists on Vol Twitter.

SUMMERS: All right, so in your opinion, what was the situation like around UT football specifically within the fan base heading into the season?

RUTHERFORD: Well, heading into the season this year, I know from covering the team and getting feedback from—because, you know, I've been covering the team since around the spring of 2014. So I got to see kind of the build-up of the Butch Jones' era. You know, things were getting better when it went from Tennessee was 5 and 7 to getting to a bowl game to the start of the 2015 season when things were starting to look like they were turning up for Tennessee and then the beginning of 2016 season. I hadn't seen that kind of excitement in a while.

But heading into this past season, the 2017 season, it was like it was—I don't want to say the excitement was lower than it had been in, you know, forever, because it was. But it wasn't to the level that it was for the Derek Dooley days or anything like that. But it was pretty low for the fact that people were just pretty fed up. They viewed Butch Jones as kind of a lame-duck coach. I think that was very true, and that's kind of how I viewed it, too.

I assumed unless he had some kind of pretty decently big year he was going to be gone, whether he would be fired or if he was going to leave on his own accord. But I assumed he would be gone, and I think a lot of fans assumed that too, A lot of fans were angry that he wasn't fired after the 2016 season when the Vols collapsed and ended the regular season losing to Vanderbilt and squandered the talents of Derek Barnett, Josh Dobbs, Alvin Kamara, and all those guys.

SUMMERS: Oh yeah, we totally missed the boat with that team.

RUTHERFORD: Yeah, oh yeah, they did. But I think heading into 2017, it was definitely…the excitement was not there. Once fall camp started, people started getting more into it because they were ready for football at that point, but everything else? The whole off-season was talking about Butch Jones being on the hot seat, talking about the different stuff on all the players that had transferred out and the injuries last year and was that going to happen again this year plus you had all the coaching changes. To me, and I meant to write an article on this and I still probably will, it felt like how the beginning of 2012.

In 2012, Derek Dooley had to make a bunch of staff changes as well and a lot of those guys left on their own accord. This time it didn't seem as many coaches were leaving on their own accord, but essentially, he replaced almost his entire staff. That's never really a good look because it looks like there's been a last-ditch effort to save your job. Obviously, it didn't work out. But I think the excitement for the season was not there because Tennessee wasn't like... they were in complete rebuild mode, at least it would seem that way.

But you also looked around at the conference and saw Georgia's gotten a lot better; Alabama's still who they are; Florida's going to be a fight even if they're not very good, they're going to be a fight; South Carolina—they beat us last year, why not again this year? So it just didn't seem like the excitement was very much there and I think a lot of people viewed Butch Jones as a guy who wasn't going to be around after that season regardless.

SUMMERS: So what do you think he needed to do to keep his job? Like, bare minimum—what record?

RUTHERFORD: I think it would have been tough, but I think if he'd gone, you know, his typical 8-4 I think he would've have been kept as long as the four losses were understandable losses, as long as they were losses to

Alabama, Georgia, whoever the other west team was this year, and Florida. But if he'd beaten Florida and maybe lost to Georgia, Alabama, but then maybe also lost to like a Carolina, Vanderbilt? I don't know. But also looking at it from a hindsight perspective, I think John Currie for sure kept would have kept him at 8-4 even if the four losses had been to crappy teams as long as he beat some of the biggest rivals. I think he was totally fine with keeping Butch Jones now that you look at it back with hindsight, but hindsight is 20/20.

SUMMERS: So, in your opinion, when did the calls for him to get fired really get charged up?

RUTHERFORD: Well, really, you know, obviously all off-season, there were people saying it, but you know, we ran different polls and stuff on Twitter and I talked to different people, and I think the negative voices are always louder than the positive. That's just how social media works. I think when you actually started seeing even people who were—I wouldn't say pro-Butch, but people who were kind of on the fence—saying no, he doesn't need to be fired, we don't need another turnover. I think the moment that happened was the Florida game this year because of how mismanaged the offense was in that game. John Kelly was not getting touches in the red zone. That one goal, he dropped the pass, but he didn't get a single carry in that entire sequence and Tennessee ended up throwing an interception that time at the goal line actually in the end zone, I think in that game—

SUMMERS: Florida couldn't stop him (Kelly) when he ran either and that just burned everybody.

RUTHERFORD: I think that game was when

everything turned, you know, that game was just a microcosm of the Butch Jones era. It was mismanagement of your best players, and then some dumb play calls, and then a defensive collapse that cost you the game. The Florida game was essentially all five years of Butch Jones in one afternoon. It was just a poor offensive showing, and a very inconsistent...I mean, they turned it on in the second half in the first quarter, they had a good...they tore up Florida on the ground and in the air, but it was inconsistent, and you had that Hail Mary that won the game for Florida. I think that game was really the turning point, because it's one thing to lose that game regardless of who it's to, but it's another when it's Florida, a team that you, you know, you should've beaten a couple years ago probably but you beat last year and you've beaten that streak. And then you're heading into this game and that was a very, very winnable game with what turned out to be a bad Florida team. That was the point that a lot of people, even the ones on the fence, were saying, "Okay, I don't think Butch Jones needs to stay in this job anymore."

SUMMERS: So, Florida was two weeks before Georgia?

RUTHERFORD: Yeah, because they had U-Mass in between.

SUMMERS: Yeah, that's right. U-Mass. The mighty U-Mass game, huh? See, that's the problem with writing this book, every time I talk about it, I get mad all over again. So, after Georgia, the 41-0, worst loss ever in Neyland Stadium—did you think Butch Jones was going to be fired the next morning?

RUTHERFORD: At that point, I was still trying to

give John Currie the benefit of the doubt. I remember we'd done our reaction show after the game on that Saturday, and I remember talking to my staff writer Will Boling about it and saying, "It would not shock me at all if he's fired." I said, "I don't think he will be, you know, it's still fairly early in the season. I don't know if they'll pull the trigger right now, but I think he should be. It would not surprise me if he is."

I remember staying up very late that night and then getting up very early the next morning in anticipation of it happening and when the letter on the date went on Sunday, I thought, *Okay, it's not going to happen.* I understand that maybe, sort of, it's not necessarily a huge deal yet that it didn't happen, but I knew at that point that it was inevitable. Once you lose that badly to your rival, at home, especially in front of a crowd that was pretty excited...I mean, the fans *showed up.* Tennessee, I didn't think was going to win that game at all. I didn't think they stood a chance, but the fans showed up, they checkered Neyland, they sold it out, and that's what they got in return. So I thought, *You know, that's it.* That team? I didn't know if they quit or what it was, but that team, when I saw them on the field, I thought, *They'll be lucky to win one or two SEC games this year.*

Obviously, they didn't win any, but I thought they'd be lucky to win one or two and that's enough to get the job done. Butch Jones, at some point in this season, is going to get canned whether it's October or November or after this season, he's going to get fired. It's only a matter of when at this point.

SUMMERS: Now, how do you think that the weeks of silence between the Georgia game and the Missouri game, what do you think that did to the atmosphere around the program, like online...fan base...and media?

RUTHERFORD: From a personal perspective and from everyone else I kind of saw and talked with that was dealing with it as a fan, it was maddening. The silence was deafening, to use that old cliché, but it really was, because usually you get to hear the nail on the coffin—like the AD gives them "support" or something like that. I mean Currie wasn't doing *anything*, and then finally, he got on some kind of interview the week or two before the Missouri game, and he did finally give a comment then, but that was weeks after the Georgia game. It was after the Georgia game, it was after the Alabama blow-out, it was after the South Carolina putrid effort that game was too... That was an ugly, ugly game. I mean, it was weeks of more embarrassing losses after more embarrassing losses and Vol fans were getting fed up with it. You could tell things were reaching a boiling point.

I don't think anyone envisioned what was going to happen with Greg Schiano and everything, but it was maddening. You just look at it and you can see from the outside looking in that, you know... just look at the body of work, look at the body of work like it was a person. You could just tell it was not a healthy situation, that the body was deteriorating, that something internally was making them sick—if you're going to use it like an actual person. There were plenty of reasons to be negative at that point in the season.

SUMMERS: Well that actually kind of leads into my next question which is: how significant do you think (VFL coordinator) Antone Davis's departure was?

RUTHERFORD: I wonder how much more we'll learn about that one as time goes on and people believe and he feels safer about saying some things about other things that have happened, but I think that was a pretty big impact. It showed you how bad things were getting because, actually… I mean, the VFL program was brought in under Dooley. I think it's a wonderful program. I think it's great. I think a lot of former players have benefitted from it and I think a lot of just people, in general, have benefitted from it. But Antone Davis, once that news came out and I think he didn't really say anything until after Butch Jones was fired, but I think when you hear about how that relationship was handled or when you hear—

SUMMERS: Yeah, it was that letter.

RUTHERFORD: Yeah, the letter, the email he sent to Currie, when you hear about all that? I mean, other stuff that came out about Butch Jones with the Marlin Lane interview, just other stuff too that people came out and said about him? I mean it was, it was eye-opening.

SUMMERS: Okay, I have been dying to ask somebody this question, so that means you get it: where in the heck was the Sports Information Department or UT PR throughout this whole situation? Where were they?

RUTHERFORD: I don't know. Because you know, you look at Butch Jones. When he first got here, he was supposed to be very good at PR, and his first couple years, he was. He was very good at handling the press, he was very good at handling the message that was being put out to everyone else by UT and by himself. But then, I don't know if it's because different people changed—you know, you got a new SID and things like that. I'm not trying to throw the new SID under the bus or anything like that. I think he's doing a good job. I know from conversations with him and other things that a lot of the stuff that was going on was (put out by people) over his head. It wasn't his fault. But there were people over his head that weren't doing their job. That's why I don't know.

Because it was not handled well, none of it. Absolutely none of it. The Butch Jones firing, the coaching search—none of it was handled well, until you finally had the change when Davenport made the decision to call back Currie and relieve him of his duties and bring back Fulmer. Once that change happened, things started to get better. But there was just such a systematic failure with Tennessee's administration for such a long time that you finally saw it starting to break down. No one in any situation at UT handled anything from about October to about late November very well at all for Tennessee. It was a very, very dark, very poor two months for Tennessee during that span.

SUMMERS: I find it impossible to imagine that a major university doesn't have an active PR department where there's somebody who can say, "Wait a second, you *really* don't want to do that, you don't want to say that, you don't want to ignore that."

RUTHERFORD: I used to joke about this with my former editor, Daniel Lewis. To me it just seemed like just talking about Butch Jones, it was very much like a Michael Scott character from *The Office*. Except not quite as lovable, because you saw him drop lines like "five star hearts" and things like that. We always joke and say there would be like the SID and the PR department that would go up to Butch

Jones afterwards and say, "Hey, you need to stop saying this" like Michael Scott when he's told not to say the "that's what she said" jokes and he couldn't help himself, he would just blurt it out the five star hearts or going out with a turnover trash can. It was just a constant thing with Butch Jones. You'd see him on script at a press conference doing well but then when he would go off script that's when disaster would strike. He would say something really stupid and you'd be like, why did you just do that to yourself? You've just made us into another internet joke.

SUMMERS: So, kind of dovetailing off of that, do you think that the whole situation with Jauan Jennings on Thanksgiving week—this is right before Schiano Sunday— do you think that amplified the discontent in the fan base? Heading into that weekend?

RUTHERFORD: Absolutely. Fans didn't expect anything great from Brady Hoke. They weren't expecting miracles, and I think fans even at that point were still feeling the Vanderbilt game as a potential loss. But that happened and it kind of came out of nowhere. I mean, Jauan Jennings comes like the day before Thanksgiving and he comes out and posts that video. Actually, I think it was the day of Thanksgiving, I can't remember now.

SUMMERS: Wednesday afternoon.

RUTHERFORD: Thank you. He went and posted that video and then, you know, it was Happy Thanksgiving from Jauan Jennings and the rest of the team. You know, the way it was handled too and it wasn't just that he was getting kicked off the team. It was that the interim head coach and the athletic director both conferred about it and kicked him off and that's what—

SUMMERS: And the AD was with the basketball team in the Bahamas.

RUTHERFORD: If they were gonna make that decision, they should have waited. It's not like he had to do it right then and there. And a lot of people, myself included, didn't think that was Brady Hoke's call to make. I also didn't agree that Currie signed off on it, for him to make the call. That was a decision that the new head coach needed to make. It wasn't something that I think Brady Hoke had the right to make. I think he could have been disciplined, you know Jauan Jennings shouldn't have done that at all.

SUMMERS: No, I agree.

RUTHERFORD: But he deserved a different type of punishment than what he got and then the whole...the way things happened afterward, the way the information was 'leaked', the way people... Jimmy Hyams, that's who I'm talking about.

SUMMERS: Yeah, I know.

RUTHERFORD: Who (Hyams) came out in an article that kind of made the piece about him testing positive for marijuana or whatever it was before the Georgia Tech game and all this different stuff. That once again was showing to me the depths that Tennessee PR had sunk, and I'm thinking—wow, this is something else.

SUMMERS: Yeah, there should have been somebody there that said, "You know what, this isn't a good thing to do the day before Thanksgiving when you're looking at the worst season in Tennessee football history, to take a kid like Jauan Jennings out of the picture because of an Instagram rant."

RUTHERFORD: Right, exactly.

SUMMERS: And yeah, I actually wrote a whole article about that because I was pissed.

RUTHERFORD: I think I remember reading your article.

SUMMERS: It was just a stupid… Okay. All right, here we go. Now we get to the fun stuff. So what were your expectations for the coaching hire? No, we're not talking about Gruden, that's a whole different chapter—

RUTHERFORD: No, I never thought Gruden was actually in play. I think there was once or twice…I thought there a couple of times when I thought maybe, but I tried not to get burned on that. But what I legitimately thought with the coaching process once Butch Jones was fired, I expected—you know, information leaked after this and kind of ended up being true—I kind of expected them to look at guys with… you know, as a sitting head coach or someone with Power Five or SEC experience or whatever, you know, kind of biggish time experience as head coach. I thought those would be there top choices and looked like there, at least for a little while, that was. Some of the guys they were looking at…Even some of the guys after Greg Schiano, they upgraded their search it looked like. They went after Gundy and Leach, who I thought would definitely be better coaches and better fits than what Schiano would've been but you look at some of the guys that were being mentioned around the program for names and whatnot. I didn't expect, you know, I thought Chip Kelly would be great but I never expected it to happen. I thought Gary Patterson would be great, he's my kind of dream guy but I didn't expect it to happen because I would just be shocked if he'd left his situation where he was to come to Tennessee.

But I thought they'd go after some bigger names than what they ended up going after. I wasn't expecting a huge hire until I was told, kind of, I was told from someone who kind of had inside information. I was told one that Currie had spoken to, I think it was a booster who was saying they expected a big, expensive, explosive hire and from that point, I think that was a couple of days before the Schiano stuff happened. I was like, "Oh, okay, if he's saying this and it's going in this direction then it could be huge."

Turns out that was definitely a misdirection unless he did expect Schiano to be a big, expensive, explosive hire. And I don't think that was the case. There was a lot of misinformation, a lot of misdirection coming from Tennessee with all of it and Currie thought he was being so coy with all of it. I don't know what word to use there, but it seemed like he thought he was....

SUMMERS: He was smirking.

RUTHERFORD: Yeah, he was smirking a lot. Seemed like he thought he was going to mislead all these people and get his guy, that's what came across and I think for the most part that's what happened. But I expected someone with head coaching experience and I'm not trying to take a shot at Jeremy Pruitt. I was expecting in the initial process someone who had head coaching experience and not like a Butch Jones coaching experience. Someone who, you know, at least if they weren't a head coach in the SEC, they had some sort of SEC experience and some kind of Power Five experience as coordinators or whatever it was. And that didn't happen under Currie.

SUMMERS: So do you think Schiano was Currie's man the whole time?

RUTHERFORD: I wonder from things that I have... and people I've talked to and what I've heard about it and everything, I think he might have been his guy the whole time. I think a lot of the stuff you heard coming out about who Currie was meeting with, and different things like that and then the stuff I was told. I've gathered it was just misdirection. He was trying to mislead people off the scent of what they were doing. Because you didn't really hear about where he was going and what he was doing until after Schiano.

SUMMERS: Ten days.

RUTHERFORD: Yeah, we didn't have a whole lot of stuff to even go off of until all of sudden Schiano was just there. He was the main guy and all of a sudden you saw stuff from (USA Today writer Dan) Wolken and from CBS, all of a sudden. "Hey look! Tennessee is going to have Schiano as their head coach." Where did this come from?

I think the night before—I remember seeing a report, I don't remember who it was, I don't think it was Mike Gundy but someone else that could have been... it may have been Mike Leach—I remember putting a report and hitting submit and Tweeting and Facebooking the article link about someone else interested in the position or somebody else... whoever it was, it was not Greg Schiano. Greg Schiano was not on our radar until that Sunday morning when all of a sudden stuff started happening and I'm like, "Whoa, wait a second. What is going on here?"

And it just kind of came out of nowhere.

SUMMERS: So take me through your Schiano Sunday.

RUTHERFORD: Oh boy. That was one of the, I mean, I think for a lot of people, one of the most hectic and interesting days I've ever had when it comes to just sports. But that day kind of transcended sports for me. I remember when the notification came on my phone, I got out of where I was, I immediately logged on to Twitter and was like, "What's going on here? I want to see what's happening."

I started looking at other sites to see if anything else had been broken or anything like that, and just all the fan reaction...I remember just thinking, *Oh God, I don't like this guy, what's going on here?* and then when...I'd forgotten that he had even vaguely been associated with the Penn State stuff. So when the reports started coming out about him, I was thinking, *No, there's no way they can hire this guy.* And then I saw the report from whenever it was he was fired from—Tampa Bay in the NFL—and guys were saying he was a kind of authoritarian coach and I was like, "God, they don't need a guy like that. That's like Butch Jones. You're hiring another guy who has the same personality type as the guy you just fired? That's not what Tennessee needs."

And then when more Penn State stuff started coming out, I was like, "Okay, there's no way they need to hire this guy, period." I remember sitting at my laptop watching more stuff come out, seeing people tweet stuff like: contact here, call the athletic director, call the department, call this person, make sure your voices are heard. Tony Basilio got on his show and went to his studio and he was on air for eight or nine hours straight or something like that. I remember going on his show with him and talking about it and he and I both—and neither one of us was joking about this. He was better off than I was because he's established—but I said if they hired Schiano that I would get a different job. I was not going to cover Tennessee sports and I was serious about it. I don't care if it uproots my whole career trajectory or whatever I'm doing, if they were going to hire Schiano, I could not and would not in a good conscience cover this team anymore. And I was serious. I would've thanked all my bosses and thanked everyone that gave me an opportunity at Tennessee, but I was going to sit out until he was gone. I was not going to cover Tennessee anymore.

But luckily that didn't happen. As the day went on, I talked about how I didn't want it to happen. I was saying this isn't from a subjective Tennessee standpoint, just looking at it as an objective bystander: there's no way I would want any university no matter who I was associated with, hiring him. And the day went on, I saw people making a move. You saw the riots on campus, the #SchiaNO kind of movement, people online, that's when you started seeing different legislators, different politicians coming out and saying, "No, this is not the type of man we want to lead our university. I graduated from there; this is not who we want to represent Tennessee." And I thought, "Okay, there's something to this. This is not just a fan base getting mad and just going to deal with it when it happens." There was so much movement, I thought, "Wow, there's a chance this could actually be overthrown. There's a chance you finally see this powerful fan base, because it is."

And most big college athletic programs and teams have a powerful fan base but I guess you can't really affect change as much and I guess this was really the first time that a fan base has rejected a coach before. This is definitely the biggest stage on which it's happened with this being in a social media era. I just remember seeing as more things came out, as time went on throughout the day, that the winds of change were blowing.

And then I think it was around five or six o'clock when I think it was John Bryce who tweeted out, "No, the deal's off." I think Basilio and Swain all confirmed at the same time too that the deal was off, that Schiano was not going to be the head coach. I remember looking over at my fiancée and I just let out this huge breath and I said, "My God, they dodged the bullet! We all just dodged the bullet on that."

And then the falloff from that was also insane. I remember wanting to double, triple, quadruple confirm that the deal was off before I really let my guard down. But when I saw the initial report from Bryce, and I think I heard Swayne and Basilio say it too, I remember sitting back in the chair that I was in and all of a sudden, the weight and stress of the day just kind of hit me and I was just like—"Oh my God! The fans just saved Tennessee."

TONY BASILIO, UNIVERSITY OF TENNESSEE ALUMNI/ RADIO HOST

"Our Own Little Tea Party"

A native of Philadelphia, Tony Basilio has been a Knoxville-based radio talk show host since 1993. He describes himself as the official voice of the common fan and does more hours devoted to Tennessee sports than anybody in his business. He does a two-hour call-in show five days a week, a post-game call-in show after every Vol football and basketball game and covers Tennessee-related stories as they are breaking. He was a leading media voice in the Tennessee fan ReVOLution surrounding the proposed Greg Schiano hire in November 2017.

CELINA SUMMERS: Okay we're good to go. Why don't you start off by telling me your involvement or connection with UT?

TONY BASILIO: I'm a 1990 graduate of the

University of Tennessee. I came here to go to school in 1987 having never seen the place so didn't even visit before going to school, I just felt like it was a place that I need to be. And I came then and basically haven't left except for six months where I lived in Southwest Virginia. I've pretty much lived here the entire time.

SUMMERS: That's actually really cool. Okay, what in your opinion has been UT athletics' primary obstacle over the last decade?

BASILIO: Oh, that's easy. That's leadership. You look at the great programs out there and I can give you a good example. You take what happened at Penn State—which should have absolutely derailed them for the next fifteen years—and they were up and running within four years. And why is that? Well, they went and they had excellent football people making their hire who knew what they were doing and in one fell swoop they flushed out a president, an athletic director, and a head coach—and the head coach was there when God handed the ten commandments to Moses.

SUMMERS: When we were born. Paterno started (as head coach) at Penn State the year I was born.

BASILIO: Yes. I mean he literally was there... I think he started as an assistant in 1950 something. That's how long that guy was on that campus. So that should have shook them to their foundation, but it didn't. And the reason it didn't is they had a couple of guys inside their infrastructure who were titans of industry including a guy that was involved in US Steel. But they went out and they talked to a ton of people before they brought in (former Penn State head coach) Bill O'Brien. And Bill O'Brien was an absolutely key hire to stabilize their situation while they fought to get their name back, which I still don't think they've got their name back but they've gotten their football program back which is…which really makes no sense.

SUMMERS: That white out game last week was something else wasn't it?

BASILIO: It was incredible.

SUMMERS: Oh man—that's what college football is supposed to be. I miss that. Okay, so in the UT document drop regarding the coaching search it seemed pretty apparent that boosters were kept out of the loop. Has that been standard practice the last ten years in your opinion?

BASILIO: That is standard practice with the Haslams. We have a group of boosters who have given millions and millions of dollars up until Schiano Sunday and just were treated like mushrooms. They were kept in the dark and fed horse crap. And I have talked with several of them through the years and said: "Why do you cede so much power to a group of people that are not good at sports and really are not very good at the university?"

What they're good at is giving money. And there's nothing wrong with that by the way, that should be appreciated…that they give money.

SUMMERS: Absolutely.

BASILIO: But money in the…money with a condition of control when it's poor control is almost money not worth taking and so for years, *years*, I've been imploring some of these people, "Step forward, own this, there's a vacuum!"

It wasn't until Schiano Sunday that they really saw what it was I saw years earlier, which was there was a level of Haslam fatigue in this community that was palpable and it finally was pushed over the edge that day. But it was brewing way before that.

SUMMERS: Also based on the document drop, in the weeks after Butch Jones's firing there were no communications with any coaches about the position at all. Does that surprise you?

BASILIO: No.

SUMMERS: Me either.

BASILIO: No because I believe that the House of Haslam had their guy circled and their guy was going to be Dan Mullen. If Dan Mullen…If Florida wasn't, or would have been slow played by Chip Kelly, Dan Mullen would be the head coach here right now and everything…and they would have had all the systems in place and none of this would have ever been exposed, the seedy underbelly of what's going among our boosters. The Haslam industrial complex would have never been exposed.

SUMMERS: So in the week between the failed Schiano hire and Currie's firing and Fulmer's hiring, what was going on behind the scenes that you were aware of?

BASILIO: I was talking about it real time. If you go back it's on my website, my shows, but I was told…Fulmer was introduced on a Friday night, is that right?

SUMMERS: Friday afternoon, 4 o'clock, December the 1st.

BASILIO: I was told that Wednesday evening that a coup was brewing. And I couldn't believe it. And when I was told that, I said: "Well, finally! Hallelujah, we're going to take this thing back!" And then the very next day was the day that we got word that...

SUMMERS: Currie went AWOL?

BASILIO: Currie was—well, Currie was going to be terminated when he came back from Washington and it was an absolute circus that...You could never make up what went on here.

SUMMERS: No, you're right, you can't. I write fiction for a living and I'm not that creative. I'll admit it. So most college football fans and especially Tennessee fans have the idea that boosters are the ones calling all the shots with major hiring decisions. Is that true at UT?

BASILIO: Yes, there's never been a hire that's happened that the Haslams in the last twenty years were not behind. Every hire.

SUMMERS: So how do you think the power of the internet like on Schiano Sunday has changed the way that big business including college athletics is done?

BASILIO: Well let's just take Twitter, and one day I'm going to write my side of this because I think people will find it interesting but you're the only person that I'm cooperating with that's written something in depth and I've decided to do that with you and Tom here in this book—

SUMMERS: Thank you.

BASILIO: But let's say this: I saw the power of

Twitter that day and the power of us encouraging people and I wasn't alone, but I was a huge part of it—

SUMMERS: Yes, you were.

BASILIO: And what's sad is that a lot of people try to take credit for it and I don't, I just say I was a part of it.

SUMMERS: Oh, don't worry. I talk about Clay Travis's attempt to take credit in the book.

BASILIO: I'm going to give you something on the record.

Celina laughs

BASILIO: Anybody that would try to sit there and try to take credit for that is a needy, sad individual because I understand that this was about a collective force of which I was a part. Now was I a large part, a small part, a medium part? I don't know, that's for other people to determine. I do know this: I had somebody literally, *literally*, LITERALLY on top of somebody that was in the room that didn't want to see the Schiano hire happen saying, "Keep the steam up, keep the steam up, pour on the steam, pour it on, pour it on, pour it on, pour it on!"

And then in the middle of that afternoon when it looked like the deal was starting to fall apart: "Continue to throw the gas on the flames, continue, continue, continue, continue! We've about got this thing knocked out, we've about got it!"

And if you go back and listen to my podcast in real time, I was giving play by play. I was saying: "This thing, trust me, people, we're having an impact, we're having an impact, keep tweeting, keep tweeting at Beverly

Davenport, keep tweeting, keep tweeting!" because I knew from a source that she was shaken.

I knew she was looking at it.

That's the power of what went on that day. That's why one day it'll be written about and I've never told anybody that but that is what happened on that day. I can't get too far in depth on it because I'll get a couple of people in a lot of trouble. Suffice it to say that Bev Davenport let it be known that she was shaken to a contact of mine and that's what happened and she put her hands up and said, "Stop. Let's think this thing through."

SUMMERS: Why do you think UT was so unprepared for what happened on Schiano Sunday and the six days afterward?

BASILIO: They don't care.

SUMMERS: That's a good, succinct answer.

BASILIO: They've always been a party of one. *sighs* One vote counts. No other votes count—it was pure hubris and the arrogance of the House of Haslam, and unfortunately Peyton Manning went with them, which was really surprising and strange. And here's the thing about Schiano, if you think...and I think Peyton Manning still to this day thinks that Schiano is a good football hire and if you think that, fine, I'm not here to change anybody's minds but culturally, culturally, that was just never going to play here with this fan base. I can tell you right now as somebody that was on the air for eleven hours that day—

SUMMERS: Yeah.

BASILIO: There might have been one, and I mean *one* caller, that said, "He's not even a good football coach." Most of it was just pure visceral, guttural offense that Tennessee would even consider it. It was just offense. It was a fan base that had been put through so much by... hey, these guys give lots of money, no doubt about it but they've been put through so much by these people, by their incompetence, which basically turned to negligence and enough was enough.

And that's what you saw. We had our own little tea party. That day that week we had our own little tea party.

Because it wasn't just the Schiano hire. It was Dave Doeren at NC State. It was a few other ones that we just said "No!" We were watching with names that got floated there as John Currie was flying around trying to close these deals and that is a powerful, powerful...

There's a lesson to learn from this which is if Tennessee was going to do that and if they were going to hire Schiano, what they should have done a month beforehand is float that out there, they should have gotten some of their minions in the media of which I'm not one—

SUMMERS: Right. Me either.

BASILIO: To prepare the fan base!

SUMMERS: Yep.

BASILIO: "Hey everybody! I hear this is what Tennessee is getting ready to do and it's not a bad idea"— you know—"and here's why." and you give your talking points. What they get is just pure hubris. "Hey, we're just gonna shit on the fans and who cares?

And that's what they did.

And the fans said, "No sir, it will not flush. Not today."

SUMMERS: So, do you think it's back to business as usual at UT?

BASILIO: No, it'll never be the same. No. The HOH's (House of Haslam), I believe, last vestiges of their unilateral role was when they terminated Bev Davenport because I don't believe that the two people that are over there now are going to be puppets of theirs. Even though it *appears* that they are, John Compton (new Vice-Chair of the UT Board of Trustees) was terminated by them (as CEO at Pilot Flying J, owned by the Haslam family)—he did not quit. And this is an interesting thing to understand to really get the dynamic of what's going on. So, tell me: if he's terminated by them then why would they float him over the Board of Trustees?

Well, they did that because that's what political people do when they know they've done somebody wrong. Let's do the guy a solid. Let's give him the Board of Trustees deal. Now I think their thought is, "We're still going to try and control him."

I'm going to tell you right now: I'm talking to people close to him, he is not going to be controlled by that, he is just not. We're talking about a guy that was a titan of industry—which I was talking about, which helped Penn State get back on track—and he's pretty damn good at what he did and what he does and he already has an ear to the ground a lot more, I can tell you this, a lot more than the Haslams did in terms of caring what people think.

And wanting people to buy in. So, I believe it's a new day.

SUMMERS: So, do you think Tennessee fans have created a blueprint for other college fan bases to follow?

BASILIO: You know, I don't know if there are other situations that were as out of whack as this one. I mean, I'm talking about a party of one, billionaires, ruling this thing basically with an iron fist, that's what you had here. *And* they were bad at sports. Look, this is nothing personal, I think that on the whole Mr. Haslam (James A. Haslam II) is a tremendous gentleman.

SUMMERS: Yes, he is.

BASILIO: Jimmy (James A. Haslam III) is a guy that many people in town wouldn't give you a dime for But the father is a wonderful guy who has helped hundreds if not thousands of people with his benevolence through the years and I think the governor (Bill Haslam) is a solid person and a solid man as well. Now, Jimmy? Jimmy is probably another story for another day. And Jimmy, by the way, was the guy that was knee-deep in the Schiano stuff. I mean knee-deep in it. Like, put your waders on knee-deep in it.

SUMMERS: Well, we're giving him a chance to go on the record. We'll see if he takes it, I don't know that he's willing to but that's just me.

BASILIO: I would agree with that.

SUMMERS: So, if you were going to describe the leadership philosophy UT has displayed, which kind of changes would you institute there?

BASILIO: Well, I think they're going do the right

thing which is: after watching the Tennessee deal under this administration just completely fall to pieces, I think the right thing was to put somebody to go outside the box for interim president which is what they're going to do with Randy Boyd. And again, my first inclination was that he was going to be a complete sheep for the Haslams. I called people that I trust in both political parties, some of my greatest sources who have always shot me straight and every single one of them—and this could not be something that was put together as if it were a campaign, these are different people that have no inkling that I know one another—and they all said, "That's going to be a solid hire for Tennessee, and if he doesn't get it fixed nobody's going to get it fixed, along with Compton."

Because I think these people are going to take the time. Both of them have had leadership styles where they take the time to listen to people. You need a lot of listening.

SUMMERS: I have a follow up with that. A significant proportion of the fan base looks at the fact that Compton worked for the Haslams and that Randy Boyd's campaign for governor was supported, at least initially, by the Haslams. And they think that the biggest power offices at UT are being given away as consolation prizes. What would you say to those fans aside from what you just did?

BASILIO: They could be right. I think John Compton was put there because he was terminated (as CEO of Pilot Flying J) and the reason he was terminated is interesting. When I talk to people, I did some research into this.

Jimmy Haslam just didn't need another chief there.

SUMMERS: Right.

BASILIO: He didn't want him there! And so, they paid him millions and millions and millions and millions of dollars to go away but it was kind of an embarrassment to him. He uprooted his family to come here. There's that inconvenience. And I think you're right. I think people that say, "Well, he got this thing as a consolation prize." Yes.

Here's the miscalculation by the HOH. I think they believe, "We're going to stick this guy here and like Raja Jubran (former vice-chair of the UT Board of Trustees) he's going to do our bidding." He's not. I'm just going to tell you, I know people close to him and I know what he's saying. He's not, he's not. So, I would say to anybody that was my perception until I talked to enough people around this thing and I've gotten an idea of what's going on which is, "Oh, you want me to have the keys to this? Sure, I'll have the keys to it. Oh, by the way, you're not going to get to drive it."

SUMMERS: *Laughs*

BASILIO: But he didn't tell them that; he just took the mantle. And if you'll look at how he took the mantle it started with Schiano Sunday and it was culminated with the elected officials repudiating the Board of Trustee appointments of Governor Haslam. That's what precipitated this. But, if there was never a Schiano Sunday, there never would have been a political environment where elected officials in this state would have felt safe doing what they did because here's the truth—the Haslams are political animals to the Nth degree, they support all candidates because the truth is: they *need* all candidates to do favors for them like all big money people.

SUMMERS: Yep. All right, we're going get to some quick questions now, we're almost done. How do you feel about the hiring of Fulmer as AD?

BASILIO: I was dead set against Phillip Fulmer being the AD in the spring of whatever year that was, it all runs together for me. Would that have been 2017?

SUMMERS: It was. "It would have been." It feels like ten years ago but no, it was just a year and a half ago.

BASILIO: It really feels like 150 years ago. Well anyway, I was dead set against that from the outset when the hire was made. I think that was the only move Tennessee had because they had to go to the family. They had to put somebody in there that they had faith in and credibility and it was almost like we were in a constitutional crisis at that point or, you know, you were the United States of America and both your president and your vice president were taken out. I mean you were really in uncharted territory at that point and it felt rudderless. It felt like something that we all cared a lot for and loved and appreciated and all these things was just teetering on the brink of extinction.

I'll never forget how it felt. And I know that sounds like I'm speaking with tremendous hyperbole—

SUMMERS: No, it doesn't.

BASILIO: But that is how it felt. And so, from that standpoint, it was almost the only hire they could've made.

SUMMERS: I agree. How did you feel about the

subsequent hiring of Jeremy Pruitt?

BASILIO: I'm back to this. That was almost the only hire they could've made. Phillip Fulmer showed me a lot there with not hiring Kevin Steele, because I know for a fact that several of his former players with whom Steele has coached, several of his friends in our community were really pulling for him and almost pushing him to hire Kevin Steele and Phillip Fulmer stood up and said, "You know what, I've got a guy in his early forties who I see something in and dammit, I'm going to gamble on him. Now, if he doesn't work I won't be here in five years. Chances are he won't be here in five years anyway. What I need to do is get Tennessee football right because it's something I love and care about."

And I think that's what he did. I think he did…I think in an era of systems and analytics that we're living in now, I think Phillip Fulmer made a gut hire in hiring Jeremy Pruitt. Just a pure gut hire.

SUMMERS: What makes it interesting is comparing his six days and the hiring of Pruitt with Currie's six days between Schiano Sunday and him getting fired. The difference in the approaches there and how that just settled the whole fan base.

BASILIO: No, you are ten thousand percent right. Truer words have never been spoken.

SUMMERS: How should Tennessee address the chaos within the administration with all the hiring and firing and interims and payouts? What do you need to do to get that ship settled?

BASILIO: End it. They need to end that and

truthfully, I think with the state that the football program is in, I think that's going to end because I think this guy will be competent enough to keep his job for at least four years. And the truth is Tennessee needs to hit a reset button. Now, the other thing is they need to go find a chancellor and then they need to go find a president and I'm telling you for president of the university long term, they need to look up there in East Tennessee State and go to Brian Nolan. And they need to hire him. Because he's the star. He is the absolute star in the state and you would really have to go some distance to find somebody better suited than he would be to take the mantle from when Randy Boyd has enough of it.

SUMMERS: Alrighty, that's it.

BASILIO: Celina you are the greatest. That was fun.

THE MASSES, TENNESSEE FANS

"I Was Moved To Activism"

AS WE set out to write this book, we were dead set on including the average fan's perspective for several reasons. First off, the Rocky Top ReVOLution is something a lot of sports journalists are going to write about. They'll talk about the university's point of view and the media's point of view—which is fine. What they won't talk about is the fans' point of view. The thoughts and opinions of the average sports fan is rarely more than a blip on the radar of the sports media. The local sports media is more attuned to the fans' opinions than the national media. Usually a national guy is too accustomed to telling the fan what to think. They don't have much interest in or knowledge of what the fans think independently.

And of all the NCAA fan bases, Vol Nation is comprised of fans who all think for themselves. To my mind, that's one of the reasons that the media consistently uses stereotypes when referring to Tennessee fans—and not just Tennessee fans but fans of any team in the South. Taking the time to learn and understand the fan base's idiosyncrasies is a lot more difficult than dismissing those fans as ignorant and uneducated brutes drinkin' shine down at the fishin' hole while talking about the day when Jon Gruden will make the Vols great again.

That's not how Vols fans really are.

As a whole, Vol Nation is one of the best-educated fan bases in the country when it comes to understanding the game and the atmosphere it survives in. Some fans can reel off stats from specific games or players—and not just UT players, but players from other teams. Only when you've experienced a football game from the middle of Vol Twitter can you understand what I'm talking about. There are average guys sitting at home who can isolate a missed call in real time, promptly make a .gif of that missed call, and have it up on Twitter with an explanation of the missed call before the "professionals" in the ESPN trailer parked outside Neyland or the replay officials can accomplish the same task.

It's really kind of impressive.

Until you understand the average Tennessee fan, you can't comprehend why the fan base reacted the way it did to Greg Schiano, to John Currie, to the Board of Trustees—to any of the major players in the story. You need a foundation of why these people who are all so different in their everyday lives come together a few times a week out of love for their university. And to build that foundation, you need to find out what makes a Tennessee Volunteer out of an average person.

So what *does* make a person into a Tennessee fan? What makes any fan stay faithful to a football—or basketball or baseball or volleyball or any athletic—

program through twenty years of decline and a decade of utter chaos? What makes them take a stand against their own university and the national media the way they did in late November of 2017?

Being a Tennessee fan takes a certain type of character, and no matter where a person grows up, or the circumstances of their youth, something about UT strikes a chord with them that bonds them instantly with people they'd never normally meet. Through the written interviews we conducted, we were able to better get a handle on who, exactly, the average UT fan is.

Some of these Vols wish or need to remain anonymous because of where they work or who they are, and we are respecting their requests. That's why you'll see some answers coming from a person's Twitter handle instead of their given names. Some people we interviewed are good friends from online, while others we've rarely interacted with on any level and still others enjoy reading our online columns and blogs. Some are multi-generational legacy fans while others are "sidewalk alumni" who never attended UT. The oldest interviewee is an octogenarian, while the youngest is in his early twenties.

These are the views of the masses, who have been repeatedly dismissed by the media, by power brokers, and by the athletic director, John Currie.

Let's start off with the easy questions.

How long have you been a Tennessee fan?

Michael Massey, from Cleveland, Tennessee, replied: "On some level, about as long as I can remember. I was a fan by proxy as a young child. My dad always had a 'Tennessee Big Orange Country' license plate on his trucks. Fandom was solidified after attending a game with my pee wee football team when I was eleven years old."

Nathan D. Escue from Milan, TN stated: "I guess my whole life, but really since about 1989. That's when I first started paying attention to college football. My father was always a UT fan, so he raised me to be a UT fan. Hell, I went to UT Martin so I could have a UT diploma. The degrees actually are identical, except it says, 'given this day in Martin' instead of Knoxville."

Bo Ransom, who lives in Knoxville, was evidently far more relaxed answering my questions than some of the other people who did interviews with us. (Understandable, since we are good online buddies.) As a result, that smart-alecky tone I engage with on Twitter leaks through to his responses. "As long as I have any real memory. I was born in Tennessee but grew up in Ohio. As you are aware, Celina, it's both difficult and easy to not be a Buckeye fan in Ohio—"

As a quick note, I currently live in Ohio and have for over twenty years. Bo understands my pain. Back to Bo's answer.

"—difficult because it's a fan base I would compare to ours as far as passion. And that's what makes it easy too. Because they are obnoxious—like us."

Bo has a way with words.

One of my favorite UT fans is Santa Vol, a jolly gentleman whose orange candy and North Pole-inspired leisurewear are the proper shade of orange (HEX FF8200, just so you know). "Entire life. Earliest season I can remember is the '79 Bluebonnet Bowl. I can also remember listening to games in my Dad's truck and hearing 'This is the Vol Network' and thinking that this was *my* team!"

Spencer Barnett, who is one of the co-founders of Checker Neyland and therefore an originator of the best graphic image of any university in the country, is another favorite of mine. Every year, the sight of a full Neyland Stadium checkered in orange and white has become one of the graphic cues of college football season—one that's a huge selling point for recruits, by the way. Checker Neyland began as a fan-driven initiative in 2014, when Barnett along with Tim McLeod and Jonathon Briehl, put together the website and seating chart, then drove the online push to get fans to participate. That first checkered Neyland was for the Florida game, and it only took the trio two weeks to make it happen. Checker Neyland was the precursor to the Rocky Top ReVOLution because it proved something absolutely no one believed possible.

The UT fan base not only could unite, they could do so quickly, online, without any help from the university, and in the process create something legendary.

That's why we asked Spencer about his UT fandom. "I was born here and I'm a 'loyalist' to where I'm from. As soon as I was old enough to realize the state of Tennessee had an official school, I became a Vol. And over the years from then on, I researched and learned about anything to do with the Vols, the Volunteer name and origin, why the orange and white colors etc, etc. That and my mom had season tickets for nearly twenty-five years starting when I was a little kid, until they flipped the sidelines back."

Tennessee fans know the little events that changed

the perspective inside Neyland Stadium. I have a UT wallet that I've carried for over two decades with leaves from the hedges down on field level.

Josh Parrott is the popular blogger associated with Tony Basilio's fiery UT radio talk show, and a compatriot of mine during later upsurges of the ReVOLution. "I have been a Tennessee fan since 1990. To be exact, my first memory of Tennessee football was the 1990 Alabama game. I was nine at the time and I can remember driving back from a restaurant with my mom, dad, and sister and hearing it on the radio. The unmistakable voice of John Ward described the carnage at the end of the game as our field goal was blocked and bounced all the way down to the thirty-nine yard line on the other end. All Alabama had to do was run some clock and kick the field goal to win 9-6. That was my introduction to Tennessee football. Little did I know that game was almost the epitome of what it is to be a Tennessee fan."

And finally, Sam Thompson expressed the feelings of many of the people I interviewed with his response. "I don't understand the question. I don't remember not being one."

Why are you a UT fan?

"I can honestly say that I first remember being hooked as a fan at nine years old, watching the Sugar Bowl against Miami (1986) with my dad and uncle. At that time in Ohio, it wasn't easy to watch Tennessee games but that experience hooked me right in. Never before had I seen anyone watch a game with so much passion as my family did that night," Travis Sweat, who's one of the most intense UT fans I've ever met, told me. "That was without a doubt when I knew I was a Vol for life. I remember going to school after that Christmas break talking so much about Tennessee, which was falling on deaf ears in Buckeye and Wolverine country. It was difficult still after that to track Tennessee football a lot, but then a local kid from Macomber High School in Toledo committed to Tennessee and the publicity grew in the area. Upon Chuck Webb's arrival, Tennessee was on the map in the northern portion of the Buckeye state. The passion I saw from my family on that one night is still the passion this fan base has today and one of the reasons I am proud to be a Vol fan."

All Tennessee fans have stories like this one, comprised of moments and memories and tradition. Many UT fans would read Travis's story and instantly know a lot about Chuck Webb—high school All-American, all-SEC in 1989, and half of the crazy and brutal Cobb-Webb connection that decimated opposing defenses with ridiculous numbers. Chuck Webb ran for 294 yards against Ole Miss in that 1989 game, which is still the most rushing yards in a single game record at Tennessee.

Let me get back on topic. Let's talk about why people are Tennessee fans.

People like Larry Hildebrand. "I fell in love with the school when I first saw 100,000 fans all cheering for the Vols. I felt there could be nowhere better to be."

For other Vols, the reasoning is different. Raynard Williams from Atlanta has a compelling story of his own. "Like many or most Tennessee fans, it's mostly because I was raised in Tennessee. Yet on a serious note, my dad is a Bammer. He told me the story of Condredge Holloway.

At the time, Holloway was the best athlete from the state of Alabama and the best quarterback. Only problem was his race. I'm African-American, so Holloway's story is a big part of why being a UT fan goes much deeper. Bear Bryant wanted Condredge to attend Alabama, but he would only offer him as a wide receiver because he knew the state would not allow him to play a black quarterback. Condredge was a *beast* and wanted to play QB. As it stands, Tennessee offered him as a QB and told him he had to earn the right to play, thus becoming the first SEC school to allow an African-American the opportunity to play the position of quarterback." Raynard paused for a moment and added, "Now, you don't have to be a black man to be a fan of Condredge Holloway. Just ask Kenny Chesney."

UT fans from all over the world followed the same path as Travis and Raynard—they liked a specific player and that player brought them to Vol Nation.

"I was born and raised in Canada before I moved to the states to play baseball in college," Kevin Cowling remembered. "My old college roommate was a UT fan and I started watching with him. I noticed a player named Paul Yatkowski, who was from Canada and had played defense for the Vols. So I went to my first game—Tennessee was playing Louisville—and brought my Canadian flag with me and waved it every time he made a play. He, of course, saw the flag and appeared to love it and appreciate the support."

What did you think about Coach Fulmer's firing in 2008?

"Even though I realized it might have been the best decision, I was devastated," Gina Lee replied. "I listened to his presser live as I drove home and cried the whole time.

I was heartbroken for him!"

Brian Gillespie of Troy, Ohio said, "I agreed that it was time for Fulmer to go, but the missteps that followed almost felt like a curse was put on us."

The "Fulmer curse" has been fodder for Vol Twitter almost since its inception.

During the nine years between Fulmer's termination and the firing of Butch Jones, what was it like to be a UT fan?

Jacob Whitehead, who lives in Georgia, was blunt. "Everyone says that the fan base they have to endure is the worst, but I promise Georgia fans can rival any. Lots of barking. Constantly. Plus with Butch at the helm, he was always saying something that just primed me to get my head kicked in. Champions of life, leadership reps, energy vampires, etc."

I thought that answer was so perfect, I let him answer the question for all of Vol Nation.

What did you think when you first heard of the Schiano hire?

Mike L., who is an active duty military man and therefore has asked for anonymity, said, "'NO.' I have a friend at work that is well-connected within the department. He had mentioned a few days earlier that he had heard Schiano was a serious likelihood. I said, 'No way. No one is that dumb.' I laid out all the reasons why that would be a horrible call. The Rutgers smokescreen, the NFL stuff, the Penn State stuff, everything. When I heard, I was literally the 'Michael Scott No' meme—"

Which, by the way, you should Google that meme

for proper context. It's hilarious.

"—And I immediately went off like never before on social media. I try to stay out of the fray on social media. Promote my work a little, be funny a little, support the team a little. Very little advocacy and try not to be an asshole. But that day was different. I was moved to activism like I've never been moved to activism before."

Jan Teal of Tullahoma, TN agreed. "I felt sick to my stomach when I first started seeing that UT was going to hire Greg Schiano. He seemed to be very similar to Butch Jones in many ways. Based on the amount of drama and his tyrant-like attitude while he was the coach at Tampa Bay, I thought the hire was just all wrong. It felt like a slap in the face."

Were you a part of the ReVOLution online or in Knoxville?

Another responder who requires anonymity— we'll just call him Pruitt—replied, "Online. Schiano was a terrible choice for hire. Completely tone-deaf to Tennessee's fan base and the situation after just putting the Title IX stuff in the rearview. Hell, we canned Lil Jon's *Third Down For What?* but we hire a guy who worked for half a decade with convicted child molester Jerry Sandusky? Dumb. Now, seeing the texts from Currie begging for PR help from Dan Wolken since 'Tennessee fans are wackos', it just goes to show you what kind of people were running the show in Knoxville. Unreal to think about how bad the leadership was from John Currie."

Dale Hutcherson from Dresden, Tn said, "I wrote a blog article about the Schiano hire in response to being singled out and called a clown on Twitter by Kirk Herbstreit—whose opinion I actually appreciate on college football. Kirk tweeted that the Schiano hire was a 'great' hire for Tennessee, and I responded in the negative—that it wasn't a good hire in the minds of UT fans, to which he responded by calling me a clown. This, of course, made me even more invested and inspired me to write a post about why the Schiano hire wasn't good for the university or the fans."

What was the week like between the Schiano deal falling through and Fulmer's hiring as AD?

"Being part of the ReVOLution was amazing. To see us actually force a change gave me a feeling of pride for our school and fans," Matthew Hays of West Point, GA answered.

Kim Davis said, "Grateful and relieved that the deal fell through, but really angry that we were being portrayed as stupid rednecks who didn't have any knowledge of anything. We were surprised by Fulmer's hiring, but felt that if anyone could settle things down and get them back on track it would be Fulmer."

"Hectic," said Zack VanMeter, from Martin, TN. "Not knowing was the hardest thing each day. Constantly scanning the internet and Twitter to try to get the latest scoop on what was happening in Knoxville just made me paranoid that we would have to see another lame hire. I am so, so happy I was wrong!"

Did you immediately believe Fulmer would benefit the university? Why?

"I absolutely did," Kyle Schmidt replied. "I felt

like he would calm a lot of nerves, unite Vol Nation, and provide some much-needed stability to the athletics department because in my mind, there is no one who cares more about the football program and the University of Tennessee than Coach Fulmer."

Ken Cowell, another good online buddy of mine, was both succinct and emphatic. "Yes, because he loves the university and he is neither a complete fool nor a Haslam puppet!"

Audrey Caylor, who now lives in Maryland, replied, "Literally the very second I found out that Phillip Fulmer would be the new AD, I was immediately calmed. I had no more concerns about our football program or any other athletic program at UT from that second. I don't know of a single living person that literally lives and breathes for the University of Tennessee more than Coach Fulmer."

Hailing from Jackson, TN, Nick Hayes stated, "I watched the press conference live when Phillip Fulmer was announced as AD. I listened to him speak several times after his firing, and the fact that he chose not to take another coaching job and how he spoke about UT and his love and passion for UT. You know that he absolutely has UT's best interest in his heart and he knows where UT (athletically) has been, is supposed to be, and he will undoubtedly do everything in his power/control to make sure that it gets back there."

Anytime you get a group of NCAA football fans together, you're going to hear everyone's origin story... how people became fans, or who their favorite player was, or what they remember most about games. That's particularly true of fans in the deep South, whether you're talking about small colleges or the sprawling, powerful state universities. That's because fans have so much to tell, to relate to other people who love the same school. And regardless of the school, you're going to hear stories with a lot of color.

Stop and think for a minute. Imagine yourself sitting in Neyland Stadium for a sold-out game. Now take a look around you at the other people in the stadium. You're looking at 102,454 other UT fans who all have similar stories about how their fandom began. Old, young, man, woman, rich, poor—doesn't matter. Being a Tennessee Volunteer almost always begins in early childhood, usually because a person's parents were themselves UT fans.

That's not some fly by night liking. People in Tennessee don't just *like* things. They are passionate about them. Their feelings for Tennessee are intense. And as a result, their loyalty is fierce and unchanging regardless of what happens.

The November 18, 2017 game against LSU was a good example of that passion. That was the first game after Butch Jones was fired and Brady Hoke was the interim coach. LSU had a pretty good team, so no one really had much hope for a victory, especially after the Missouri debacle the week before. During the game, a veritable monsoon hit Knoxville. People were wrapped up in soaked UT gear during a bitterly cold November rain slashing them sideways in a howling wind and dodging debris that was launched like missiles at the crowd. Probably one of the most miserable game experiences imaginable.

And in the middle of that monsoon, Tennessee

scored. I was working so I wasn't watching the TV, but suddenly *Rocky Top* blared through my speakers. Despite the weather, despite the horrible situation the team was in, despite everything stacked against them the Tennessee fans were singing *Rocky Top* defiantly...proudly as the storm winds shrieked around them.

That's just the way Tennessee fans are.

There's a reason Tennessee is called the Volunteer State, and the state university's nickname is the Volunteers. Tennesseans are infused with courage, always the first ones to step up and the last to leave. They are fearless and bound together by ties that are incomprehensible to outsiders, thanks to a combination of independent thinking, generous spirits, and kindly natures.

Tennesseans have one other characteristic that the national sports media and people high up in the athletic department and administration of UT found out the hard way. If the Tennessee fan base unifies for any reason, it's going to be one hell of a fight. Attack one person and you'll find yourself fighting them all.

On the morning of November 26, John Currie was in the middle of a text message exchange with USA Today sportswriter Dan Wolken. One of Currie's comments really sticks out.

"Gonna need some help on the PR. Our people are wacko."

The Tennessee athletic director who sent that text was blithely going on about his business, insulting the people whose taxes paid his salary, and preparing to foist a head coach on the Vols that he knew the fan base would hate. Currie knew he was going to have to spin the hire to make it palatable, even to the point of colluding with the national sports media to force acceptance down the throats of the Tennessee faithful.

John Currie was about to find out the hard way what happens when you try to impose your will on Rocky Top, and that resulted in a series of events so fantastic that it's still difficult to believe. But in order to understand the events that followed, the views of the fans quoted in this chapter had to be seen in order to put all Tennessee fans in context.

You know.

The masses.

Part III | ReVOLution

By Celina Summers

BEHIND THE VEIL

LEADING UP to the 2017 football season, Tennessee fans were invested in their now-annual internal struggle—optimism, blended with absolute negativity. This emotional mash-up was probably the fan base's most prevalent new trait, developed over the past decade and a half of disasters. Coming off two reasonably good seasons, the fan base was primed for greater glory than a 9-4 season but was also aware that replacing the talent lost to attrition the year before was going to be nearly impossible. Most reasonable fans expected a 6-6 or 7-4 campaign.

Should Vol Nation have been prepared for a 4-8 season and going 0-8 in the SEC?

No.

For one thing, Tennessee had *never* gone winless in the SEC, and there was no reason to think that they ever would. The Volunteers shared the distinction of never going winless in conference play with the Ohio State Buckeyes—one of several as-yet unknown connections with Ohio State that would unfurl over the space of the next year.

For another, UT had a coach that had won more games each year than he had the year before. Confidence should have been steady in head coach Lyle "Butch" Jones, but for some reason that confidence wasn't shared by a fan base that had been tearing itself apart since 2008.

Throughout Vol Nation, a sentiment was growing that something wasn't quite right.

Fans were thinking uncomfortably about those previous coaching searches before the season in 2017. Now Butch Jones was facing a season of transition, which brought all the insecurities back to the surface of the always-churning fan base as the Vols squared up for the year. He had the number one recruiting class in the nation heading into the year, but also had to replace a slew of big-time players. Despite the fact that at almost any other school, the fans would have trusted a head coach who so far had improved his program in each subsequent year, UT fans were divided about what the season had in store for the Volunteers.

Many UT fans and the local media pointed to the strange number of injuries that had shot down the previous two years' teams. By the end of October in both 2015 and 2016, the Vols had twenty-five or thirty players on the injured list—or who'd left the program for mysterious reasons—which led to UT's end of the season collapses. For the 2016-17 squad to defeat both of their primary SEC East rivals, Florida and Georgia, and then lose to South Carolina, get stomped by Missouri, and end the year on a soul-sucking loss to Vanderbilt was incomprehensible.

Plus there was a newly dangerous element to consider as another embattled coach neared the start of the football season at UT.

Social media.

Social media had been in its infancy when Fulmer

had been shown the door. But in 2017, online fandom was a constant twenty-four hours a day, seven days a week, fifty-two weeks a year presence that was always talking, always dissecting, always analyzing what was going on at Tennessee. Social media was no longer an infant.

Social media was all grown up.

Online fandom reflected the breach in the fan base almost perfectly. Most of the Facebook groups established for UT fans were more optimistic and initially supportive of Jones. Vol Twitter, however, was not. If there was one thing Twitter Vols were agreed upon, it was a nearly universal dislike of Butch Jones. They hated his use of clichés, and his apparent inability to answer a simple question. They didn't like his behavior on the sidelines. They despised his gimmicks.

The local media was pretty much in the same boat. Just as with the fan base, there was a breach between the older journalists and the younger ones covering the UT beat. This conflict would become more evident as the season wore on and would result in the exposure of several long-standing, festering wounds within the community on Rocky Top.

So as a long, dusty Tennessee summer waned and Georgia Tech loomed as the Vols' foe in the Kickoff Classic, fans argued and chattered online, slapped up videos of Jauan Jennings breaking Jalen Tabor's ankles when he torched the Gators for a touchdown run to Florida fans and the Dobbs-Nail Boot catch to Georgia fans. But everyone—fan and student, alumni and media— wondered what kind of product Butch Jones would manage to put on the field. Unfortunately, Jones answered that question almost immediately during the September 4 opener against Georgia Tech by debuting his latest embarrassing gimmick on the sidelines.

A trash can.

A turnover trash can.

No, I'm not kidding.

A trash can.

The University of Miami had a massive turnover chain that any defensive player who caused a turnover was allowed to sport on the sidelines as a symbol of their feat. But on Rocky Top, Butch Jones thought a *turnover trash can* was a great way to inspire his team.

Little did he or anyone associated with Tennessee know at the time, but that turnover trash can became a metaphor for the entire football season…and the coaching search that turned the University of Tennessee into a running gag once that season was over.

Being a Tennessee fan has never been easy.

Until the mid-1980s, maybe two Tennessee games a year were shown on television. Once cable finally showed up in my hometown, the additions of ESPN, TNT, TBS, and Fox meant that number of game broadcasts doubled. Sometimes we got as many as five Vols games a year, but the Nashville stations were our local TV and more often than not they opted to telecast Vanderbilt games. By the time ESPN expanded and cable sports packages guaranteed most Tennessee games could be watched on TV, I was already an adult and Tennessee was already a bruising team with probably the biggest home field advantage in the NCAA. The football team started to gain a little respect.

But the fans? Not so much.

Back then, Vol Nation didn't really care. By that point, the Tennessee fan base didn't need the media's respect anyway. Fans sold out Neyland week after week, traveled en masse to wherever the Vols played their away games, and ignored media snubs with a home-grown lack of concern. There wasn't yet an avenue that a sprawling group of college football fans could utilize to make those opinions known aside from talk radio on the local level. That's why the sports media could and did stereotype and insult fans—or athletes, coaches, and schools—with impunity. There weren't any consequences for their actions. Even when Tennessee legend Peyton Manning was under center on Rocky Top, the media focused on Tennessee's faults.

In those days of Tennessee's success on the football field, the fans' opinions didn't matter. The fans had no voice and carried no power, so they posed no real threat to the national sports media.

That all changed drastically when personal computers created a platform everyone could use. Suddenly, fans from all over the world and all walks of life could talk about what they loved online. They could respond instantly to games...or the latest snide remark from some sports analyst who thought it was funny to broadcast his depiction of UT fans as uneducated, stupid, and incapable of understanding big money sports.

And once those insults made it onto the internet,

they never went away. For example, Outkick the Coverage's Clay Travis screeched his opinion of the typical UT fan in a January, 2015 article "The Ten Dumbest Fan Bases in America"[1]. Travis ranked Tennessee as the tenth stupidest fan base, supporting his claim with the following laundry list of stereotypes:

> *Despite living in a single wide in a holler thirty-eight miles north of Knoxville, he vacations in Pigeon Forge — making sure to book a room in a hotel with a Jacuzzi — where he proceeds to screw his overly plump 'fiancee' while eight of their kids — three are his from his first shotgun marriage, four are from her first shotgun marriage, and one is his from a different woman when he was sixteen and it slipped — sleep in the bedroom outside. They will spend the next three days riding go-carts, feeding bears bananas in concrete pits, eating funnel cakes, and talking about the time he saw Tee Martin in the Wendy's on Kingston Pike. ("He ordered a frosty. Paid with a twenty!")*

> *Before leaving Pigeon Forge, he will buy each of his kids a tie dye t-shirt that says, "Go to hell Gay-tors."*

> *He has worn a Peyton Manning jersey every Saturday in the fall for the past 21 years. (On Sundays he wore a Colts jersey until Peyton moved to Denver and then he became a Broncos fan). He named his first son Peyton and his second son Manning. And he has a VFL tattoo on his arm even though he never took the ACT and thinks the F in Vol For Life stands for "fer."*

1 "The Ten Dumbest Fan Bases In America #10 Tennessee" by Clay Travis, *Outkick the Coverage*, January 2, 2015

*He did take the GED though. Twice. Much like the 2013
Vanderbilt game, he prefers not to talk about it.*

*His most prominent trait is his ability to immediately
suspend all disbelief and believe every word that a new
football coach tells him.*

That's how a member of the sports media who
now claims to be a Tennessee fan (despite his George
Washington University and Vanderbilt degrees) described
the fan base, and he wasn't alone. This opinion was
generally shared by his peers in the national sports media,
as will be demonstrated when the Schiano protests began,
and Travis's diatribe was just a regurgitation of all those
prejudices.

Certainly makes his claims of outrage during the
UT fan uprising seem a little...convenient.

So at the time of the BCS era, there was nothing
the fans could do or say about the stereotypes, the slurs,
the generalizations based on outdated mythologies about
the people who were born and raised in Tennessee or who
supported the state's flagship school. All Tennessee fans
could do was seethe, because they had no legitimate voice
to do otherwise.

But during the decade between 2008 and 2018,
the way that people communicated underwent a drastic
change. The UT fan base embraced social media early,
and tens of thousands of people came together under the
Volunteers' unifying brand. Major cities across the US now
have groups of Tennessee fans who met via social media
and come together weekly to watch UT games. There
are Vols in foreign countries as well, notably in France,

the UK, Australia, and Canada. All of those Volunteers interacted daily with fans in Tennessee and elsewhere, forming a far-reaching and voluble community online. By the time Lyle "Butch" Jones was hired to replace the woeful Derek Dooley as the head football coach, Vol Nation's social media platforms were firmly entrenched in Tennessee culture.

Coinciding with all that and the beginning of the Butch Jones era as Tennessee's head football coach, a major power player exploded on the scene...a thought-influencing platform that would become instrumental in the fates of not only Jones but everyone involved in the program.

Vol Twitter.

Anyone who's waded into the shark pool known as Vol Twitter quickly learns the value of social media in today's society.

Social media is a dog eat dog world anyway, but when you add in the volatile emotions of college sports the online world can get downright scary. Vol Twitter is the most outrageous, aggressive, keen-edged fan base on social media.

Period.

Vol Twitter quickly began to drive public opinion about everything UT. The Tennessee fans who came together to create Vol Twitter came from every walk of life. Former UT athletes built relationships with farmers halfway across the country while business executives bonded with housewives. There were no social class lines in Vol Twitter. Every individual within that tight-knit yet inclusive online society was equal. Vol Twitter grew increasingly sophisticated to the nuances of the sports they followed, sharing knowledge about NCAA regulations and rules on the court or the field, Watching a game while on Vol Twitter soon became almost ridiculous because Tennessee fans missed nothing.

Nothing.

Every call was analyzed and argued. Every misstep was under the immediate glare of the fan base's spotlight. Every snafu was dissected. Vol Twitter was so practiced at breaking down game film that some members could do so in real time and much faster than the pros in the television trucks. Fans immediately interacted with local media, and the younger journalists who covered the UT beat became expert at working with and within Vol Twitter. This extraordinary relationship changed the way that Tennessee sports were reported and tore down the walls between the fans and sports reporters at all levels of coverage. With the local Knoxville media, Twitter turned journalists into friends.

Or enemies, depending on the journalist.

Vol Twitter was very much in tune with whatever was going on with every sport on Rocky Top. And while UT fans congregated on other mediums, like Facebook, Vol Twitter became the online face of the fan base.

As with any large group of people, the Tennessee fan base has always fought within itself. Online was no different. There have been spats and cliques within Vol Twitter that made for some very interesting off-season nights. Facebook groups, like the immense Vol

For Life Facebook group, were soon in conflict with the more volatile personalities of Vol Twitter. That conflict also exemplified a major divide within Tennessee fans. Facebook-connected fans were more forgiving of Jones's missteps initially; Vol Twitter, on the other hand, neither forgave nor forgot a single inept act. But at the beginning of the 2016-2017 football season, Vol Twitter was fairly united on one thing they thoroughly disliked about Tennessee football.

Butch Jones.

Before the 2017-18 football season, there was a strong sense that this was the last gasp chance for head football coach Butch Jones. On the surface, that speculation seemed way off-base to people outside Vol Nation. After all, Jones had walked into a serious dumpster fire left by Derek Dooley and Lane Kiffin. He'd recruited well, he'd rebuilt the program, and he'd seemingly kept his promises.

But beneath the surface, the UT community's suspicions of Jones were increasing. In 2016, Tennessee fans had watched in horror as the most talented team to run through the T in twenty years had crashed and burned. Instead of the college football playoffs or a major bowl game, the Volunteers had gone 9-4 and subsequently played Nebraska in the Music City Bowl on December 30 while much of its roster watched from the sidelines or from home. For the second season in a row, a baffling rash of injuries had deep-sixed the season with more than twenty-five players out of commission by the end of October, and disturbing rumors had begun to circulate as to why so many athletes were hurt.

On top of that, many one-time prized recruits and

star players had quietly left the program and UT for other schools. Stories were circulating about the alienation of former Tennessee players, and rumors that Jones had struck players or attempted to destroy the credibility of players who bolted mid-season. Also, pro scouts or players' top choices for transfers were reportedly being told negative things about UT players by their head coach. So the rumors were swirling, but they never quite reached any sort of level where the media would pick up those rumors and run with them.

During that summer of 2017, those stories created an unusual level of disquiet among the fans after the successes of the previous two years. Now the Vols were facing a new football season, and the matriculation of talent on top of the rumors subsequently resulted in a great deal of uncertainty about what was in store for Tennessee. The Vols were picked to finish third in the East division at SEC Media Days, with most prognosticators predicting a seven- or eight-win season as the pinnacle of what UT could hope to accomplish.

From that moment on, Jones was on borrowed time.

The 2017-18 season was the fifth year of the Butch Jones era. Every player on the roster was recruited and coached by Jones and his staff. And while everyone, both in the media and within the fan base, was aware 2017 was a rebuilding year, the success of the team would determine once and for all if Jones really was the coach Vols fans had been waiting for.

No doubt about it. Vol Twitter was agitated and uncertain as the inaugural game of the year rolled around.

The fan base was anticipating an unacceptable season from their coach and subsequently, the team.

If he wanted to keep his job, Butch Jones needed a legendary season.

He got one.

THE 2017 FOOTBALL SEASON

BUTCH JONES'S legendary season began much quicker than anyone could have expected, but *legendary* did not necessarily equate *good*. Seeing as so much of the fan base was already turned against him, the odds of him surviving the year must have looked grim even to him, and within three weeks he appeared to be a lame-duck coach to all but the most optimistic fans.

Two games in particular solidified Vol Twitter's repudiation of their coach, well before they were faced with the unthinkable results of the season. The Florida game, and the Georgia game.

The Tennessee-Florida game in 2017 was a massive strategic battle between Butch Jones and Gators head coach Jim McElwain. Unfortunately, they shared the same strategy. They both called the most ham-fisted, poorly coached game imaginable for a pair of SEC coaches. Regrettably for the Vol faithful, Jones won the "I'm the worse coach" battle, losing to McElwain at the Swamp. What set Vol Twitter off in particular was the abysmal play-calling in the red zone.

The Volunteers possessed one of the top running backs in the nation in John Kelly, who led the NCAA in yards after contact. Opponents found it almost impossible to tackle Kelly once he'd found his lane. In a tight game against one of the Volunteers' most universally loathed rivals, John Kelly was an invaluable weapon in the red zone.

At least, for any other coach.

In addition to the two touchdowns Tennessee scored, the Vols made two more trips to the red zone. Once inside the five yard-line with a first down and four attempts to score—twice—the play calling should have been easy.

Rush.

Rush.

Rush.

And then, evaluate and decide.

Kelly was having a great day, averaging 7.4 yards per carry—and most of those came after contact. Kelly was—and still is—a tackle-breaking beast.

But no. Inexplicably, Butch Jones called *three passing plays in a row*. Both times. First down: pass. Second down: pass. Third down: pass! On one trip, UT settled for a field goal. On the other, Tennessee threw the ball to a Gator, not a Vol, and that was all she wrote. Jones's winning strategy couldn't have affected the game worse if he'd deliberately set out to lose the game. The final score was heartbreaking for fans, at least.

Florida 26, Tennessee 20.

That was the *first* loss UT football had to Florida in 2017. Another came later in the season. We'll get to that in a minute.

The second game that sealed Jones's fate came two weeks later, when the Volunteers welcomed the Georgia Bulldogs to Neyland Stadium.

Georgia was flourishing in Kirby Smart's second year at the helm, so much so that they would eventually end up facing Alabama in the national championship game. But historically, whenever UT and UGA played each other, fans would throw the record books out the window. That game was always hard-fought. There have been so many iconic upsets when one team was expected to do great things that year and a double-digit underdog decided to shatter their dreams. That's just the way the Vols and 'Dawgs play. Tennessee had come away with victories in the previous two meetings between the schools. In particular, Georgia was still smarting from the Dobbs-Nail Boot play exactly 364 days before, when quarterback Joshua Dobbs had heaved a forty-three yard Hail Mary with four seconds left in the game and WR Jauan Jennings had soared higher than the six UGA defenders to snag the winning ball.

Vol Twitter had enjoyed torturing Georgia fans with that play for almost a whole year. As the game approached, the glee started to sound a little forced. Tennessee fans were nervous about playing a newly intimidating Georgia team, but most expected the same annual slugfest...a game that would go down to the wire.

In the week leading to the game, Butch Jones had chosen the absolute worst time imaginable to alienate the local media. After star defensive tackle Shy Tuttle had missed the Massachusetts game on September 23, rumors began to swirl that Tuttle had received an orbital bone injury during a fight with a teammate. When asked about the story during his September 25 press conference, Jones denied the report stating, "The injury was caused not by a teammate. He landed on a helmet, and that's the truth."

Then, apparently oblivious to the incredulity of his audience, Jones launched a rant against the Knoxville media. "I think we have to understand—what do we want out of our media? This place with the drama? I love our kids, and I'm going to protect our players, and I'm going to protect our program. And sometimes the negativity is overwhelming. If everyone is Vol fans (sic), how do we let our opponents use this in the recruiting process with fake news?"

Not exactly the best way to garner the goodwill of the local press for a coach whose seat was already uncomfortably warm. Nick Saban at Alabama, perhaps, could get away with such a diatribe. Winning gives a coach a lot of leeway to complain.

But Butch Jones needed more than leeway by that point. He couldn't have picked a worse week to lecture the Tennessee sports media if he'd tried. Five days later, the Georgia Bulldogs annihilated the Volunteers, administering a 41-0 beating in the worst loss in Neyland Stadium's ninety-six year history. The Vols looked strangely apathetic before the game...and during it as well. Jones and his staff had no answers, no strategies to employ against a well-coached Georgia team wanting vengeance for 2016.

What Jones *did* have was an outraged fan base, sportswriters who'd come away from his ill-timed lecture of their faults with a bitter taste in their mouths, and a team that was already out of the race for the SEC East crown by the first day of October.

After the Georgia game, Tennessee fans had very little doubt that the Butch Jones era was over. Heading into the game, UT had the top recruiting class in the nation for 2018. Those recruits started disappearing like teenagers usually do at chore time. If Tennessee wanted to have a hope of retaining those commitments, the coaching change needed to come sooner rather than later and the new coach needed to be an elite coach.

The Tennessee athletic director, John Currie, shouldn't have had one iota of trouble firing Jones after the Georgia debacle. Currie was a young athletic director, one who'd been hired away from Kansas State after a ridiculously long six-month search for a suitable replacement for the unlamented Dave Hart. He'd managed to gain the goodwill of many Tennessee fans because he was instrumental in returning the Lady Vols nickname to all women's sports just a few months before. And Currie had once served as an assistant athletic director at UT and was part of the coup that had ousted Phillip Fulmer as head football coach in 2008.

If Currie acted decisively and quickly, Jones would be let go immediately after the most humiliating loss at home the Vols had ever suffered. There were several high profile coaches like Bob Stoops and Chip Kelly on the market so to speak, and if Tennessee could hire one of them to replace Jones the recruiting class might be saved and the fan base appeased. With a couple of former head coaches on Jones's staff and former Tennessee coach

Phillip Fulmer serving as a special advisor to Joe DiPietro, UT's president, the football team could be safely guided through the remainder of the 2017 season. The whole process could have been completed before any other major program jumped onto the annual coaching carousel, and that's what many people expected to have happen.

But they were wrong, and Butch Jones continued to coach Tennessee while the athletic director remained apparently unfazed. John Currie didn't make one statement about the Georgia game or Butch Jones or a coaching change, however.

John Currie remained completely silent, ostensibly ignoring the entire situation for the next six weeks. At the time, no one could understand why he wouldn't address the growing disquiet among the fans or the swelling criticism by at least acknowledging that the situation was dire. Instead, he didn't say a word.

Currie, therefore, set the stage for Florida's second victory over Tennessee in the process. On October 28, Tennessee lost to Kentucky—once again in humiliating fashion and as the result of ridiculously poor coaching. On October 29, Florida fired head football coach Jim McElwain after he began to make bizarre claims about receiving death threats from fans, and the worst possible scenario was then in play. One of Tennessee's most hated rivals had fired their head coach and they instead of UT were the first school to enter the annual feeding frenzy over the coaching carousel.

Tennessee had lost the advantage when it came to hiring the best possible available coach, and it was all John Currie's fault.

Vol Twitter, which had started off the season seething, had been boiling since the Georgia game. Each subsequent loss cranked the heat up higher. Fans began to black out their avatars on Twitter, making timelines look like targets at the shooting range, or to change their user names. Tennessee fans were outraged that Florida had fired McElwain while Butch Jones remained on the sidelines in Neyland Stadium.

The week after the Kentucky loss, Vol Twitter initiated the #EmptyNeyland movement—a threatened fan boycott of everything Tennessee football including letting the fifth-largest stadium in the country sit unoccupied during games.

Each subsequent loss forced even the most loyal Tennessee fans to acknowledge that the Volunteers were no longer even a *mediocre* team. For the first time in the modern era, Vol Nation understood that the football team was just plain *bad*.

The local media had come to that realization before the main core of Tennessee fans and were getting more vocal in their demands that John Currie and the administration do something...anything to address the situation.

After all, Currie obviously didn't have a problem with firing coaches mid-season, considering that he had been part of Mike Hamilton's athletic department staff and helped to orchestrate the Fulmer dismissal nine years earlier. But what emerged from the UT athletic department was...nothing.

For six weeks, through a woeful October and half of

a disastrous November, John Currie took no action, made no comment, and didn't visibly care that the Tennessee football program, the pride of the university for decades, was being utterly destroyed. For a month and a half, Currie smirked his way through a Volunteer nightmare, while local sports media crucified both Currie and UT for its inaction, and the rest of the college sports world turned UT into a laughing stock.

On November 16, Missouri massacred a woefully undermanned UT roster—with only fifty-five players available...a loss of *thirty* players from the team—50-17. Mizzou dropped 659 yards of total offense on the Vols, and things were so bad that the Pride of the Southland Marching Band played *Rocky Top* for a blocked extra point, to the outrage of the fans.

And at last, frustration and rage brought all the scattered elements of the Tennessee fan base together. The groups on Twitter and Facebook, the people who called in to local and national radio shows, the local media, the alumni and students, and the former players were all in agreement that the status quo of Tennessee athletics was no longer acceptable. While all these elements were stewing together, the recipe for a fiasco was created.

Only then did Currie finally act. Butch Jones was terminated as the head football coach at the University of Tennessee. Brady Hoke, formerly the head coach at the University of Michigan, was named the interim coach for the final two games of the season.

John Currie set the parameters for the head football coaching hire in his official statement announcing Butch Jones' dismissal—a process the university and its athletic director would undertake without the services of a search firm.

"Meanwhile, we now turn our attention to an exhaustive search to identify a coach of the highest integrity and character with the skills and vision to return Tennessee football to championship form. Our commitment to doing what it takes to hire the absolute best coach for the University of Tennessee is resolute…

"…To protect the integrity of our process, following the press conference I will have no further public comments until such time we announce our new coach. This search will be my sole focus and I will be in regular contact with Chancellor Davenport. Naturally, there will be great interest and speculation across the college football world. As I reminded our student-athletes when I met with them earlier today, unless you hear news directly from me, do not assume it to be accurate."

At the end of the day, John Currie set the expectations for the fan base himself—not just for the coaching hire, but for his behavior and involvement as well. If he deviated even the slightest bit from the course he'd publicly charted in those first few hours, then he'd set the stage for disaster.

In the end, the debacle of a John Currie-run coaching hire was inevitable. Currie maintained a strict silence over the search. In fact, when his texts and emails were released due to a Freedom of Information Act in March of 2018, the fans learned to their dismay that there really wasn't a coaching search at all. Apparently, the only candidate for the position was Greg Schiano all along. Not one other name was mentioned regarding interviews or vetting, and Currie obviously wasn't focused solely on finding the top available coach for the job. As a result, there wasn't a snowball's chance in hell that resentment in the fan base wouldn't boil over when news of the Schiano hire got out.

So when the news was leaked intentionally on that Sunday morning of November 26—reportedly by a heroic yet anonymous UTAD employee who thought the hire would be disastrous—that John Currie's man of the "highest integrity and character" was Greg Schiano, Vol Nation exploded.

The Rocky Top ReVOLution had begun.

SCHIANO AND THE REVOLUTION

NOVEMBER 26, 2017 dawned as a sunny, cold day in central Ohio. A couple of states away, the day was a bit warmer as Vol Nation readied itself for church and the rest of its day. Nothing seemed amiss. I sat down at my laptop with a cup of coffee and, as usual, checked Twitter first thing. That's the only place a writer watching a coaching search from another state is going to glean any pertinent information.

That morning, Twitter was relatively calm. After all, it was Sunday and most people were either at church or sleeping in.

Easy to tell what camp I'm in.

But before long I noticed a trickle of messages from Vol Twitter, and rumors that UT was about to hire Greg Schiano, the Ohio State defensive coordinator and former head coach at Rutgers University and the Tampa Bay Buccaneers. I wasn't particularly concerned. I had been told the night before by a reliable source that Dan Mullen was UT's primary target. So as I drank my first cup of morning coffee, I sent out my first tweet of the day.

"I have this mental image of Currie sitting at his breakfast table, orchestrating all the controlled leaks like

Machiavelli, with Wile E. Coyote's evil genius laugh, planning to trot Greg Schiano across the stage at a school that just paid dearly to settle Title IX cases."

Granted, I don't get up early but the smart-alec in me never sleeps. So it was still early in my day when I saw the first credible tweet regarding Greg Schiano and the University of Tennessee flicker across my timeline around noon. The tweet was from USA Today writer Dan Wolken with an apparent scoop.

Greg Schiano and John Currie were settling the final details in Columbus to set the Buckeye Defensive Coordinator up as Tennessee's new head football coach.

I spit coffee all over my laptop. *Greg Schiano? Greg Schiano is what John Currie thinks is a homerun hire? You've got to be kidding me—*

Had to be a joke, right? Only...only Wolken was a legit journalist.

Living half an hour away from Ohio State, I knew more about Greg Schiano than I ever wanted to know. I had followed Rutgers a bit while he was their head coach— primarily because of Ray Rice—and then had shaken my head in disbelief when he'd turned his head coaching stint at Tampa Bay into a totalitarian regime that included an outbreak of the severe staph infection, MRSA. Pretty much the first thing he'd done after being hired at OSU was to accidentally hit a guy on a bike with his car, and...

Something else. Something was niggling at my brain about Schiano, but for the moment it escaped me. So at first, I honed in on John Currie's psychology over anything else.

What was the man thinking?

Currie had promised to open up the checkbooks of the most profitable athletic program in the SEC to bring a man of integrity in with the skills to win championships. He'd announced there was no searching firm involved in the hunt, and that all his attention would be fixated on bringing UT a coach the program needed to move out of the cellar of the SEC. Then he'd taken his family to a basketball tourney in the Caribbean that weekend, which bothered a lot of Tennessee fans including me. And he'd settled on...Greg Schiano?

Something wasn't right, and Vol Twitter roared to life.

Took only a few additional minutes for me to recall Schiano's nebulous connection to the Jerry Sandusky scandal at Penn State. Former PSU assistant Mike McQueary testified that Schiano, when he was a graduate assistant at Penn State, had come to him after seeing Sandusky "doing something to a boy in the shower. That's it. That's all he told me." The allegations hit the Washington Post[2] when court documents in the case were unsealed in July of 2016, soon after Schiano was hired as the Ohio State defensive coordinator.

For me, that Sandusky connection was unimportant. It was a he said/he said situation between two men that were in differing power situations in the makeup of the Penn State staff regarding an event that had occurred decades ago. If any graduate assistant had raised a stink about Jerry Sandusky at the time, he would have crossed

2 Boren, Cindy,"*Greg Schiano, Tom Bradley knew of Jerry Sandusky abuse at Penn State, documents show*", *The Washington Post*, July 26, 2016.

Joe Paterno, the most powerful coach in college football, and probably would have been drummed out of football in short order. The allegation was unsubstantiated except for McQueary's sworn testimony in court, and Schiano was never deposed or questioned in regard to the case.

Heck, in that situation at twenty-two or twenty-three, I wouldn't have known what to do either.

That being said—

The University of Tennessee had settled a Title IX lawsuit alleging sexual assault by college football players for $2.48 million three weeks before McQueary's testimony broke in the Washington Post. Under those circumstances, why would anyone at the University of Tennessee think hiring Greg Schiano a little over two years later was a good idea? Make no mistake, for all the fire and brimstone sportswriters hurled at UT fans in the coming weeks, if Schiano had been hired as the highest-paid employee in the state of Tennessee, the national media would still have blasted UT and all that hellfire would have had substance.

In the media firestorm—pardon the pun—regarding the ReVOLution, what national journalists apparently couldn't comprehend was why Vol Nation was so angry. Currie's hiring of Greg Schiano exemplified the severe and growing disconnect between the decision-makers at the university and the fan base. That Schiano announcement was the first lethal bomb thrown publicly onto the dumpster fire the university's high-profile athletics department had become. For a decade or more, major hiring decisions had allegedly been brokered by big money athletic boosters in the shadows, bringing a succession of poor if not downright incompetent coaches into the spotlight and dragging a perennial top ten football program—along with men's basketball and women's basketball—into mediocrity.

A word of warning here. What Tennessee fans consider mediocrity, fans at other schools (like Rutgers, for example) would consider successful.

The 2017 season had been one of the most humiliating tumbles from the rafters of any NCAA D1 program ever. In thirteen months, the Volunteers went from a top-ten team to a squad with a winless SEC season, a 4-8 record, and thirty players out due to injury or mid-season departure. Volunteer Nation had been watching to see how—and when—UT was going to respond. That watch began officially on October 1, the day after the Georgia defeat.

I wrote a column that day for the Orange and White Report, and halfway through it, I'd said: "As Tennessee heads uneasily into a sorely needed bye week, Currie's actions in the days ahead will set UT on a course that will either trend up or down. There aren't any leeway or gray areas to hide behind, no middle ground to safely rest in. Vol Nation has made its stance very clear. Tennessee is a storied, legendary football program with one of the largest and most vocal fan bases in the nation. Mediocrity is unacceptable."

But throughout that October and halfway through November, the athletic department and its director had said exactly...nothing. Butch Jones continued as the head coach, the football team continued to lose, and the fan base evolved emotionally from frustration to fury. On October

1, UT had looked like it was at the head of schools facing the annual coaching carousel with a top recruiting class and its pick of big-name coaches. On October 29, UT had been shoved out of the way by one of its most-hated rivals. That recruiting class evaporated—Tennessee's *second* loss of the season to Florida for anyone keeping score. There'd been a strong sense that Mississippi State head coach Dan Mullen was atop UT's prospective coach list. Surely John Currie would see the necessity to secure his top guy, fire Jones, and try to take the momentum, right?

And while some people thought that UT's silence meant Currie already had his man lined up, the majority of UT fans and press were apoplectic that six weeks had passed since the Georgia debacle and not a single move had been made or even publicly discussed by Currie. Anyone with even a modicum of knowledge in the field of public relations would have told the University of Tennessee that allowing the weeks to pass without a single comment regarding the hire was a bad idea.

But, no. The silence continued, to the shock and consternation of everyone outside of the shadowy corners of Knoxville where big-time hiring decisions were actually being made. It's interesting to speculate what was going on in those corners at the time. I know there were lots of people who were approaching Knoxville journalists at the time—including me, and I'm just a columnist—with a lot of crazy stories about the power brokers of UT football. Who was on what side, who wanted what and whom, and who was being tossed around as potential successors to Butch Jones. That why I'd penned a satire on my blog about a mega-booster vampire and Grumors—so I could get all those off the record stories out there and have a little fun.

That Butch Jones's career at UT was done was obvious to everyone in football, so obvious in fact that on November 3 an athletic department employee had texted John Currie with: "Mike Leach wants to speak w/you about coaching the Vols."

Problem was, Butch Jones hadn't been fired yet, and Mike Leach's overtures were ignored by Currie until it was too late to salvage anything about the situation.

On October 30, I'd penned a column that said, in part: "It's time for John Currie, the administration, and the board of regents to demonstrate that they have actually listened to the peasants for a change and intend to make the kind of coaching hire that we, their employers, demand them to make. Not soiled goods or a flash in the pan coach who's had one year of success, but an experienced, successful coach from a D-1 background, who has demonstrated his abilities at all levels of the collegiate game—recruiting, training, and developing elite athletes; creating teams who are winning on the field and in the classroom; achieving success without violating NCAA rules or common morality; and who can keep the goodwill of the fans and—dare I say it?—the media. Tennessee needs to make that hire *now*, to keep key players from transferring, maintain the recruits we have left, and flip a few decommits back to Rocky Top—something that can absolutely happen with the right coach. Nothing else will do. Nothing else is acceptable. And UT's recent tendency to ignore what its fans want is disturbing."

After the loss to Vanderbilt to close out the 2017 season, I wrote my last pre-ReVOLution column. Entitled

"The Night The Lights Went Out In Neyland", this story was penned the day *before* Schiano Sunday. What's strange about that column now is an eerie sort of prescience, a gut feeling that came across in those lines that really strikes home hard a year later.

"A look at the Tennessee football program as the 2017 squad left the field on Saturday night was the saddest ongoing disaster in college football. To watch helplessly as one of the great, storied schools floundered and bumbled and fumbled and blustered its reputation and history away like a used hot dog wrapper felt like some kind of Greek tragedy, where hubris and arrogance collide in some horror-fest two weeks after the title character died.

"The tragedy of Butch Jones. In almost but not quite five acts.

"The nightmare that was UT this football season is, obviously, unprecedented and therefore uncharted territory for Vols fans and athletes both. So now we ask ourselves this. What's next? There's only one way to make this nightmare bearable, and that's the right coaching hire. God help Tennessee if they trot out a new head coach without the resume or cachet to pacify the fan base. No room for error with this search. Not anymore."

I had no idea how disturbing UT's behavior—and decision-making processes—really were when I penned that last line, and less than twenty-four hours later Tennessee exploded.

Looking back at the ReVOLution almost a year later, what resonates most strongly is the instantaneous and simultaneous engagement of thousands of voices online, voices so insistent and outraged that they could not be ignored. Not by sports fans. Not by the media. And ultimately, not by the University of Tennessee. The sheer volume of Tweets with the #SchiaNO hashtag is mind-boggling.

All of this was what the sports media had missed. So had Currie and UT. So instead of a triumphant press conference introducing the new head football coach to the Volunteers community, Tennessee was astonished when the fans launched a ReVOLution on Rocky Top.

Within ten minutes of seeing the Dan Wolken Tweet with his scoop (courtesy of the UT athletic director whose back pocket he'd taken up residence in), Vol Twitter was unified, outraged, and blowing up the internet. Within a few minutes, Knoxville local radio took notice. Tony Basilio was the first to go on the air and his show remained on the air for eleven straight hours. Other stations followed suit. Local media, gobsmacked by the Schiano announcement coming through USA Today instead of the UT sports beat, was frantically chasing down sources. Many of those sources were just as shocked as the media and the fans.

As the furor increased, the country's attention focused on Knoxville, where protestors were beginning to gather around Neyland Stadium and the athletic department. Inside of an hour, videos of the protests blew up the internet. In Columbus, Ohio, I was anxiously keeping up with social media on my phone, digging through flight plans at John Glenn International Airport, and heading toward the Ohio State athletic department to see if there was anything to see.

The sight of not-quite-Tennessee orange in a shopping bag heading into the OSU athletic department, along with confirmation from a contact who was inside the building, was enough to convince me that Wolken was horrifyingly correct. A flight plan had just been filed for Knoxville using a prominent local physician's plane, and while that plane might have been taking a doctor's family to the Smokies for the weekend the coincidences were too lined up.

Horribly, I had to confirm the report was true. The University of Tennessee really was going to hire Greg Schiano! How was that even remotely possible? Any undergrad taking a public relations degree could have foretold the fan base's reaction. The fact that the university was so tone-deaf as to think the hire was a *good* idea was incomprehensible.

In the meantime, the national sports media started to take notice. The majority of football pundits and analysts—and keep in mind these were well-known, credentialed journalists—came down heavily on the fans who'd dared to interfere.

Dan Wolken, who should have recused himself from the fray seeing as he'd just been texting about "the wackos" with the Tennessee athletic director, said in an article on the evening of November 26: "What Tennessee fans don't understand is that their behavior Sunday hurt the program. If Schiano and Tennessee indeed finalize an agreement…it's a marriage that starts out on terrible footing. If they go their separate ways, Tennessee's fan base will forever carry the stain inside the profession of being crybabies for whom nothing is good enough."

Pat Forde from Yahoo Sports weighed in as follows: "And then came the lynch mob to destroy the deal. You people are ridiculous. Not all of you, but the delusional loudmouths who somehow think a program with a 62-63 record over the last decade is too good for Schiano. The internet vigilantes who want to bully their way into running the school's coaching search. The piling-on politicians. The protestors. The rock painters. The rubes who still are waiting for Jon Gruden to slide down the chimney. But the worst among the Tennessee lunatic fringe are the disingenuous liars who say this Schiano backlash is about Mike McQueary's testimony regarding Jerry Sandusky and things that happened at Penn State, when in reality it's because they don't think Schiano is going to win a Southeastern Conference tile."

Pete Thamel, also from Yahoo, agreed. "The outrage of Tennessee fans over Schiano's hire was rooted in their football preferences and fueled by a tenuous and uncorroborated second-hand link to the Jerry Sandusky scandal. It provided a perfect storm of uncomfortable modern realities, where those screaming the loudest ended up getting their way without much regard to factual realities."

ESPN's Stephen A. Smith said, "I think this is a travesty, and I want to go on the record saying that. This is a travesty of justice and that needs to be pointed out adamantly."

Booger McFarlane, of ESPN and the SEC Network said, "What kind of spineless, no backbone thing is that? Tennessee is a program that I thought had a lot of tradition. It's a program that I thought stood for something...but right now, they look bad. It's a shame; it's a travesty...Bill Belichick vouched for Schiano. Urban Meyer vouched for Schiano. All these people vouch for Schiano and now all of a sudden Tennessee's too holy and they don't want Greg Schiano? Who the hell does Tennessee think they are right now? I think they're disillusional (sic) and I think they're going to ultimately pay the price for it."

FOX Sports's The Herd Analyst Joel Klatt chimed in with a spiteful, "I hope no one takes that job because that fan base doesn't deserve anybody. And you know why? Here's another part of this: who wants to go there knowing the first time you lose two or three games you're going to get that type of mob mentality?"

And let's not forget CBS Sports's Dennis Dodd with his bigoted spewing of inaccurate stereotypes talking about the "social media lynch mob" comprised of "Bubbas from the Pidgeon (sic) Forge trailer park".

All of these men—educated, well-respected journalists of some standing, despite Dodd's inability to spell Pigeon—blasted Volunteer fans for disapproving the hire of the highest-paid state employee in Tennessee.

Here's a question for you: who else *but* Tennessee fans had the right to speak out on that hire, subsidized by Tennessee taxpayers, at a land grant university that is the flagship school of the state? Was that the role of sports pundits in Bristol, CT or NYC or LA to determine who got hired at Tennessee?

No, it wasn't, despite Dan Wolken's collusion with the UT athletic director.

At the end of the day, only Tennesseans—

residents, alumni, boosters, former athletes, long-time family fans—only the people intimately involved with the University of Tennessee have that right. From the onset, journalists should have realized that. Booger McFarland's faux-indignant, "Who the hell does Tennessee think they are?" is easily answered, so let me answer the media on Vol Nation's behalf—because the ReVOLution firmly established who the hell Tennessee fans think they are— with a very non-journalistic "we".

We are Tennessee. We, the people who love and financially support the university. Not you. Not you who went to LSU and now makes tons of money as a national football analyst. Not you, who hovers around athletic department striking quid pro quos with ADs and exchanging scoops for PR support to spin a bad hire. Not you, with your multi-million-dollar contract and a show on ESPN, where you act like your opinion is the only one in sports. Not you.

Us. We. Tennessee. Until you've spent the money to be one of the 102,455 at Neyland Stadium on a crisp fall afternoon and stay until the end, win or lose, you don't get that right. You can't take that right away from the fans. You, who never make a move without calculating how that move could best forward your goals, your aims, your agenda, your checking account?

That right is not yours to assign. Unless you are part of the Volunteer family or a citizen of the state of Tennessee, *you* don't get to tell us, the we known as Vol Nation, what *our* place is in the process. We'll decide that ourselves, thank you very much.

The national sports media—save for a few rare

exceptions like Bleacher Report's Barrett Sallee or syndicated radio host and former USC and San Diego Chargers quarterback Sean Salisbury—made critical errors on Schiano Sunday.

They allowed themselves to get pulled into kneejerk reactions at least as egregious as the ones they accused Tennessee fans of. If they were interested in actual facts, they would have pointed out that Tennessee fans were not the first to protest against a proposed Greg Schiano hire. Oregon and South Florida fans had reacted much the same way Vol Twitter did during the 2016 coaching carousel when Schiano's name was floated as a candidate. A simple search informed Vol Twitter of those fan protests after about five minutes, so it's not like they were hard to find.

Were those protests as public or widespread as the Schiano-Tennessee deal? No.

But those other fan bases cited the exact same reasons Vol Nation did for disliking the hire. Are they Pidgeon (sic) Forge trailer park-dwelling Bubbas in Oregon, too? Or Florida?

Popping your opinion out there without researching the facts can have unforeseen repercussions. Relying upon ancient stereotypes and applying them to the multitude of educated, tech-savvy fans who support the University of Tennessee is the worst sort of pseudo-intellectualism and laziness.

For example: everyone's aware that the Rock at UT is a free speech space, right? And yet, every single one of these journalists at some point referred to the "Schiano

Covered Up Child Rape At Penn State" painted on the rock early, and not what was subsequently painted over it. Why didn't they accurately point out that most Tennessee fans were outraged because Greg Schiano is about as close as you can get to Butch Jones without hiring Butch? How his former players felt about him? Why did none of these things make an impact?

Also, UT claimed that Bill Belichick and Urban Meyer both vetted Greg Schiano extensively, and Currie had accepted their comments as statements of fact. But, McQueary's testimony in which he claimed Schiano had gone to an assistant coach at Penn State and witnessed Sandusky "doing something" to a minor in the shower came out after Schiano was hired at Ohio State, not before. Until those court documents were unsealed and released, there was no reason for OSU to exhaustively vet Schiano regarding the Sandusky case, regardless of what Meyer and OSU athletic director Gene Smith claimed. He was already on staff and accepted. That's much different than a head coaching hire at a traditional powerhouse in the Southeastern Conference like UT.

Perhaps that extensive post-hire vetting has a lot to do with why OSU didn't name Schiano as the interim coach when Urban Meyer was benched for the first three games of the 2018-19 football season. And at the end of the day, that action on Ohio State's part validates UT fans' objection to Schiano heading up the Tennessee program.

And finally, let us be clear. The Tennessee fan base was not the cause of any embarrassment on Schiano Sunday. If anything, the direct opposite is the case. Vol Nation exposed a seamy, ugly side of big money college athletics. You know. The shadowy slums of amateur sports, where athletes are disposable commodities and everyone makes a fortune off the game except the athletes themselves. The slums where big-name donors control the decisions and big-name journalists make deals for insider information and the no-name, anonymous masses sit meekly down and shut up and eat whatever they're fed.

So what really scared the sports media so much about the UT fans saying, "No!" to yet another bad coaching hire? And why did so many of them stick to their guns when it became obvious that the fans, at least, had a better handle of what needed to happen than the university did?

Was it because the ReVOLution revealed that the sports media had agendas of its own? Stripped away the fallacy that those journalists are impartial observers? Made them betray a bit too much interest in the outcome of the hire? Was it because the fans of a major university stood up and for the first time demanded that their school was not going to hire any coach that was not first acceptable to *them?*

Answer me this: if Greg Schiano was such a knockout hire, then why did UT Athletic Director ask USA Today's Dan Wolken for help spinning the hire to the fans in the first place? If Currie was aware the hire would be unacceptable before he announced it, then why would he move forward with Schiano? And if Wolken was genuinely surprised at the reaction of Vols fans against the hire, why would he agree that spinning Schiano was even necessary?

I'll wait while you think up those answers.

In the meantime, while fans grew even more perturbed and media coverage doubled, another aspect of the incompetence making decisions about UT athletics was scrambling around in the background, unsure of what to do. The University of Tennessee Board of Trustees was shell-shocked and reeling. Their utter contempt for the masses had caught them off-guard, and now the ReVOLution was not only uncontained but beginning to be supported by prominent lawmakers throughout the state.

"I have reached out to *@John_Currie* and others in administration at UT expressing that WE as a TN Community do not approve of Schiano. *#higherstandards*" State Representative Jason Zachary tweeted.

"Our Tennessee standards mean something, and a Greg Schiano hire would be anathema to all that our University and our community stand for. I sincerely hope that these rumors are not true, because even serious consideration would be unacceptable." said State Representative Eddie Smith.

"Absolute wrong choice and I hope these reports are incorrect. As a supporter and season ticket holder, I know UT can do better." Diane Black, at the time a GOP Gubernatorial candidate, and sitting member of the US House of Representatives added.

"Honestly I don't know this rumored UT coaching hire from *#JohnAdamsHousecat*. But judging from my tweet line, Somebody at *#UTAthletics* should be answering questions quickly."

Sen. Frank Niceley chimed in with the political

zinger of the day with that last tweet.

Clay Travis of Outkick the Coverage, whose opinion of the Tennessee fan base we've already discussed, underwent an astonishing change of heart on Schiano Sunday. Evidently incapable of passing a dumpster fire without throwing a propane tank on it, Travis tweeted at 2:48 pm, during the height of online outrage and offline protests on campus: "I'm told Browns owner and Tennessee booster, Jimmy Haslam, has been personally calling members of the Tennessee legislature who were critical of Schiano hire and telling them: 'You don't make the Tennessee hire, we do.'"

This was never confirmed by any Tennessee lawmakers. Although Diane Black did admit to receiving a call from Jimmy Haslam, her office did not release any details of what was discussed. Interestingly, according to USA Today, a spokesperson for Haslam also confirmed the call, stating it was a "private conversation."

That brings us to a series of events that requires analysis if we're going to arrive at a conclusion. Let's discuss the elephant in the room for a minute...Jimmy Haslam.

The fact of the matter is that the Haslam name, and particularly that of Jimmy Haslam, has been consistently tied to every major move in the athletic department since Doug Dickey retired in 2003. That's why for this book, we requested interviews not only with Jimmy, but his father, Big Jim.

And honestly? I was surprised they both agreed. As far as I know, neither has been on the record regarding the

Schiano hire save for Jimmy Haslam stating at a Cleveland Browns presser that he had nothing to do with it. Tom and I felt—and our publisher Joe McCamish agreed— that offering the Haslams the same platform we'd offered other prominent boosters was the right thing to do. They merited a public pulpit to go on the record and relate exactly what their involvement was, if any, and what their thoughts on the hire and the resulting chaos were. So their interviews, like all the other donors, are related word for word so their comments cannot be taken out of context.

I do not have any qualms in stating that I unequivocally believe that both men, father and son, genuinely love the University of Tennessee. Their generosity has been unparalleled. No one should ever question that.

But by the same token, Jimmy Haslam's own story regarding the Schiano hire reveals that of all the phones blowing up on Schiano Sunday, only his was being blown up by the people involved in the process. His people confirmed he called Diane Black that afternoon, which is the only link supporting Clay Travis's tweet about him calling lawmakers to yell at them. Schiano's agent, Jimmy Sexton, called him to help facilitate the contract that morning before the hire was leaked, and asked for his help reassuring the Board of Trustees, who were concerned about Schiano's alleged link to the Sandusky case. Haslam called Raja Jubran, who headed up the BoT, and told him how to handle those concerns. John Currie called and asked to borrow a plane to fly Schiano to Knoxville. And a few weeks earlier, they met for lunch in New York City, and John Currie asked him about Greg Schiano then.

Odd, really, that of all the interviews we conducted with people close to the program, only one donor seemed to be actively participating in the decision-making process that led John Currie to Greg Schiano. And then, too, his reaction when Currie backed UT out of the deal and his opinion of the fans and social media makes his assertion that he had nothing to do with the hire at the very least, suspect.

Does that mean that Haslam dictated the hire? No.

But it does make it difficult to accept Haslam's assertion that he wasn't part of the process at face value. Obviously, he was, just like he admitted in the same interview that he was involved in the hiring of John Currie as athletic director.

As the five o'clock hour neared on that Sunday afternoon in November of 2017, everyone who was paying attention to the Rocky Top ReVOLution was in an uproar. The fans were revolting. The local media was agitating and encouraging the fan base to keep it up. Vol Twitter broke the internet. Politicians were weighing in from the state capitol to the White House press room. The national media was intent on persecuting the fan base. The major donors were taken completely off-guard, first by the hire and then by the backlash. The Board of Trustees was scrambling as Knoxville radio was urging the fans to keep up the fight, and Chancellor Davenport was reportedly shaken by the fans' anger.

"More steam! More steam!" Tony Basilio was shouting.

At 4:58 EST, I tweeted: "Just was told by an Ohio

State source that Schiano is intimidated by fan backlash in regard to any UT hire."

The pandemonium spiked even higher as rumors that the deal was falling through began to trickle through the fan base. At 5:23 EST, I followed that first tweet up with: "Looks like the deal fell through. Schiano's 'courage' may have failed him. Again."

And finally, around 7:30 EST, Mark Schlabach from ESPN tweeted: "Tennessee has backed out of a memorandum of understanding that would have made Ohio State defensive coordinator Greg Schiano its new head coach, according to ESPN's Chris Low. Schiano and the Volunteers had reached an agreement earlier Sunday, but UT officials changed their minds after Schiano's anticipated hiring was met with sharp criticism by UT fans."

Against all odds, Vol Nation had been galvanized by the local media and spearheaded by Vol Twitter...and won. Guess Dan Wolken's PR help hadn't been all that helpful.

But that didn't settle the fan base. Not by a long shot. Victory was just a temporary reprieve. John Currie was still running the athletic department and, presumably, the coaching search. The administration had been AWOL throughout the upheaval on campus and online. Tennessee had been vilified and villainized by the national media.

But Vol Nation knew the fight was not yet over. Now, none of the fans trusted the university to do the right thing. There was a reason the hire was going to be announced at eight pm on the Sunday following

Thanksgiving. There was a reason John Currie had asked Dan Wolken to help him spin the Schiano hire. There was a reason that Tennessee mega-donors and local media were astonished by the announcement that Currie had settled on Greg Schiano.

Basically, UT's athletic director was trying to sneak Schiano in. On that particular Sunday a lot of people were on the road, returning home after the holiday. College football season was over, save for championships. Schiano would have been hired before the coaching carousel really heated up, which would have made John Currie appear proactive instead of reactive. And incredibly, he permitted the Jon Gruden rumors to continue unchecked, using that pipe dream coaching hire as a smokescreen for what he was really doing.

He was trying to pull a fast one.

What was most interesting about the University of Tennessee texts and emails that were released in response to a Freedom of Information Act request in March of 2018 is a strong thread of...contempt that was running through some of the Board of Trustee communications, along with a continued inability to comprehend the fan base's reaction.

Even *after* the Schiano debacle...even though Tennessee was getting eviscerated by the local, regional, and national media...even though there were protesters outside the UT athletic department...even though Twitter had exploded...even though there were hundreds of emails from UT alumni, donors, and boosters imploring the university not to hire Schiano, the vice-chair of the UT Board of Trustees, Raja Jubran told a large group of trustees that: "I need to also let you know how impressed I was with John Currie the past three weeks. He is doing a great job with all the vetting and due diligence."

You read that correctly. Jubran thought Currie had done a great job even though that condemned the University of Tennessee to have its lack of leadership and tone-deafness exposed in the most public, most humiliating manner possible.

But not all of the Board of Trustees was on board with Jubran's assessment. John O. Foy wrote, "What is troubling to me is that this is such an incredibly high profile and that not to have others or a search firm is troublesome. It is even more troubling to me that the members of the athletic committee have not been involved. Why have a committee if they are not involved? It is troubling also that our Athletic Director has been on the job a short period of time and to not involve the committee is not understandable. The UT football coach is a state-wide position and the politics of this is so sensitive and should be something that folks who have been around the state for years and knows some of the politics should have been involved."

Common sense. I like it.

When you think about the interviews we conducted with boosters, media, and university insiders, those stories provide even more context for Foy's censure. Everyone we spoke to was taken off-guard by the Schiano hire and the resulting backlash.

Everyone.

But...one.

Chalk one up for the masses. But more was still to come. And a new sentiment began to drift through Vol Twitter.

We are the caretakers now.

You don't appreciate the savage beauty that is Vol Twitter until you watch them taking on the entirety of the national sports media.

You also don't appreciate the dangers of living in a golden tower until the mob is at the gate. Make no mistake—when that happens, the peasants with the pitchforks *always* win. Vol Nation, in the space of six hours, destroyed Currie's plan to bring Schiano to Knoxville, and sent the athletic director into a desperate five-day scramble to save his job.

Currie needed to appease the fans with a home-run hire he'd promised them ten days earlier. What ensued was farcical for the rest of the country, but UT fans were wearing paper bags over their heads. Currie's headlong rush into career suicide was the real embarrassment in the whole fiasco.

The Tennessee athletic director proceeded to throw offers and money at coaches across the country, leaving upgraded contracts in his wake. Monday, he went after Mike Gundy at Oklahoma State, who now earns $5 million a year thanks to Currie's offer. Tuesday's coaching buffet featured Purdue first-year coach Jeff Brohm, whose subsequent raise netted him $3.3 million a year. Wednesday's humiliation included North Carolina State University coach Dave Doeren, who used an offer from UT to leverage a new five-year, $3 million contract.

Wolfpack fans had spent that day begging Tennessee to take him. Vol Twitter handled that little impediment by redirecting their campaign at the embattled coach for two hours, politely informing him he wouldn't be welcome in Knoxville.

Then the search was elevated from farce to slapstick comedy piling out of a clown car. The University of Tennessee *lost* their athletic director. He disappeared—went right off the grid. Jubran's continued concern for Currie was displayed when he texted around one o'clock that afternoon, "Have we confirmed that John is safe?"

No one knew where he was until reports started to surface that Currie was meeting with Washington State coach Mike Leach.

Vol Twitter was intrigued. Bringing the pirate to Rocky Top was a move they could get behind.

But the Leach deal disintegrated when John Currie was ordered unequivocally to return to Knoxville without moving forward on a contract or MOU. The Tennessee administration finally ended the school's mounting embarrassment. The next morning, it took eight minutes for Chancellor Dr. Beverly Davenport to relieve Currie of his duties, setting the stage for a moment of sweet vindication.

Later that day, on December 1, 2018, one of the most extraordinary press conferences in college sports history was held at the University of Tennessee. UT's Chancellor, Dr. Beverly Davenport, sat next to Phillip Fulmer who had just been named interim Athletic Director. As Coach Fulmer spoke about bringing championships back to

Tennessee, the camera lights set off a sparkling flash on his hand.

His 1998 BCS championship ring, proof of the promised land.

That flash kept my attention throughout the presser. Hearing Fulmer's familiar, calm voice soothed the edges away from my anger. And as a novelist, I couldn't help but appreciate the vindictive beauty of Coach Fulmer's story line. He'd been a giant at UT, brought down by a cabal of people inside the athletic department, allegedly with the collusion of one or two mega-donors. He'd remained loyal to the school that had wronged him, never coached elsewhere, and continued to avow his undying loyalty to UT. And then, when the ReVOLution led to the ouster of the athletic director who had purportedly served as the smirking hatchet man in his own firing nine years earlier, Phillip Fulmer had stepped over the twitching remains of John Currie's career and taken the AD chair for himself.

Sweet justice.

For a fan like me, who never got over Fulmer's farewell address nine years earlier, his return felt like a victory.

And as soon as the press conference was over, all the tumult around the University of Tennessee stopped cold.

Vol Twitter was satisfied. The athletes were reassured. The university stopped making knee-jerk decisions. Fulmer's presence had released the chaotic energy surrounding the program. Fulmer conducted a thorough but swift coaching search, hiring Jeremy Pruitt six days later.

Vol Nation had won.

The sports media, which is heavily invested in big time college football, wanted the world to believe that the ReVOLution was created by a bunch of ignorant, borderline illiterate idiots on Twitter because they didn't like the coaching hire.

But the uprising was much more than that.

The ReVOLution changed the landscape of NCAA football, when the fans of a major and storied program like Tennessee seized a portion of authority over the university and wielded it themselves. An unprecedented alliance of fans, boosters, students, alumni, former players, and local sports media had forced positive and necessary changes in the institution they loved.

A blueprint for other schools.

Forget what you might have seen on ESPN. Forget what national sports media said. Forget about the condescension and insults you might have heard.

Unless you were a part of the Rocky Top ReVOLution, you have no idea why it went down the way it did.

As we near the one-year anniversary of that crazy week at the end of November, looking back at those six days should be empowering for all UT fans. Vol Nation did something no other fan base in the country was capable of doing.

I had an appointment with my doctor in the spring.

We always end up arguing football. He's a graduate of the University of Miami and I was laughing about the 'Canes experience with Mark Richt's annual end-of-season collapse, which I'd warned him would happen after Richt returned to his alma mater.

His nurse said kind of rudely, "Well, *your* team had an awful year."

My doctor shook his head. "No, they didn't. Tennessee won the football season over *everybody*. They not only got rid of Butch Jones, but they saved their program."

Vol Nation. Still undefeated.

However, unbeknownst to the fans celebrating their victory, there was still more of the story to be told. The darkness that had surrounded their beloved football program had masked a nightmare that would be difficult for anyone to fathom.

TENNESSEE'S HIDDEN NIGHTMARE

Player Injuries and Mistreatment

THIRTEEN MONTHS.

Thirteen months was all Butch Jones had needed to destroy his previous four years of work. Thirteen months.

Thirteen months was the span between the Tennessee Volunteers being an undefeated, top ten-ranked team who'd beaten their two biggest rivals in the SEC East and were heading into College Station to play a formidable Texas A&M squad...and a 4-8 record, winless in the SEC, and the laughing stock of the football world thanks to a turnover trash can, one of Jones's inexplicable gimmicks.

Thirteen months.

Tennessee's utter collapse and subsequent plummet into the gutter wasn't expected by anyone—not the fans, not the university, not the team, and most certainly not the media. And while suspicion and distrust of Jones' ability as a coach was growing, few people outside the program had any real understanding of what was actually happening on his watch to the young men who wore

Volunteer orange and white.

Over the course of those five seasons, one disastrous problem of the Butch Jones era was glaring. Injuries. In 2016 after the Texas A&M game, twenty-five players were on the injured list. By the time Jones was fired in 2017, only fifty-five players were still able to play out of an eighty-five man roster. Throughout those seasons and particularly in 2015 and 2016, injuries had plagued the Volunteers, keeping some outstanding squads—and players—from reaching the full potential they had, on paper at least.

So was it realistic to believe that all these injuries were just some karmic retribution on Tennessee? Or was there another reason? Was there something going on in the program that contributed to the plague of injuries, the plethora of transfers, the players leaving mid-season, all the fights that were dismissed as accidents? The number of injuries and transfers and odd occurrences should have aroused my suspicions.

But even more importantly, they should have aroused someone's—anyone's—suspicions in the UT athletic department or the administration. I mentioned earlier that when there's a vacuum of leadership in an organization, something external invariably steps in to fill that vacuum. With the constant turnover and chaos surrounding both the athletic department and the administration, no one had any oversight of the football program. No one was keeping an eye on the practices of the coaching staff, and especially not what Butch Jones was doing.

During the summer of 2017, disturbing rumors began to reach fans' ears regarding the way Butch

Jones treated his staff, his players, and the strength and conditioning staff. I started to hear whispers about how many players had transferred quietly from Tennessee, and how some of them were mysteriously not able to play for other universities. So I started to poke around to see if there was anything to some of these stories.

I interviewed Marlin Lane for the first time in October of 2017.

Marlin Lane came to Knoxville as a highly recruited four-star running back from Daytona Beach, Florida. He played for the Vols from 2011-2014, spanning the stretch between the end of Derek Dooley's tenure and the early periods of Butch Jones's five-year stint. Marlin chose UT over multiple schools including Miami (FL), Florida State, and Auburn. A bruising north and south rusher with deceptive agility and the ability to unleash an incredible burst of speed had rated him as one of the nation's top running backs in the 2011 class. He made an immediate impact on the Vols, scoring two touchdowns in his first game as a true freshman and becoming the first Tennessee RB to score a touchdown in each of his first three games since Reggie Cobb did it in 1987. But when Derek Dooley was fired and Butch Jones was hired, the freshman star was uncertain if his future included any other seasons on Rocky top.

"When Coach Dooley left, I was going to transfer to Florida State," Marlin remembered. "I ended up coming back to UT because of my running back coach (Rick Graham). He told me the new coach was going to run a pro-style offense—run the Power I and all that—and that's what I wanted to do. My first meeting with Coach

Jones, he sounded like a good guy. He started off with a big brother/little brother thing so we thought he was good."

I have to admit. When I look back at the early days of Jones's tenure, what I remember is a smiling, genial man who appeared to be one hundred percent invested in turning around the University of Tennessee football program. Back then, there weren't any uncomfortable stories being related about what was going on with the football team...or its coach.

"My running back coach left (for Florida State) because he'd been told we were running a pro-style offense, then when he opened up the playbook it was all spread offense," Lane said. "Then, Coach Jones started showing himself as he really was...how he treated the players. He wasn't the guy that he'd put on the front to be. He didn't treat us like he was supposed to. He treated me okay at first, but after a while he figured I wasn't going to do things his way."

By the end of the spring semester in 2013, after being suspended from the team and missing the Orange and White game due to unsubstantiated and subsequently dropped sexual assault allegations, Lane was ready to transfer from UT.

"So after that first spring with Coach Jones, I wanted to transfer and they wouldn't let me. I talked to Tennessee State and Akron—I wanted to go to Florida State, where my running back coach had gone."

I interrupted with a question. "What do you mean they wouldn't *let* you? They can't stop you from changing schools, right? It's your education."

"They can hold your transfer papers. People don't realize we had the most transfers at UT but it was under the table because he didn't want to stop recruits," Lane replied. "When they found out I was going to transfer, Coach Jones sent coaches to pull me out of class. They told me, 'If you transfer, we'll make sure you don't play for another school.'

"They tried to blackmail me too. They said they'd tell other schools I had a bad character…about the rape accusation even though the girl took it back and said I didn't do anything. I had a minor drug charge from high school. They said they'd tell other schools that I couldn't read the playbook. Heck, I played for four years and every year the playbook was different. I knew them all." For the first time, Lane sounded a little angry. "But when I got back home, they'd talked to my momma and stepfather. They were blowing everyone's phone up—my momma, my stepdad, my dad, my brother—to get me to come back. I didn't want to go through that."

So Marlin Lane stayed at UT, and that's when the real man behind the head coach's façade was exposed. There had been a long-running rumor in the Tennessee community surrounding Jones's micro-management of the program. But the story that emerges now is much more explicit and damning than expected. In fact, the picture that emerges of the former Tennessee coach is disturbing.

"He picked on players that he knew couldn't defend themselves. Kind of tough seeing that from a coach. You can't fly off on a coach. Can't say what you want to a coach. His character—it was unreal what he would do to guys,"

Marlin said. "The assistant coaches did what they had to do because of the head coach. He'd get in coaches' faces in front of the team and threaten to fire them on the spot if they didn't do things his way. The coaches started treating players the way Coach Jones treated them. If Coach told you to do something, you were going to do it. The last time I talked to Coach Jones was my last day of college, about a former player that transferred. I kind of talked to him then. He was talking about that situation to try to get me to cover for him. But what's right is right and what's wrong is wrong. I just felt like he got rid of people the wrong way."

You have to wonder why no one talked about this, why no one protested this treatment. Marlin Lane addressed that question as well.

"When people did speak about it, they were run down," Marlin said. "You had to be mentally strong to deal with that guy. My four years in college were hell. There were times I didn't want to be here anymore. I did all I could to keep from going back home and becoming another statistic."

In hindsight, that kind of coaching culture explains the constant turnover at UT, not just among the players, but the staff as well. The picture Marlin paints of his time at UT is a devastating tapestry of micro-management, abusive player and staff treatment, and in some cases, outright negligence regarding player injuries and careers, all of which leaves particularly devastating aftereffects for not just people, but the program.

"I feel like I never reached my full potential at UT. My freshman year—I wish I could have redshirted (post

ACL/MCL injury) and played correctly—but I earned my time. I played, I performed very well, I had fun. I felt like I did what I did and my dream was coming true. Then Jones came and the conflicts started happening." Marlin's voice was low, and I could hear the regret when he said, "I didn't have the college career I wanted. I tried but I was held back from having the college career I wanted."

When we started writing this book, Tom and I decided to interview Marlin again. I felt like he was completely sincere, but his story was so alarming and so thoroughly damning of the coaching staff and athletic department that I found it difficult to believe no one had come forward and addressed what was happening. How was it possible that *nobody* knew? So, I needed to ascertain whether his story remained consistent a year later.

But I also wanted to have someone present who could perhaps put this type of story into perspective. Tom and I asked a mutual acquaintance, Dr. John Staley, to join us while we interviewed Marlin for a second time. Dr. Staley—Doc—was a former athlete whose football career was ended by injury in high school. He subsequently attended and graduated from college and med school at UT, becoming a prominent critical care/ER physician and UT booster in Knoxville. He also co-founded Team Health, a medical corporation that staffed hospital emergency rooms. Team Health grew into a Fortune 500 company, the largest medical company of its kind in the world.

If anyone could evaluate Marlin's story, we thought it would be Doc.

So after going through some of the same material we'd covered the year before—Marlin's story was unchanged, by the way—I introduced a line of questioning that I was particularly focused on. All those injuries. Year after year, watching as UT starters dropped like flies and the team went into November burning redshirts and losing to inferior opponents.

And of all the people seated at the table, I knew there was one man who shared my interest in how that plague of injuries had occurred. Doc had his own theories on what might have happened but didn't have any inkling of what had really gone on. I wanted to see what happened when he heard Marlin's story and needed his perspective as an ER physician regarding the medical side of those events.

"So, all the injuries—was that just bad luck?" I asked, starting the questioning off. "Was there a reason for them?"

"We were treated just enough so we could practice or play in a game," Marlin replied without hesitation. "Ever since 2013—that's what happened. The team was always beat up and injured and hurt because they were not getting treated."

"How many players were hurt or had ruined careers as a result of this policy?" I asked.

Marlin Lane didn't hesitate. "A lot."

"Like who?"

"Dylan Bates, Devrin Young, Antonio ("Tiny") Richardson, trying to think of… there was a lot."

"What about Jalen Hurd?"

"Jalen's shoulder gave him problems all...he was getting rehab probably more than he was sitting in meetings because his shoulder was that bad and...Marquez North, I still talk to him to this day."

Doc interjected. "Can I ask you one question there? You had a miraculous career in high school and you had some surgeries prior to coming to UT. Not many people can do what you did. Of these players that you named, did they have pre-existing high school injuries before they got to UT?"

"No," Marlin answered. "No sir. I know Marquez North didn't hurt his shoulder until he got to UT and I'll never forget—me and Marquez were standing in the middle of the field and I was talking to him and Coach Jones walked up to him and said, 'Yeah, you thought you were going to the NFL after this year. No, I don't have to stop you now you got hurt. You're mine now and I own you.'"

Shocked, I blurted, "He said what?"

"'You're mine now and I own you.'"

I honestly thought I hadn't heard him right. The odds of a football coach saying this and particularly to an African-America player had to be astronomically small. So I repeated his words. "'And I own you?'"

"Was he talking to you or Marquez?" Doc asked.

"Marquez North," Marlin replied. "So that's probably why y'all never saw Marquez North come back and play another college down because he said to me, 'Nah, I'm not gonna play for him. I'm just gonna stay here and continue getting my rehab.' Until he got well enough and he entered the draft. His freshman year was his last year of really playing after he messed his shoulder up."

I turned the questioning back to Marlin and his own injury situation. Perhaps the most damning stories revolve around player injuries, Tennessee's ongoing nightmare over the past five seasons. Lane's condemnation of the Jones regime is absolute, and the picture he paints is damning.

"Playing football is not one hundred percent healthy," Marlin said. "If you were injured, you'd hear, 'If you don't play, you're not going to play at all the rest of the season.' That's what made a lot of players force themselves to play and that led to bigger injuries.

"This time at practice—we were going to play Bama, my junior year. We were practicing without pads but we had helmets. I was running the ball and had a player come at me full speed and tackled me when he wasn't supposed to. I had a headache and the coaches said, 'Don't tell the trainer or they'll sit you.'" He paused and then added, "The team was playing Alabama...the coaches were not caring about the kids. I had a problem with concussions since high school—blood on the brain—but they didn't care."

Okay, I've been around football for a long time. I know how practice and training are conducted. I don't expect coaches to be soft-spoken and polite. But what I do expect is for the players' health and ability to play to be evaluated accurately and fairly. That has to be the top priority for any coach, not just because it's the right thing to do but because there's no way to make it through a grueling four-month SEC schedule without your top players on the field.

Football 101, right?

Particularly when it comes to concussions. With the recent awareness on playing football, concussions, and CTE (Chronic Traumatic Encephalopathy), how was it possible that a coach at an NCAA institution was that… well, frankly, *stupid?*

"Were there other players with concussion issues?"

"We got a running back. We used to call him Bender. He was from North Carolina. Good running back; he was real good. Number twenty-four. Derrell Scott. He had a concussion for about four weeks. He failed the concussion test and all that, so Coach Jones came in and told him that they felt like he was faking because no one had a concussion for that long. Coach said something about, 'I don't know what's going on but you need to practice or go take that concussion test and pass it.' Because they were saying he failed it on purpose."

"How do you fake a concussion protocol?" I asked.

"I have no idea. They were saying it because they thought he was failing the test on purpose."

"How do you fail on purpose?" Tom asked.

"It's a computer test you have to take. Because he missed the whole fall camp, he missed the whole of fall camp because he got a concussion that first week. I know how concussions feel and sometimes like now I have memory problems. Sometimes I'm in the middle of a conversation and I forget what we're talking about. Later,

Bender transferred to ECU (Eastern Carolina University).

"We were stuck in the maze—we just had to do what we had to do to get our stats up and make a career (in the NFL). I still have a torn ligament in my right foot—south Alabama—but I was still forced to play, no redshirt, no proper medical treatment. Trainer treatment was a coaching decision—you'd get a treatment that had you okay to practice."

It's difficult not to be drawn in by Marlin Lane. He's a soft-spoken, articulate young man. Doc questioned him closely, delving into practice protocols, the injury treatment process, and the chain of command. After the two-hour conversation was over, we had so much information from Marlin that we couldn't use it all. At that point, we knew we needed to talk to other players or people close to the program.

That led us to Mykelle McDaniel, who I interviewed a couple of weeks later along with his mother, Shawnte-Amoure Simmons. Mykelle was another highly touted recruit, a four-star strongside defensive end who had thirty-one offers coming out of high school—including offers from twelve of the fourteen schools in the SEC: Alabama, Florida, Georgia, Auburn, South Carolina, Mississippi State, Texas A&M, Kentucky, LSU, Missouri, Ole Miss, and Tennessee. Mykelle and Marlin did not know each other, and Marlin's full story is only being revealed now, in this book. So there was no way that these two young men somehow coordinated their stories. Marlin is in Knoxville; Mykelle is in Hutchinson, Kansas.

I spoke with Ms. Simmons before she and her son committed to an interview with me. The first thing she said struck me hard and made me feel slightly sick. "My son's father hasn't been a role model in his life. My second husband never had that bond with Mykelle either. The reason I felt comfortable sending my son to Tennessee was because Coach Jones presented himself as that father figure I always felt my son needed. I thought he was going to go to Tennessee and have that mentorship I'd always wanted for him. But I was a single mother going through his recruitment period with him, and I had no idea what to look for."

I don't think I'll ever get over hearing the tragedy in her voice. Her voice was lovely anyway, soft and low-pitched, and she spoke with such sincerity and eloquence that as soon as she finished that comment, I started to get angry because I thought I knew what was coming. I just hated it for her and for her son, who I'd not yet spoken to. The bond between them was so touching. I mean—think about it. Before she would allow me to interview her son, she had wanted to talk with me first.

I don't blame her for that. I admire her for it. She'd learned her lesson about trusting strangers with Mykelle.

As I said, I thought I knew what was coming. In actuality, I had no clue how bad that story was going to be. The next day, I interviewed Mykelle with his mother sitting in on the call.

During the pre-training camp physicals, the UT team doctors detected popping in one of Mykelle's knees. They soon diagnosed a torn meniscus—an injury I can empathize with because I've had the same injury myself—and recommended that he have surgery to correct the issue. Because he'd finished a math class late—and not because he failed it. He had a score of 26 on his ACT—Mykelle already had an academic redshirt for the 2016 season, his freshman year. So his path seemed clear. He would have the problem surgically corrected, which was a fairly minor procedure, and would redshirt that season.

But the coaches didn't agree. They were appealing the academic redshirt and thought there was a chance he could play that season. So Jones and his staff were pushing Mykelle to go ahead and play the season—with his injured knee. Of course, Mykelle, at eighteen, was anxious to start playing too. But a torn meniscus isn't an injury to be ignored. The torn meniscus in my knee had led to a total knee replacement. I couldn't imagine any responsible coach or trainer trying to get a young man to play with a torn meniscus and particularly not in the SEC.

"We had like a team advisor. You know, you go to him and just talk to him, you know what I'm saying? Just talk to him. The guy's not supposed to tell anybody what you talk about at all. I did find out later on, the more I talked to him, the more I told him, the more he was going back to coach and telling him everything," Mykelle explained. "So I got to talking to him and I was just going back and forth, getting his opinion and expressing my opinion as far as how I feel about playing on my knee right now and thinking about whether I wanna fix it or whether I want to go ahead and have the surgery. And the first day I actually tell him about it, later on that day in a team meeting, Coach Jones was...he didn't say my name, didn't mention any name at all, but he started saying that: 'If you're thinking about having surgery instead of playing, don't be a bitch. Man up and help your team out.' Didn't say any names but I'm not stupid. I clearly know who he was just talking about."

"So, after you decided to go ahead and have the surgery and that was with Knoxville Orthopedic Clinic, correct?" I asked.

"Correct."

"Okay, were the trainers, the assistant coaches, or Coach Jones pushing you to not have the surgery and to go ahead and play even though they knew the doctors had recommended it?"

"Everyone except the doctor himself," he replied. "When I approached everyone else about it, they said, 'Don't have it. There's a chance you could burn your redshirt. We need you...' And so on and so on. When I went to the doctor about it there was one thing consistently on my mind. It's my career. I need to be smart about it. So I go see the doctor and I explain to him that the coaches have not been allowing me to have my surgery for a couple of weeks now and he says, 'They can't do that. I had no idea they were doing that. It's illegal for them to do that. No one can pick and choose when you have your surgery but you.' When he told me that, and once they (the coaches) were *aware* that he told me that, that is when they permitted me to have my surgery."

Now there were all sorts of alarm bells going off in my head. Marlin Lane had also stated that the physicians at KOC were outstanding and provided great medical care, but that he had to go to them outside of the normal injury protocols with the trainers. Now, we have an eighteen-year-old freshman being told by a KOC physician that the coaching staff was making medical decisions on his behalf although that was illegal. That goes well beyond Jones and his staff micromanaging the program. If not outright abuse, that's downright negligence.

Butch Jones was trading the health and future prospects of his players for wins on Saturdays in the fall and no one at UT had stepped forward as an advocate for those young men.

Mykelle's mother put her foot down. Her son's surgery was scheduled and successful, thanks to the Knoxville Orthopedic Clinic physicians. Three weeks later, Mykelle was back on the practice field, training with the team. Because he wasn't active on the roster, he was working with the scout team. Six weeks into a fourteen week season, it would have been ridiculous to burn his redshirt. Clearly, the smart thing to do was to let him sit out the remainder of his redshirt year, and then join the active roster the following season.

On his first day back at practice, Mykelle was wearing a green no-contact jersey that the trainers had told him to wear.

"I was back on the field. I came back. In my mind, I'm one hundred percent. I still have a green jersey on but I'm still working. I'm still practicing on the scout team. I walk onto the practice field and I'm like, 'How you doing, Coach?'

"And Coach Jones says, 'I'm doing good but I'd be better if you wasn't in that green jersey.'

"I said, 'It's not me, it's the trainers that got me in it.'

"And he said, 'Yeah, you being a little bitch.' His exact words."

I have to admit that at that moment, I kind of lost my temper. What made it tough was that I was on a three-way call with Mykelle and his mother. The last thing I wanted to do was to follow my initial instincts, which would have involved cussing. So I took a moment and then asked, "Okay, so he called you a little bitch because you were wearing the no contact jersey when you first got back out on the field after your surgery, correct?"

"Yes ma'am."

"So what did you do?"

"I chuckled and said, 'Yes sir. I hope it gets better.' and I continued on with my stretches. And he walked past."

Always just a little embarrassing to realize a teenager is more mature than I am at fifty-two. But that's the kind of young man Mykelle is. Like his mother, he's articulate and extremely courteous. In this day and age, it's positively refreshing to hear an eighteen year-old just being polite. Those "yes ma'ams" told me more about his character than any amount of background research could have. These were good people, who could never have anticipated what was going to happen next.

"It's South Carolina week," Mykelle went on. "The next incident was South Carolina weekend and we come out for practice Monday and I'm pass rushing this particular day, against this person...a new starter on the o-line. He tore his meniscus before I tore mine. He had surgery before me but his body didn't heal as fast as mine.

He took his good time coming back, so he was literally just now coming back off his meniscus injury and they put him in the starting lineup and line us up to go to work. And I'm going against him and he's shooting his hand… he's heading for my face mask. He's shooting his hands and he's aiming for my throat, slapping me in my face and whatnot. I turn and Butch Jones is literally just standing right there.

"We had officials at every practice and they would throw flags and, you know, break up every fight before they happen. Literally. Every practice there would be twenty officials out every single practice. There'd be twenty officials. And he's slapping my face mask and he's doing it for so long and it gets to the point where I turn to Butch Jones and I say, 'Are you just going to sit there and watch him do this?'

"He doesn't respond to me, he just head nods. I don't know what that means but I said, 'Are you just going to sit here and watch him keep playing me dirty like that?' He just nods his head. So I go back, and I come off the ball, and at this point, I do a post move. That's a move that you don't do at practice. You're not supposed to do it against a teammate. At that point he grabs me and he throws me on the ground. Once he throws me on the ground, everyone else hops on top of me. I mean the offensive line was on the bench. They wasn't even in the game or in the play. The line's just jumping and stomping and beating me and nothing is happening. Officials just standing there, not running onto the field. Coaches standing there, not doing anything. I was cool with all the running backs, the only people jumping me were the offensive line. Running backs just standing there watching. Wide receivers just standing there watching. Everybody just stood there watching.

"I talked to a couple of people afterwards, one of the running backs that I was cool with, his name was Jeremy Lewis, he tried to hop in, but his coach cussed him out and said, 'Don't you hop in. That's your o-line. You leave them alone.' I talked to Jauan Jennings. He told me he was running a fly route. He was way down the field, he didn't even know what happened until he got all the way back. Everyone was asking, 'Where were you when it happened?' Everybody had different reasons but they all were saying it was just the offensive line when they did what they did.

"I went back and looked at it. I saw it on camera that same night, you can pull it (practice film) up on camera. I watched the offensive line just run in and jump in, I watched Jauan running the fly route, I watched the coaches just standing there, I watched the coach cuss the running back who tried to hop in to help me, I watched Butch Jones stand there, I watched the officials just stand there. The next day when I go back, everybody is in the locker room looking at it on their iPads. Everyone on the team gets it. Once Coach Jones comes in and sees everyone's on their iPads in the locker room watching it, they take the film off of the site. They take that play off of the team thing (practice video site), they took that whole play off. It's no longer there. I don't know what they did to it but it was no longer there."

When writers are conducting an interview and things like this come out, it feels almost like a double gut punch. The first response is a human reaction, visceral and raw, to what you've just heard. The second is like getting slapped across the face or punched in the jaw with adrenaline. That feeling is like leveling up right before a boss fight in a video game. You don't know exactly what's coming, but you think to yourself that now might be a good time to head to the closest save point. You recognize the feeling that you're getting close to something really big.

"So how many...when you say jumped, are you saying they physically pummeled you? They hit you?"

"Stomped, punch, beat. I was beat. By the entire offensive line. If you need me to go into names, as far as the offensive line, I could name the entire offensive line on the 2016 player roster."

"Now were they instructed to do so by the coaching staff?"

"If you ask me? I know nothing as far as they did it. I do not know nothing for a fact. If you ask me, I'm no fool. I've seen other fights happen all through the season. I've seen other scuffles happen, the referees break it up, I mean within a second, like instantly. The officials are over there and then it's over with. This particular fight, they all just sat there and watched."

Mykelle's mother was still on the line so I asked, "Ms. Simmons? You saw that entire fight on film, right?"

She'd told me that during our conversation earlier.

"Yes. I saw the fight but when I tried to go back the next day after my mom was saying you need to find some way to download it, the next day when I tried to go back it was gone."

"How long would you estimate that scuffle went on before it ended?"

"I would say about at least ten minutes?"

Although nothing should have shocked me at that point, I found myself gobsmacked yet again. "That long? *Ten minutes?*"

"Oh yeah."

Now, I cannot imagine she was running a stopwatch while she's watching that film of her son being assaulted by a group of football players. I also am aware that during a traumatic situation, witness descriptions are usually inaccurate—over- or underestimated because of the stress those witnesses are coping with. That's enough to make two minutes feel like five, or five like ten for most people. Regardless, her testimony makes it clear that the incident went on much longer than an unplanned scuffle between football players in the heat of the moment would have. Keeping in mind that coaches and officials were standing by and watching—*allowing*—this to happen indicates to me that this assault continued for some minutes before it finally ended, and that is disturbing.

"All right. So what kind of physical shape were you in after that Mykelle?"

"My adrenaline was running so I don't feel anything at the time. I get up and I grab my helmet. Coach Jones tried to go to the next play and none of the scout team players ran in to replace me. So he's like, 'Who's supposed to be here right now?' And then I'm putting my helmet back on and running back onto the field, and he grabbed me and was like, 'No, you go to the sidelines.' That's when he started cussing out the scout team players. 'Why the f*** are you out of the game? Get out there, you're not doing nothing, or I'm gonna take your scholarship!'

"So he went out there and that's when I calmed down and realized that every time I moved my shoulder, my collarbone was popping out. Literally. I showed the doctors, they took me into the training room with the doctor to take a look at it and he said I needed to go to the emergency room immediately. And they put me in an ambulance and I went to the emergency room. He said the way my collarbone was moving, it was too close to my throat. They didn't want my bone to cut anything, you understand what I'm saying? So, they took me to the emergency room immediately. They took me there, they X-ray'd it, put me inside the CAT scan, they said—they basically came up with the conclusion I got a contusion in my collarbone and they can't fix it, because if they go in and fix it, nine times out of ten they would do nothing but make it worse. Just gotta pray it falls back into place."

"Okay, at this point Ms. Simmons, you have documentation from the hospital that he went to. Was that UT medical center or somewhere else?"

"I'm not sure about what hospital it was because they never gave me documentation so everybody was telling me that Butch Jones had it, and I scheduled meetings with him. First of all, he wouldn't take a phone call with me. I scheduled two meetings with him after that, both of which he cancelled. I was able to... Coach Strip (Steve Stripling) connected me to the doctor, and I don't remember the doctor's name. I have emails, I'm gonna go back through my emails and see what I can find."

"So after that event, and I saw the text message exchange you had with Butch Jones on your Twitter feed. Did you ever discuss the incident more with him?"

Just as a note—that text exchange was just about what you'd expect from an angry eighteen-year old football player who just found out his coach was glad he got injured as the result of a fight. The language was probably cleaner than what I would have used if that had been my son on the field.

But not by much.

"Oh yeah, he called me after that and when he called me his exact words were, 'I understand you're frustrated, I understand you're upset, but there's a certain way you can't talk to the University of Tennessee head coach.'"

"Oh wow, that's just arrogant. My God."

"Yeah, he said, 'I apologize for what happened. I didn't mean for that to happen. You won't need to focus on getting any revenge from anybody. I'm gonna get the revenge for you. I'm gonna talk to them. I'm gonna get on to their coach. I'm gonna make sure they're in trouble for this. They will pay for this.'

"So, I got off the phone and thought, 'I'll sleep better tonight.' And nothing happened to the offensive line. Nothing at all. Yeah."

"Some of my teammates—Taeler Dowdy, and Jauan Jennings, and John Kelly—they told me at the end of practice that Coach told the whole team that he was glad that what happened, happened. You got to understand that at the time, the whole starting defense...I'm the only scout team player on scholarship so everybody who's on the field knows that I'm honestly there because I want to be on the field with them. So they respect me. I'm chill with them; they understand that's who I'm with. So the whole defense has no idea that this happened to me when Butch Jones said, 'I'm happy that happened because when we play South Carolina this weekend it's going to be a street fight and that's just showed me that y'all are ready for a street fight.'

"That's why I texted him and I said, 'Did you say you were happy it happened?' That's when the text messages started because right when I found out I texted him and I asked, 'Did you say you were happy it happened?'

"He was trying to say that I was twisting his words. 'I was happy that you got out there.'

"I don't understand how you can even switch that. You were happy that I got out there? Or you happy that it happened? I don't know how...I don't really understand what he's talking about on that."

"Yeah, that's not something any normal person would say."

"Yeah, not at all. So, while I'm in the emergency room—I'm in the hospital when the defense found out. That's when Derek Barnett, Corey Vereen, Kahlil McKenzie, Jonathon Kongbo—all of them, the whole defensive line—that's when they went to the offensive line in the locker room and basically there was a fight in the locker room about what happened. A little scuffle, not really a fight because the offensive line wouldn't fight back. They were like, 'We don't wanna fight, we don't wanna fight, we didn't mean for it to happen.'"

As soon as I heard that, my mind instantly flashed back to the 2017 season when Shy Tuttle had his orbital bone broken and Butch Jones had claimed in a press conference that he'd fallen on a helmet. Obviously, fights on and off the practice field were a pretty standard event though—something these players were accustomed to under this coaching staff. Here again—I've been around football for a long time. I know how frequently tempers flare up on the field, both during practice and during games. But something like this?

How often was this type of thing going on? And how out of line was that with other teams?

Preferred walk-on Taeler Dowdy was one of the players that Mykelle had mentioned in regard to the incident. I spoke with him a week later.

"Okay, so you witnessed the fight that ended up breaking Mykelle's collarbone, right?"

"Yes, I was actually in the locker room with him after it."

"Okay, why don't you tell me about what went down as far as you could tell with that whole thing?"

"I won't say I saw the whole thing but I definitely heard from everybody, because everybody was talking about it. I think it was a play, and it's funny because the coaches, like, I was a practice player at the time and, Mykelle, he was a scout player too. And they (the coaches) would like for real yell at us if we would beat the first stringers, like if we, I guess, went too hard and we actually beat them they would get mad. And Mykelle, he would just always beat the o-linemen and I guess they just all get mad and they jumped him. When he came into the locker room, it was just him when he came into the locker room, and I had to help him take his shoulder pads off and stuff. And then like five minutes of him being in pain, the trainers finally came. I don't know, I just felt like they definitely dealt with that wrong. And then after that practice, Coach Jones says, 'Good job to the offensive linemen for like sticking together and having each other's backs' or something."

"What were other players saying in the locker room about what happened? After it happened?"

"Well, a lot of the defensive players were mad and, I mean, the linemen, them and Mykelle kinda like— they just didn't like Mykelle because he would do good. He would do good against them at practice so they were gloating about that. I don't feel like they felt bad that they did what they did."

"Did anybody on the coaching staff, strength coach, GAs, other players, did anybody step forward and say what they did was wrong?"

"Not that I heard of honestly because that wasn't the only fight. I mean, there were fights after that and I believe that because of that situation went so wrong there was more after that...*because* of that. There wasn't a punishment for that or something."

So, let's take a minute to assimilate what's been said. Another player has just corroborated Mykelle's story. Keep in mind, too, that Mykelle's account dovetails with what Marlin Lane had said earlier—not only about injuries and how the coaches demanded their players continue to play, but also about how Butch Jones used players against their teammates, setting some guys up as almost a gang in order to enforce his rules and expectations upon the others.

"While you're playing, if you don't perform to the way he wants you to perform, or basically carry a jug of water or do this and do all that, he was basically saying, 'You're not performing up to your abilities so I'm going to give you a year probation on your scholarship. If you don't perform or do what you came here to do that's...you're done.'" Marlin had said two weeks earlier. "And what kind of had me up in the air with the last interview I did, which I did not with you guys, but with some... I can't even remember, who... I think it was SB Nation, I'm not sure but they quoted something that I said in the wrong—"

"Yeah, I remember that."

"It almost kind of messed my career up with jobs or...and everything else. But by me, you know, just knowing certain people that they gave me a chance at my job now. By them (SB Nation article) saying he had me threaten kids' lives, which I never did. I never said that. What I said was he would use me, because of my background, where I come from, my environment. On player staff meeting one day which is—we sit at a table like this of probably fourteen players that pretty much can have a voice to other players—and we were sitting in his office conference room and he literally told me, 'I'm going to tell you why I got you on player staff because you got street in you and so you could go up to certain players and say this to certain players and they won't react to you because of...' Basically he was saying where I was from, you know, and I kinda laughed it off but at the same time I'm like...where is that going? Even Justin Worley, like they all... 'Why would he say that?'"

"When I hear you talk or watch the way you are, I don't instantly think street, am I wrong here? I mean you're a very well-spoken young man, how could anybody get street off that?" I said.

"That's what...'The reason why I'm in here is because you want me to go to certain players and tell them that if they don't act right, you're gonna kick them off the team.'"

So now, all the pieces are starting to fall together. I'm getting a clear picture of what had happened to those earlier teams, those earlier players. I understand better what the environment must been like, and why those squads that looked so good on paper didn't live up to their potential. I can see why so many injuries decimated the Volunteers, and why so many players transferred. I have three players on the record now: Marlin Lane, who was gone before Mykelle McDaniel and Taeler Dowdy arrived. I have a parent on the record. And thanks to Ms. Simmons, I have documentation of what happened between her, on her son's behalf, and the university.

As I write this now, I have a strong hunch that these stories are just the tip of the iceberg. Too many other players have been named by these three. And I know that for me, this story is just beginning. There are months of research ahead of me as I track down other players, staff members and former coaches, trainers and physicians and university officials.

And obviously, the person I want to talk to the most is Butch Jones. I would be shocked if he wasn't restricted by a tight non-disclosure agreement after his termination from the University of Tennessee. I'd assume almost every high-profile coach in the country is. That being said, he should be given the opportunity to discuss these claims on the record and I'd be more than happy to provide him that platform.

But I think it's essential to understand the following as the foundation of what we've been discussing: a football coach is in a position of near-absolute authority over the players on his team. A coach must administer that authority in such a way as to not needlessly endanger a player's safety, or to negatively impact their prospects. Jones was responsible for his players' welfare on multiple levels, whether they were superstars or on the scout team. Regardless of how you look at these stories—and this is just a fraction of what I was told by these interview subjects—at the end of the day, any coach that jeopardizes the players on his team must be held accountable for his actions.

That's why the Maryland decision to retain head coach DJ Durkin after the investigation into the death of player Jordan McNair due to heat stroke caused such a backlash among students, media, and fans. The investigators had censured the coaching practices that led to these same kinds of repercussions on the Maryland football team, citing a culture where players were afraid to speak out, a athletic department that was deeply dysfunctional, a strength and conditioning program the university failed to supervise, and an overall lack of oversight warding the players' health, safety, and well-being.

Being suspended for a few games isn't true accountability. That's a slap on the wrist. The University of Maryland had no option but to terminate Durkin the day after they had reinstated him as head football coach.

And let's be honest—the similarities between Maryland under Durkin and Tennessee under Jones are striking. Considering the type of injury Mykelle McDaniel received, the two programs were closer than anyone, including me, would ever have guessed.

After I wrote this chapter, I sat back and thought for a few minutes about what I'd learned. When I first heard Marlin and Mykelle and Taeler tell their stories, I was kicking myself for not knowing what was happening to them even though I live hundreds of miles away. Like I should have possessed some sort of insight superpower. Then, I felt disturbed that Vol Nation revolted against UT because we were mad that the university was ignoring what we, the fans, demanded and expected from them when it came to hiring a football coach.

Coaches. The highest-paid, most-visible state employees with their multi-million dollar contracts subsidized by taxpayer dollars. And as I thought the above sentence, something clicked in my head.

The fan ReVOLution wasn't just about winning football games after all. Without the uprising, none of these stories—or the ones we'll pursue after this book is finished—might ever have come to light.

That's how important it is for fans to hold their universities accountable for their decisions. Not just to win games, although that's a big part of it. We must require them to discharge their responsibilities toward all students. If colleges don't adequately safeguard their students, then it's everyone's absolute duty to hold them accountable for it, whether in Baltimore or Waco, East Lansing or Knoxville.

We really are the caretakers now.

WE ARE THE
CARETAKERS NOW

THE WORD "ReVOLution" has a special meaning to Americans. The word conjures up images of the Founding Fathers, of the resistance to taxation without representation, and a firm commitment to liberty. In particular, Tennesseans respond instantly to such a word. There's a reason the University of Tennessee chose the "Volunteers" for its nickname, and why the state of Tennessee is called the Volunteer State. When America forth a call to action, the sons and daughters of Tennessee are and have always been first in line.

Always.

The origins of Tennessee being nicknamed the Volunteer state are murky—and disputed. Legend has it that the term "Volunteer State" began with Andrew Jackson's men in the War of 1812, when he led 1500 Tennesseans to decimate the British in the Battle of New Orleans in 1814. Historians can pinpoint how the nickname stuck, though. The Tennessee Volunteer really began when iconic Tennessee legend Davy Crockett wasn't re-elected to the House of Representatives. At his leave-taking speech to his constituency, Crockett finished with, "You may all go to Hell, and I will go to Texas!"

And he did, dying for the promise of what would

become Texas, at the Alamo in 1836.

So when the Mexican-American war began in 1846, the US government asked each state to raise 2,600 men to serve in the army. Within a week of the call going out, over 30,000 Tennesseans showed up to fight—all volunteers. The first Volunteers, fulfilling the promise that Davy Crockett had exemplified.

So perhaps it's unsurprising that we call what happened in those six crazy days in November of 2017 the Vol ReVOLution. Once again, Tennessee is leading the way. In a country where everyone profits from the marquee players in college football except the players themselves, what other fan base was going to head up the charge for accountability and input into the decisions that affect the schools they subsidize? Who but the people of Tennessee, whose everyday existence is conducted in the spirit of the Volunteers, were going to step up, put their feet down in a spontaneous and unplanned outpouring of unity and absolute defiance, and say *No, we are no longer going to blindly accept decisions that cheapen who and what we are.*

No one would. Not unless they were a Volunteer.

In the year since the Vol ReVOLution, the Tennessee fan base has been vindicated in so many ways. When Ohio State University head football coach Urban Meyer was suspended for three games because of his complicity in enabling alleged domestic violence of one of his assistants, the school did not name Greg Schiano the interim head coach—despite the fact that he was considered Meyer's second-in-command on his staff. The university, athletic director, and coach who so vilified the UT fan base for not accepting their "thoroughly vetted" assistant coach in Knoxville turned right around and rejected him in Columbus as well.

Members of the national sports media who colluded with former UT athletic director John Currie have undergone immense scrutiny for their role in the debacle, and several have been decidedly conciliatory to the fan base in the months since. Once the FOIA documents were released by UT, the scope of the problem was exposed and the proof easily available that the fan base's suspicions and fears were justified.

In Knoxville, things are very different. The Vol ReVOLution resulted in sweeping personnel changes from the Board of Trustees to the UT president to the chancellor to the athletic director to the football coach—a total reset of the Tennessee system, compelled by the atmosphere of strong scrutiny from fans and citizens alike.

As for the football program, a serious culture change is underway. New head coach Jeremy Pruitt is installing a mindset that hearkens back to the glory days of the mid- and late-nineties under the supervision of new athletic director Phillip Fulmer, who was vindicated thoroughly by being swept into power in place of a man who'd been part of the conspiracy to remove him nine years earlier.

For the first time in a long time, someone in the UT administration—the new athletic director Phillip Fulmer—is taking accountability for what happens in the athletic programs on his watch. No way that abusive practices can go on under that world-wise and shrewd regard Fulmer has shown for the past decade.

As I write this, it's the morning after the Tennessee Volunteers upset the twenty-first ranked Auburn Tigers in Jordan-Hare Stadium. The Vols, a 14.5 point underdog heading into the game, took the elements that had started to come together in Athens against Georgia two weeks before, and brought Jeremy Pruitt his signature win in only the sixth game of his head coaching career. The victory stopped an eleven game losing skid in the SEC, dating back to the end of the 2016 football season and was the first win over the Tigers since 1998.

It's too soon to say if Jeremy Pruitt is the coach who'll lead Vol Nation back to the promised land, but in the press conference after the Georgia game Vols fans witnessed their new coach choking back tears as he discussed what he'd seen from his players—an event that made most fans feel he was a step in the right direction. That feeling was confirmed with the subsequent win, turning a Saturday that had begun with such ambivalence into a sense of confidence that the Vols' future course had been laboriously turned from over a decade's worth of disaster into a future that looked much brighter and a lot more familiar to Tennessee fans who'd grown to adulthood basking in the reflected glory of a program that was a source of pride to the state.

After all, Jeremy Pruitt is legitimately Phillip Fulmer's hand-picked successor, delayed by nine years, three head coaches, over $24 million in buyouts, and a 57-56 record. In a sense, Tennessee had come full circle and had rounded the last turn before the Volunteers' inevitable and welcome ascent on the path back to greatness.

And why not? On that beautiful Saturday afternoon

on the plains of Alabama, Tennessee faithful were rewarded with the first validation of what *they*—not the football players or coaches—had accomplished. That first seminal victory of the Jeremy Pruitt era at UT had only taken six games to attain and announced what all of the sports world would be forced to admit.

Tennessee fans were right in refusing to meekly swallow yet another attempted hire of a mediocre coach, one whose track record and reputation was patently unworthy to be associated with the University of Tennessee and its fan base.

Tennessee fans were right in forcing the ouster of an athletic director whose behavior during the coaching search had been so patently dishonest and embarrassing to the University of Tennessee and its fan base.

Tennessee fans were right in standing up to the condescension of the majority of the national sports media, whose opinions were based upon the type of intellectual laziness that led to the propagation of bigoted stereotypes that were insulting to the University of Tennessee and its fan base.

Tennessee fans were right in their belief that their insight and opinions should carry more weight than the agendas of a sifted few in and around the athletic department that ultimately resulted in the near-destruction of the legacy of the University of Tennessee and its fan base.

Tennessee fans were *right*.

No one knows if it's possible for any fan base to accomplish what Vol Nation did during the Vol

ReVOLution. Those six days in November of 2017 were unprecedented, yes. But they also created a precedent, a blueprint that other fans from other schools can look at and think, "We can do that too."

More importantly, perhaps, is the fact that other universities now know it is entirely possible for their fans to revolt against them as well. In the current atmosphere of collegiate sports, with scandal after scandal rocking the foundations of traditional athletics powerhouses, the Vol ReVOLution blueprint can be used for so much more than affecting the hiring of a coach.

Imagine what would happen, for example, if fan bases across the country united to force the NCAA to implement changes that would benefit all athletes and all schools. Imagine what good could be accomplished if the NCAA was forced to penalize programs with gross mishandling of power—like forcing Baylor University or Michigan State University to make reparations for the sexual assault scandals both universities ignored and then tried to cover up? Or compelling North Carolina to pay a significant penalty for the fake classes it created to keep their athletes eligible?

Or establishing severe penalties upon any football program with a culture that encourages an environment of abuse or neglect toward the athletes?

What if the fan bases of America insisted that the NCAA actually *govern* university athletics programs, enforce penalties upon guilty universities uniformly, and focus upon the real issues facing college sports in this day and age instead of whether a recruit's parents paid for breakfast on an official visit?

Pipe dreams? Once, perhaps, but not anymore. The Vol ReVOLution has changed everything because the tens of millions of college fans in this country have been shown that yes, they do have power if they choose to exercise it.

More importantly, the universities now know this too. The last thing any major powerhouse program wants some Sunday in November is to face an uprising like UT did on November 26, 2017.

And yet, I'm not sure such a perfect storm of events and personalities could ever have been orchestrated anywhere other than Tennessee. At least, not initially. Even if other uprisings occur at other schools, they'll be the result of organization and a conscious effort to duplicate what Tennessee fans did spontaneously and simultaneously. There may be other ReVOLutions, but they'll be planned and coordinated.

The ReVOLution was created and fueled by the people of a state that's been renowned for its volunteer spirit for two hundred years. The ReVOLution was conspicuously free of leaders. Instead, as they've done for centuries, the people who love Tennessee came together in spontaneous unity as a response to a call for action and overwhelmed their enemies with the sheer volume of those who showed up prepared to fight for what they believed in. In the process, they toppled an oligarchy, deposed dictators, compelled a political shift, and took back for themselves something no one ever thought they had.

Power.

Only Volunteers could have pulled that off.

After the Auburn victory, I ran across a Tweet from Bleacher Report journalist Barrett Sallee, who was one of the few in the national sports media who'd sided with the ReVOLution on Schiano Sunday—a rare voice of understanding and approval in what was arguably UT's darkest hour. He said:

"Greg Schiano would be a great fit for Tennessee, they said.

"Jeremy Pruitt can't handle this, and Tennessee would have been in great hands with Greg Schiano, they said.

"They were wrong then. They are wrong now."

Barrett Sallee always understood why the Vol ReVOLution happened and why it was so important. What he saw and almost none of his peers did was that the empowerment of a fan base like Tennessee's would change more than just a coaching hire or a school's culture. He understood that empowered fans could potentially change the way college sports are run not just at Tennessee, but at every university in the country.

When I interviewed UT fans about the ReVOLution, I also sent out a few interviews to fans from other schools and some media contacts I had who were covering other SEC schools. One of those sports guys was Michael Rose, formerly of the Thom Abraham show and now the co-host of the Smarks Pod show out of Huntsville, Alabama.

Bless his heart: he's a Vols fan born and bred, and he's trapped in Alabama dealing with Tide fans.

At any rate, Michael was one of the guys I was

feverishly DMing with during the ReVOLution. Just a great guy to talk to. I asked him a different set of questions from everyone else—this was early in my research process, when I had planned to write an entirely different book—and something about that interview kept niggling at me. So I'd kept it on my desk, hoping that whatever was making me fixate on that interview would hurry up and let me know why it was so darn important. Today, futzing with this concluding chapter, I picked it up and read it again. My five hundredth re-read of that interview proceeded without interruption until I got about a third of the way through. Beginning with that question, here's what was said.

CELINA: What did you think about the way the national media was covering the uprising?

MICHAEL: Now this is something I'm glad I received after the info was put out with the text messages with Currie/Wolken. This is one situation that showed why local media is better than the national media. As Bruce Lee said, "I do not fear the man who has practiced 10,000 kicks one time; I fear the man who has practiced one kick 10,000 times."

The man that practiced that one kick is the local media. They are there every day. National media is only there if you are good or in trouble, and UT was not good last year. First time ever 0-8 in the SEC. The national media try to use their connections to sway people and get insider access but the local media is where you should be going for your news. I am so thankful for Twitter. I can follow all my local Vols media people and get their thoughts on what is happening around UT.

The national media weren't there to tell a story. They were creating one. Let me ask you—after the announcement of Jeremy Pruitt as head football coach, how much has the national media talked about the Vols?

Good question.

CELINA: As a member of the sports media not working/covering UT sports, what was your assessment of how the university handled the crisis?

MICHAEL: One word—shitshow.

CELINA: Take me through your Schiano Sunday.

MICHAEL: Once Wolken tweeted that news break, all hell broke loose and no Vols fan was having it. Bama fans tried to ask me, "Why are you so against it?" That was the day I logged the most minutes on Twitter, because once I saw "UT backtracking Schiano hire", two words came to mind that are now a common phrase for Vols fans: more steam! And that steam came through everyone. Seeing all the local media, along with fans, unite and say "Hell, no!" was the greatest thing.

Vol Twitter does a whole lot of in-fighting because we had Butch supporters/haters, protected accounts because you don't want to hear someone else, etc etc. That day, though, was the only time Vol Twitter was united and it was something amazing.

CELINA: So what were Bama fans thinking down in your neck of the woods? Did they think the fans had made UT a laughing stock? Or did they think Currie and UT had done that themselves?

MICHAEL: Bama fans always make fun of UT

fans, but during this time they were more sympathetic. They weren't blaming Vols fans. Bama fans want UT to be good like they want Auburn to be good. That way when you beat your rival, it's that much sweeter. Besides, let's see what happens when Nick Saban retires and who Bama gets and how their fans act.

CELINA: How big of an impact was the announcement that Fulmer was the new AD?

MICHAEL: *He is one of us. You see most Vol profiles now and they say, "We are the caretakers now." That is why Fulmer was the best choice to be AD.*

Michael's interview had sat on my desk for over six months. I loved what he'd said but hadn't figured out the best way to use it...until today. Today, everything clicked for me and it was because of Michael. His answers weren't long—there were a few fans who sent me novellas for their answers—but his unique point of view made those answers sing. Here's a Tennessee guy, born and bred, working in sports media in Alabama. Michael was both an observer and a participant in the ReVOLution; he knew what was driving UT fans and what Bama fans were reacting to; he'd analyzed the media's reaction, both nationally and locally, and he had summed up everything that was really important with that one, last response.

He is one of us. You see most Vol profiles now and they say, "We are the caretakers now." That is why Fulmer was the best choice to be AD.

Regardless of how the rest of the world views the ReVOLution, the usually churning masses of the University of Tennessee fan base have settled back into their customary volatility. The squabbling is just as intense as always. The NegaVols are at war with the sheep—anyone who displays optimism regarding any UT sports team is a sheep and anyone who doubts is a NegaVol—in a never-ending sequence of escalating then ebbing friction. The Knoxville media has settled back into its normal battle for information.

But something is different about the Tennessee fan not even a year beyond Schiano Sunday. There's something changed about the way Vols fans hold themselves, a certain glint in the eye that can shift swiftly from humor to forbiddance. Those eyes are fixed upon the university, monitoring closely what happens there. While the culture at Tennessee seems to be shifting and everyone is currently walking the same path, there's a definite sense that the fan base is still meticulously sensitive to what's happening at UT.

Leadership. Oversight. Accountability.

All three words have popped up in this story over and over again. The University of Tennessee didn't have constant leadership over the past decade and a half. As a result, there was no oversight on the part of the athletic department over the football program, and therefore no one stepped up and claimed accountability for the disasters that took place there. By Butch Jones's last season at UT, his absolute dictatorship led the Volunteers into uncharted and unexpectedly dark waters. And when those waters threatened to drown the entire athletic department, the fan base stepped forward. The insistence upon doing things the right way led to the ReVOLution, and the ReVOLution led to UT hitting the reset button.

With a clean sweep of the chain of command from the football staff on up, Tennessee is beginning to right the ship. Now there is additional oversight over all these processes as well.

The fans and media trust Coach Fulmer to steer the athletic department ship back into Tennessee's familiar waters.

Because he is one of us, and we are the caretakers now.

In Knoxville throughout this transitionary year of 2018, things are once again calm...but they'll never be the same. The new leadership has settled into their offices, but they cannot keep from being aware that always...always... the eyes of Vol Nation are on them. Not in a censorious way but warily. Protectively. On Rocky Top, it's like hundreds of thousands of people are standing completely still, focused upon the same sight, and together, they proclaim the truths they learned from the ReVOLution in a single voice that splinters the darkness threatening to engulf them.

We will not fail this university or its students. That's not UT kowtowing to the masses. That's UT's recognition, finally, that the core of the connection between this school and its fans, students, alumni, boosters, athletes, former athletes, and local media isn't confrontational. That's the Tennessee family's understanding that we cannot and will not leave one of our own behind anymore. That's the Volunteer spirit, and we will no longer desert our own to straggle along behind us, limping and battered. Instead, we will go back to lend our strength to our own much-wronged family. We will bear their weight until they no longer need our help. Those who are not part of the crazy, volatile, unpredictable family that gathers around the University of Tennessee cannot possibly understand what caused the ReVOLution.

They probably think this is just about football, and that the loudmouth rubes have hurt the university. Nothing could be further from the truth. The ReVOLution didn't hurt the University of Tennessee.

The ReVOLution *saved* Tennessee.

We are Vol Nation. We will not forget, and we will not fail. We learned how much power our raw determination has won for us. We will not cede that power to anyone in the future. The University of Tennessee is our school, part of our family. Our family needs to be nurtured by our own—by the men and women who have always loved Rocky Top, who have known its secrets and where the bones are buried.

Vol Nation is a partnership, an alliance that has surpassed any outdated paranoia about the fans' "proper place". We are the 102,455.

Together we are the Volunteers and the Lady Vols.

Together we are a proud, storied athletic powerhouse in the toughest conference of the NCAA.

Together, we are building Tennessee's legacy as an institute of higher learning where every student is a valuable asset to the school and not a disposable commodity.

Together we are moving forward as a trailblazing university, bearing our torch to shine a light on the shadowy edges of our national culture upon issues of equality and diversity.

Together, we stand side by side in our thousands… in our millions, globally. We have united to preserve the mission and heritage of the University of Tennessee as we work to better our society and our world. We are proud to stand shoulder to shoulder, because in Vol Nation's darkest hour, our unity saved us from the vultures circling us as if we were already dead. We are linking our purpose, hand to hand, acknowledging that our Tennessee family was not whole a year ago and hadn't been for a while

But look at us now.

Together, we are Vol Nation. We remembered our heritage on November 26, 2017. We remembered our purpose. We remembered our mission. We remembered our obligations on December 1, 2017. We had forgotten that the University of Tennessee is a family—a family of Volunteers and the state is our campus. No matter where we reside our hearts live on in Tennessee.

During our darkest hour, we needed someone to light our way. So when Phillip Fulmer stepped up as the Torchbearer to show us our path, our anger and fear calmed.

Why, you ask?

Because we are the caretakers now—we! The sons and daughters of Tennessee—and he, Phillip Fulmer, is one of us.

The sons and daughters of Tennessee are home now, to lead our younger brothers and sisters as we once were led by our elders. Pat Summitt—she was one of us. Phillip

Fulmer—he is one of us. Randy Boyd, Wayne Davis—all the leaders on our campus—they are one with us. Those who we bring to UT who embrace our culture, who treat our student-athletes or teach them. Rick Barnes—he is one of us. Joe Johnson and Doug Dickey and Johnny Majors—they are each one of us as well.

We are Tennessee, and we are the caretakers now. So either stand with us?

Or get out of our way.

AFTERWORD

by Dr. John Staley, Jr. M.D.

WHEN CELINA and Tom asked me to hear Marlin Lane's story, as a physician and UT donor, I was surprised by what I learned. I found Marlin to be a refreshing, enlightened young man who was frank about his experiences at Tennessee. Now he-is trying to establish himself in the business world. Like many young adults right out of college, he wants to be successful and support himself and his family.

I could identify with his struggles to make ends meet. When I graduated from the University of Tennessee Medical School, I had already undergone two major abdominal surgeries. At twenty-nine years of age, I was struggling.

But there were several big differences between Marlin and me. I had a medical degree, I received excellent medical care, and I had a support system I could lean on as I started my residency. My dream to pursue a career in emergency medicine would come true.

Marlin's dream to play professional football would not.

I was astounded to hear about the sheer number

of UT players who spent time daily in rehab, nursing injuries. The coaching staff demanded that athletes force themselves to play while hurt, using playing time as a threat. That turned minor injuries into major ones, leading to the end of the season breakdowns Tennessee squads suffered under Butch Jones. That's why many are now sitting at home, working menial jobs with unresolved physical issues, instead of playing in the NFL.

Marlin described how he has just two courses remaining to graduate from UT. But Marlin has two children to support, while dealing with lingering physical ailments from giving his all for Tennessee.

What I couldn't understand was how it was possible that any UT athlete would be left in that condition after school. The UT football program's team physicians are the Knoxville Orthopedic Clinic. Personally, I have experienced five major orthopedic surgeries—knees, hips, and wrist—all performed by KOC. All of my operations resulted in successful outcomes and with appropriate rehabilitation I'm living a normal life. I find it difficult to believe that any physician, and especially those at KOC, would have left any athlete's injuries untreated.

For some reason, Marlin didn't receive complete or proper medical attention while a student-athlete at UT, and he's not the only former player in that situation, as young Mykelle McDaniel and the stories of dozens of other players prove.

These stories stirred deep emotions in me, including disturbing questions about player health and safety issues and how they could have ultimately affected game outcomes during the period from 2009 to 2017. It's obvious the athletic department suffered from a lack of leadership while the university showed no oversight over what was happening in the football program. Given insight from Marlin and several other players, I finally found the answer to the question that has puzzled us all for almost a decade; why did the University of Tennessee football team have so many injuries? Tennessee's ineptitude forced our student-athletes to pay a steep price.

An NCAA five-year study released in 2015 stated that an average of 8.1% of a football team's roster was injured for every 1000 exposures—a combination of practice and games each season. At times over the past decade, Tennessee had 25-30% of its entire player roster unable to play. Think about the 2016 double-overtime Texas A&M game, in a year where Tennessee led the nation in missed starts with fifty-two. That game on Kyle Field was the turning point of the 2016 season. You can't line up and win if you don't have enough healthy players.

From a personal standpoint, I empathized with Marlin, but I felt sickened upon hearing a premier athlete left my alma mater in such poor physical condition. Today, Marlin has a distorted foot because of a blown and torn ligament resulting from an injury in the game against South Alabama in 2013.

Marlin's perseverance, resilience, and pride despite all of these setbacks inspired me. At one time he had the physical talent, drive and the ambition for a promising NFL career. I'm certain Marlin will find a way to succeed, and I want to help him, and Mykelle, and all the student athletes who may have suffered the same fate.

Legendary UT Coach Pat Summitt, who was my inspiration for many years, once said, "Leadership is really a form of temporary authority that others grant you and they only follow you if they find you consistently credible." We've seen ten years of bad leadership decisions at the University of Tennessee. So in 2017, Vol Nation smelled another bad decision coming and rose up against the university, particularly on social media. Social media is our society's most direct and immediate form of communication. Online, people are not always held accountable for their actions.

However, a state university *must* be held responsible for what it does because of the sheer number of people it affects.

What I found compelling about the ReVOLution is that on Schiano Sunday, Tennessee fans found a unified voice and compelled the university to reject a hire the fans felt was inadequate. Simply put, after ten years of bad choices and losing results, the Vol Nation said enough was enough. The "masses" knew UT leadership was failing from the top down.

As Albert Einstein famously said, "The definition of insanity is doing the same thing over and over again and expecting a different result."

After the ReVOLution on November 26th, the University of Tennessee began replacing their top administrators. Within the year, they overhauled their entire chain of command. Now, under the guidance of the people's choice for athletic director, Phillip Fulmer, Tennessee has started the daunting task of rebuilding the culture around what just twenty years ago was one of the most prestigious athletic programs in the country.

As we all know, leadership determines the success of any organization, business, or university. We've had strong leadership in the past at the University of Tennessee. The last such period was when Coach Doug Dickey was the athletic director, and Dr. Joe Johnson was president. Not only did we win on the field, but we were also doing the appropriate things to take care of players when they weren't performing, as well. We seem to be getting back to that now with Phillip Fulmer overseeing the athletic department, and Jeremy Pruitt as head football coach. They are invested in doing things the right way and providing both the oversight and accountability that was lacking.

Student-athletes deserve to have a proper education and to be healthy when they graduate or leave the University of Tennessee. I'm determined to help our student-athletes and future players when their careers at the University of Tennessee come to an end. These Vols for Life deserve our support. All of us want to ensure that things are done in an appropriate manner, particularly for these student-athletes who are our gladiators. We all want them to go into the world healthy, educated, and prepared for whatever their adult lives bring them. Some people have called me an agent of change, and now I'm going to take the initiative to help these young men.

As one of the co-founders at Team Health, we created a leadership evaluation system using scorecards that gave us the opportunity to evaluate our performance each month. In my previous role as one of the Presidents of Operations, some people called me an agent of change.

Now, I'm going to take the initiative to help these young men and bring about positive changes to the Tennessee community. Tom, Celina, this book's publisher Joe McCamish, and I are working on a scorecard system everyone can use to evaluate a university's actions regarding academic, athletic, career, and health issues. This system will empower fans, students, and citizens to hold every university accountable for its decisions. Then, we will develop a foundation to support the UT student-athletes injured or otherwise adversely affected during this dark period from 2009 to 2017, when for whatever reason, they were never given the proper physician's care.

I'm taking steps to start this foundation now. We want this foundation to be a recruiting tool for Jeremy Pruitt, Rick Barnes, Holly Warlick, and our other coaches. We want our coaches and athletic director to be able to approach the moms and dads and families and be able to say: "When you come to the University of Tennessee, you're not only going to get a great education, but you will achieve your dreams of playing to the best of your ability. And if something unfortunate should happen along the way, we're going to have a support system to help you."

I'm not sure there are any other programs in the country can give a young athlete all these options.

On my birthday, October 24th, I attended an event honoring one of my co-founders at Team Health. I didn't realize I would have another epiphany as the result of the ceremony—just like I had after talking with Marlin Lane. The event was held at a Philadelphia, Pennsylvania Boys Club where I and a room of adults listened spellbound to two teenaged girls sharing their success story, 'Building Bridges and Improving Lives.' The Building Bridges Initiative is a movement to improve the bonds between youth and their communities.

If you think about it, improving the life of someone else is what we do as physicians. As ER doctors, we never ask for any money, never check the financial background of patients before we treat them.

People don't care how much you know until they know how much you care.

So, this foundation is going to create bridge builders, and we're not going to give up on these student-athletes. We will harness their competitive natures and give them every opportunity to be our future bridge builders. We're going to help this foundation raise money so our student-athletes can have the opportunity to change their lives, to make a difference in the adult world, and to nurture their entrepreneurial objectives so they can be productive role models long after they leave the university.

The Vol ReVOLution taught us that the fans do have a powerful voice. They demanded and took control of a situation rendered chaotic by poor leadership. The common man...the masses...stepped forward and said with one voice, "We are the caretakers now."

That statement was true. We *are* the caretakers now.

As we build bridges for our student-athletes' continued success in life, it is our responsibility to continue to be the caretakers of past, current, and future

Tennessee Volunteers. After any ReVOLution comes recovery, and healing, and a new path toward success. That's the bridge the University of Tennessee has started to erect. We, the members of Vol Nation, have a responsibility to help the university bridge the divide not only between our student-athletes and their futures, but between Tennessee and us.

That mission begins now.

BIBLIOGRAPHY

Bebb, Russ, "The Big Orange," Strode Publishers, Fifth Printing, 1981.

Bebb, Russ, "Vols: Three Decades of Big Orange Football," Champaign, Illinois 1964-93," Sagamore Publishing, 1994.

Epps, Darren, "Orange Crushed," Lookout Mountain, Tennessee, Jefferson Pres, 2006.

Fulmer, Phillip, "A Perfect Season," Nashville, Tennessee: Rutledge Hill Press, 1999.

Fulmer, Phillip, and Gerald Sentell, "Legacy of Winning: It Doesn't All Happen on Game Day, " Knoxville, Tennessee: Pressmark International, 1997.

Gilbert, Robert W, "Neyland: The Gridiron General," Savannah, Georgia, Golden Gate Publishing Company, 1990.

Glier, Ray, and Phillip Fulmer, "What It Means to be a Volunteer," Chicago: Triumph Books, 2008.

Gossett, Ward, "Volunteers Handbook: Stories, Stats and Stuff about Tennessee Football." Wichita, Kansas: The Wichita Eagle and Beacon Publishing Company, 1996.

Greeson, Jay, and Stephen Hargis, "Game of My Life, Tennessee Volunteers: Memorable Stories of

Volunteer Football." New York: Sports Publishing, 2013.

Harris, Haywood and Gus Manning, "Six Seasons Remembered: The National Championship Years of Tennessee Football," Knoxville, Tennessee: The University of Tennessee Press, 2004.

Harris, Haywood, Tom Mattingly, Rob Hardin, and Donnell Field, "Celebrating 75 Years of Neyland Stadium 1921-1996, June 17, 1996, through Aug. 30, 1996." Knoxville, Tennessee: University of Tennessee Sports Information Office, September 1996.

Hyams, Jimmy, "Peyton Manning: Primed and Ready," Kansas City, Missouri: Andrews McMeel Publishing, 1998.

Kozar, Andrew J, "Football as a War Game: The Annotated Journals of Gen. R. R. Neyland," Nashville, Tennessee: Falcon Press, 2002.

Majors, Johnny, and Ben Byrd, "You Can Go Home Again," Nashville, Tennessee: Rutledge Hill Press, 1986.

Manning, Gus, and Haywood Harris, "Once a Vol, Always a Vol," Champaign, Illinois: Sports Publishing L.L.C., 2006.

Mattingly, Thomas J., "Tennessee Football: The Peyton Manning Years," UMI Press: Charlotte, North Carolina, 1999.

Mattingly, Thomas J., "The Tennessee Football Vault: The History of the Tennessee Volunteers, 1891-2006," Whitman Press, Atlanta: 2006.

Mattingly, Thomas J., "The Tennessee Trivia

Book." Hill Street Press: Athens, Georgia, 2007.

Mattingly, Thomas J., "The University of Tennessee All-Access Football Vault." Whitman Press: Atlanta, 2009.

Mattingly, Thomas J., and Earl C. Hudson. "Smokey: The True Stories behind the University of Tennessee's Beloved Mascot." Knoxville, Tennessee" The University of Tennessee Press, 2012.

Montgomery, James Riley, Stanley John Folsmbee, and Lee Seifert Greene, "To Foster Knowledge: The History of the University of Tennessee, 1794-1970." Knoxville, Tennessee: The University of Tennessee Press, 1984.

Nagi, Mark, "Decade of Dysfunction," Knoxville, Tennessee: Mean Streets Living, 2018.

Nelson. Lindsey, "Hello Everybody, I'm Lindsey Nelson." New York: Beech Tree Books, 1985.

Parker, Barry, and Robin Hood, "Neyland: Life of a Stadium." Chattanooga, Tennessee: Parker Hood Press, 2000.

Siler, Tom, "Tennessee: "Football's Greatest Dynasty," Knoxville, Tennessee: Holston Printing Company, Revised, 1962.

Siler, Tom, "Tennessee's Dazzling Decade, 1960-70," Knoxville, Tennessee: Hubert E. Hodge Printing Company, 1970.

Siler, Tom, "Through the Years with the Volunteers: Tennessee Football, 1890-1950." Knoxville, Tennessee: Archer & Smith Printing Company, 1950

The (Memphis, Tenn.) Commercial Appeal, "Great Moments in Tennessee Vol Football History." Knoxville, Tennessee, and Memphis, Tennessee, The Knoxville News Sentinel Company and the Memphis Publishing Company, 2004.

Travis, Clay, "Dixieland Delight: A Football Season on the Road in the Southeastern Conference." New York: HarperCollins Publishers, 2009.

Travis, Clay, "On Rocky Top: A Front Row Seat to the End of an Era." New York: Harper Collins Publishers, 2009.

West, Marvin, "Legends of the Tennessee Vols." Champaign, Illinois: Sports Publishing L.L.C., 2005.

West, Marvin, "Tales of Tennessee." Sports Publishing L.L.C.

Williams, F.M., and Jeff Hanna, "Majors of Tennessee." Nashville, Tennessee, The Tennessean, 1976.